ARCTIC CONVOYS

David Kenyon is Research Historian for the Bletchley Park Trust. He has worked on numerous historical television and film projects, including acting as historical advisor to *War Horse* in 2010. His books include *Bletchley Park and D-Day* and *Horsemen in No Man's Land*.

ARCTIC CONVOYS
Bletchley Park and the War for the Seas

DAVID KENYON

YALE UNIVERSITY PRESS
NEW HAVEN AND LONDON

For information about this and other Yale University Press publications, please contact:
U.S. Office: sales.press@yale.edu   yalebooks.com
Europe Office: sales@yaleup.co.uk   yalebooks.co.uk

Set in Adobe Garamond Pro by IDSUK (DataConnection) Ltd
Printed in Denmark by Nørhaven

Library of Congress Control Number: 2024932060

ISBN 978-0-300-26944-4 (hbk)
ISBN 978-0-300-27935-1 (pbk)

A catalogue record for this book is available from the British Library.

10 9 8 7 6 5 4 3 2

CONTENTS

CONTENTS

PART III ATTACK: THE JW–RA CONVOYS, 1942–1945

ILLUSTRATIONS

PREFACE

Like its predecessor *Bletchley Park and D-Day*, this book started life in 2019 as a research project for an exhibition at Bletchley Park. A permanent display was being created in Block A, the former home of the Naval Section of the Government Code and Cypher School (GC&CS), telling the story of what went on in that section and its effect on the war. (The resulting *The Intelligence Factory* exhibition opened in 2022.) Naturally this led me to investigate the wartime occupants of the building, and the work of Naval Section more widely. In hunting for an example of the influence of signals intelligence (SIGINT) on the war at sea I was immediately drawn to the events of July 1942 and the catastrophic damage inflicted on convoy PQ 17 in the Arctic, a story dominated by the influence of SIGINT. As my investigations continued, however, I came to the conclusion that the events around PQ 17, despite their firm place in the mythology of the Second World War, were not representative of the Arctic convoy campaign as a whole. The wider effort to supply the USSR by sea around the North Cape was a much more complicated and interesting story. Five years later, after interruptions from COVID, and distractions by other projects, this book is the result of those investigations.

As always, I am grateful to the Trustees and Executive of Bletchley Park Trust, and Head of Programmes Nicola Ayrton for allowing me to work on this project as part of my 'day job' as research historian at Bletchley Park. I was also greatly assisted by our archivist Dean Annison, who provided access to the significant collection of unpublished Naval Section materials on loan from Government Communications Headquarters (GCHQ) and held in the BPT Archive. Bletchley Park's Oral History Officer Jonathan Byrne was also instrumental in providing the veteran testimony of Block A staff collected via the Bletchley Park Oral History Project, and Exhibitions Manager Erica Munro assisted with image research. Further documentary materials from Naval Section, along with transcripts of the tens of thousands of German wireless messages deciphered by GC&CS during the campaign, are held in The National Archives (TNA), Kew, London, and the assistance of their staff is acknowledged. Had it not been for the digitisation of much of the relevant message traffic by TNA and its availability online via their website this project would have been much more difficult.

Individual advice, guidance and appropriate criticism were also provided by my fellow Bletchley Park historian, Research Officer Dr Tom Cheetham, and by naval intelligence expert and fellow author Andrew Boyd.

David Kenyon, June 2023

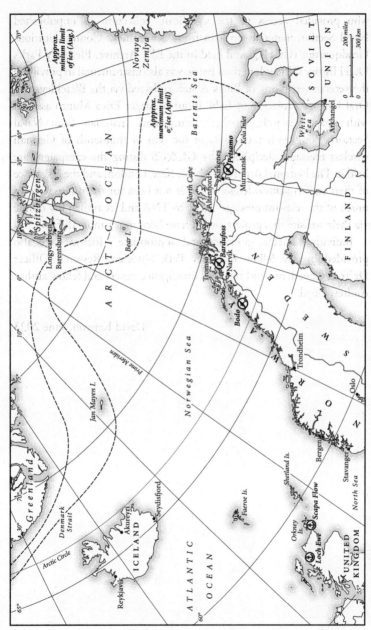

The Theatre of Operations

PART I
CODEBREAKERS

CHAPTER ONE

THE WAR IN THE ARCTIC

A SIGNAL CATASTROPHE

In 1914, as the First World War was beginning, John Broome was sent to Royal Naval College, Osborne. At the age of thirteen, 'Jack', the son of a failed Klondike gold prospector, began his studies to become an officer in the Royal Navy. A few years later he joined the elderly battleship HMS *Colossus* as a midshipman. The captain under whom he served was one Dudley Pound. Jack's name was to be linked to that of Pound twenty-five years later, in ways neither could foresee. Between the wars, Broome served as a submarine captain, but when war broke out again in 1939, he was deemed to be too old to continue commanding submarines and was moved onto destroyers. He spent the next few years applying his knowledge of submarine warfare to catching U-boats as a convoy escort commander in the Atlantic; in his own words, 'a thief to catch thieves'. In 1941 he was appointed to the command of Escort Group 1 (EG1) as the captain of the destroyer HMS *Keppel*.

In 1942 EG1 was allocated as close escort to the Arctic convoy PQ 17. On 4 July 1942 Broome received a fateful wireless message from his former captain, now First Sea Lord, Dudley Pound. It read: '2136: Most Immediate. My 2123. Convoy is to scatter.' It was the First Sea Lord's belief that the convoy was about to be attacked and potentially destroyed by the German battleship *Tirpitz*. Broome was

3

otherwise unaware of this threat to his charges but was obliged to pass on this command to the merchant ships of the convoy. This he did by flag signal, and by sailing alongside the cargo ship *River Afton* in order to communicate directly with the commodore leading the convoy, merchant captain John Dowding. Broome recalled this conversation as follows:

| *Keppel to Commodore*: | Sorry to leave you like this. Goodbye and good luck. It looks like a bloody business. |
| *Commodore to Keppel*: | Thank you. Goodbye and good hunting.[1] |

Broome, HMS *Keppel* and the rest of EG1 then turned away from the convoy to engage what they assumed to be the German battleship and its consorts, approaching from just over the horizon.

In fact, *Tirpitz* had yet to put to sea, and Pound's message instead condemned the ships of the convoy to piecemeal destruction by German submarines and aircraft. *River Afton* would be sunk by a U-boat the following day. Only eleven of the thirty-five ships in the convoy reached their destination, in what became a notorious maritime disaster. Captain Broome carried the burden of that day for the remainder of his life, and when in 1968 David Irving wrote a book about PQ 17 blaming Broome for the disaster, Broome sued for libel. He won damages in court and was inspired to write his own account of events. The case hinged on the testimony of those involved, but also on a mass of evidence in the form of signals, those sent to and from the convoy and its escorts, and to and from the Admiralty and Home Fleet. These messages were not only the key to understanding what had happened on 4 July 1942 but were in many ways the direct cause of what took place. Broome made this point repeatedly in his book, commenting: 'Most important of all were the signals; the vivid authentic framework on which that melancholy episode was built. Signals which created, operated, sailed with, and eventually killed PQ17.'[2] And later: 'PQ17 was just another splendid convoy, ploughing along with no claim whatever to history or fiction until those signals arrived from the Admiralty. The order given in the final signal had to be obeyed or ignored. To my dying regret I obeyed it.'[3]

Broome's point was that, after the advent of wireless, signals, and the orders and intelligence they conveyed or did not convey, were a fundamental part of naval warfare. No sea battle could be understood without reference to the wireless traffic of the belligerents. This is a truth which must be acknowledged by all historians of the wars at sea in the twentieth century.

SECRET HISTORY

There is, however, an additional layer not revealed by Broome. The lawyers in Court No. 8 of the High Courts of Justice were denied a significant part of the evidence relevant to these proceedings in that they only saw the operational signals (those sent from the Admiralty to ships at sea). The signals intelligence (SIGINT) on which those decisions made at the Admiralty were based remained a secret until the following decade. Pound made his decision sealing the fate of PQ 17 on the basis of 'Special Intelligence' – information gained by the interception and decryption of the messages of the German navy and air force. Much of this material was available to Pound as a result of the work of the Naval Section of the Government Code and Cypher School (GC&CS) at Bletchley Park in Buckinghamshire. It was not until the mid-1970s that the existence of this organisation was revealed publicly, and it was only in 1977 that versions of the original intercepted messages that had been passed from Bletchley Park to the Admiralty back in 1942 were released.

The result of this secrecy was that, in addition to Broome's own narrative, several of the other influential accounts of the Arctic campaign do not acknowledge the full role of SIGINT. The official history of the campaign, which occupies several chapters in Stephen Roskill's *The War at Sea* (published in three volumes by HMSO between 1954 and 1961) makes no reference to codebreaking or 'Special Intelligence', as the whole subject remained a closely guarded secret. It is highly probable that Roskill was aware of this material, as he had himself served as Deputy Director of Naval Intelligence Division (NID) just after the war, but he was not able to reference it overtly in his writing. A similar official publication was the Naval Staff History *Arctic Convoys 1941–1945*, issued in 1954. This document was subject to restricted circulation, being classified 'Confidential' for many years, but that level of security was not sufficient for any information about Special Intelligence to be included. This work has now been declassified and was published relatively recently in 2007.[4] It provides a key source for events at sea but remains silent on SIGINT. Early popular works suffered in a similar way. Brian Schofield's *The Russian Convoys* (Batsford, 1964) was for many years a key popular work on the topic. Given that Captain Schofield had been Director of the Trade Division at the Admiralty during a large part of the relevant period (he held the post April 1941–January 1943), he was likely to have been party to much of the key intelligence, but again his duty of secrecy concerning Special Intelligence was maintained.

Works published after the 'ULTRA' secret was made public in 1975 have acknowledged the role of SIGINT in Arctic operations but have yet to investigate the matter in detail. Richard Woodman produced a substantial account of the whole campaign in his *The Arctic Convoys 1941–1945* (John Murray, 1994), but its focus is on the convoys themselves, and on the experience of the Merchant Navy. While he referenced intelligence fed to the relevant commanders, he typically relied on the Admiralty signals to the fleet and did not seek to interrogate the process by which the information in those signals was actually derived. More detail was provided in the official history of British intelligence written by Harry Hinsley between 1979 and 1981. As will be examined in later chapters, Hinsley worked at the heart of the naval SIGINT operation at Bletchley Park during the war, but, again, his focus in writing his history was on the application of the intelligence rather than the details of its production, and he in any case had a much wider field to consider than just the Arctic.[5]

More recent publications on the Arctic convoys have tended to fall into two groups: there are those works which focus on the human experience, drawing on letters and diaries, or on the oral testimony of veterans, and there are those which take a wider historical approach but do not consider the campaign as a whole. The first group represents a flourishing genre of books on the Arctic convoys, and indeed the Second World War more broadly. The experience of the merchant sailors in particular is viewed as one of the worst of all those involved in the conflict. Each journey was a battle against the elements: stormy seas, and extreme cold, with the added burden of waiting constantly for the sudden shock of a torpedo hitting a nearby ship, or worse still your own, and sentencing you to a perhaps mercifully quick death in the freezing waters. Part of the perceived horror comes from the lack of agency these men had in their own fates, forced simply to hold station in the convoys and await events. These stories make for stirring reading and have an important place in the historiography of the war, but they do not provide any strategic analysis, and do not touch on SIGINT.[6]

Partly as a consequence of the inherent drama of certain parts of the story, brought out in the works just mentioned, there has also been a tendency to publish works describing only parts of the campaign. Allied losses were not evenly distributed through the war. Many of the ships lost were sunk in a few particularly costly incidents. Other convoys sailed without interference. The most notorious of these incidents of loss is of course convoy PQ 17. Unfortunately, this has led to a significant body of literature (as well as television)[7] concentrated solely on that episode.[8] While it is a gripping and tragic story, the events of July 1942 were by no means typical of the Arctic campaign as a whole. Continued focus on that disaster has led to a skewed perception of the wider campaign. The signals sent during that operation and the intelligence on which they were based have been subject to minute scrutiny; however, the commanders concerned were not making one-off decisions. To understand why Pound thought *Tirpitz* was at sea in July 1942, it is necessary to look at the other occasions on which similar intelligence had required similar decision-making (such as *Tirpitz*'s sortie three months earlier in March 1942). Only when the SIGINT picture around each convoy is examined in the context of the longer campaign can the decisions taken by the leaders on both sides be properly assessed. By focusing on this one event, these books fail to do justice to the campaign as a whole from 1941 to 1945 and, if anything, contribute to the mythology surrounding the convoys. Since the story broke in the 1970s, a good deal of ink has also been expended on the story of Bletchley Park and the breaking of Enigma. The story of how Alan Turing and the inhabitants of Hut 8 at Bletchley Park found their way into naval Enigma has been well described in several works.[9] However, while these works provide a thorough account of the breaking of naval Enigma, they make no attempt to examine the impact on the war of the intelligence gained via Enigma, concentrating only on the cryptanalytical process.

This book is an effort to place the naval battles in the Arctic from 1941 to 1945 in their proper SIGINT context. Only by doing so can the history of these battles be properly told. In addition, this book will examine how that intelligence was produced – how the enemy's signals were intercepted and decoded, and then distributed to those that needed them, all the while maintaining the secrecy vital to the continuing success of the operation. Central to this story is the Naval Section of the GC&CS, whose break into German naval Enigma in 1941 came at a crucial time for the defence of the Arctic convoys. A section which started with five people and four chairs grew into an intelligence-generating machine employing over five hundred people. Thousands of messages were successfully delivered to the Admiralty, revealing vast quantities of detail on the German navy's movements and intentions. How that intelligence was used or not used, and the consequences in terms of ships sunk and lives lost, lies at the heart of this story.

At the time of writing, a large body of unpublished archival material is available concerning SIGINT in the Arctic, and it is this material which forms the basis of this study. The trail starts with the decrypted enemy signals teleprinted from Naval Section at Bletchley Park to the Admiralty's Operational Intelligence Centre (OIC). As will be explained later, these are not an exhaustive reflection of what was intercepted or deciphered at Bletchley Park, but they are a complete collection of all the traffic that was considered important enough to be passed on. This material was declassified and supplied to The National Archives beginning in 1977.[10] In the land and air campaigns of the Second World War, the equivalent teleprints were typically passed directly to commanders, including those in the field (for example, Field Marshal Montgomery in his headquarters in Normandy in 1944). In the case of the war at sea, however, this intelligence passed through a further filter at the Admiralty, and only some of it was passed on to commanders in the form of Admiralty Signals. These latter messages are also preserved in The National Archives, and a comparison of the content and timing of the two series is often instructive.[11] Further signals information is contained within the reports of individual convoy sailings compiled at the time, as well as other contemporary after-action reports and documents.[12]

In addition to this immediately contemporary material, the GC&CS produced a large quantity of analytical and historical documentation at the end of the war. As the organisation scaled down in 1945–1946, staff in all the various branches were ordered to produce accounts of their work to avoid loss of knowledge as staff left, and to preserve lessons learned for any future conflict. It is fortunate for naval historians that this process was supervised by Frank Birch, then Head of Naval Section, and while other teams at Bletchley Park seem to have paid only lip service to this requirement, Naval Section produced a profusion of histories and analytical documents. These include the substantial fifteen-volume *GC&CS Naval SIGINT*, much of which was written by Frank Birch himself. This work has not been published and survives as a bound typescript which was not made publicly available until 2014.[13] Numerous other reports on Naval Section activity, from cryptanalysis to captured documents, have also been released at various times since the 1970s. In addition to studying their own activities, Naval Section also produced a series of volumes on the activities of their enemies, as learned from SIGINT and other sources such as captured documents and prisoner interrogations. These were titled the *GC&CS Naval History* and ran to twenty-four volumes covering the German, Italian and, to a lesser extent, Japanese fleets and their activities.[14] These were compiled by Lieutenant Commander L.A. Griffiths, RNVR, and of particular interest is Volume 23, 'Northern Waters', which covered the Arctic operations and was written by Griffiths himself.[15] With the benefit of these now publicly available but not yet published sources, a more rounded assessment of the role of SIGINT in the Arctic can be attempted.

It is also hoped that this study will stand alongside the increasing body of scholarship which questions the popular mythology not only of the Arctic convoys but of the wider Battle of the Atlantic and the war for Britain's trade routes as a whole. The story of the Arctic convoys sits within a wider mythology of the convoy wars. Typically, the story is framed as one of defenceless merchant ships, constantly at the mercy of omnipotent U-boat 'wolfpacks' hunting them down, while under the meagre protection of Royal Navy corvettes and other small escort vessels. Much of this myth-making can be attributed to Winston Churchill, who during the Second World War served both as First Lord of the Admiralty (a role he had performed in the First World War) and as Prime Minister. He famously remarked in his history of the Second World War: 'The only thing that ever really frightened me during the war was the U-boat peril.' He called the news of the PQ 17 disaster 'One of the most melancholy naval episodes in the whole of the war'.[16]

Part of this fascination with convoys on the part of the Prime Minister was due to his service as First Lord and his interest in all things naval, but it also had a political dimension. Churchill was keen, in 1940 and 1941, to emphasise the threat to the UK for the benefit of public and political opinion in the US. This was done in order to gain as much help as he could from his neutral trading partner across the Atlantic and ultimately bring them into the war on the side of the Empire. Latterly, once the Arctic convoys began in the summer of 1941, Churchill was engaged in an equivalent propaganda campaign directed at Stalin and the Soviet Union; only by emphasising the effort and cost of the Arctic convoys could he counter the Russian leader's incessant calls for a second front on mainland Europe and more help to defeat Germany. The result of these efforts was to frame the convoys both as critical to the ability of the UK to continue the war against Germany and as a fight where the enemy held many of the strategic and tactical advantages. This framing was necessary to wartime politics but has also cast its shadow over the way the campaigns have been viewed in popular memory.

A contribution to this mythology was also made by the Nazi regime itself, which lauded its submarine captains and their crews on the same level as ace fighter pilots and offered them up in the media as icons of national prowess. Historian Michael Hadley, in his study of just this phenomenon, remarked: 'During both wars, and during the interwar years as well, the U-boat was mythologised more than any other weapon of war.'[17] This point was reiterated by Clay Blair in his seminal two-volume history *Hitler's U-boat War* as follows: 'The myth goes something like this: the Germans invented the submarine (or U-boat) and have consistently built the best submarines in the world. Endowed with a canny gift for exploiting the marvellously complex and lethal weapons system, valorous (or alternatively, murderous) German submariners dominated the seas in both world wars and very nearly defeated the Allies in each case.'[18] Recent scholarship, however, has questioned these legends. It is now widely acknowledged that the threat of British defeat by the U-boats was probably never as severe as Churchill claimed. Also, far from being invulnerable hunters, the German submarines became increasing prey to Allied ships and aircraft equipped with sophisticated anti-submarine technology, including ASDIC (sonar), radar, depth charges and homing torpedoes. To quote Blair again: 'Contrary to the accepted wisdom or mythology [. . .] U-boats never even came close at any time to cutting the vital north Atlantic lifeline to the British Isles.'[19]

It is not the intention here to suggest that the convoy battles in either the Atlantic or the Arctic were insignificant, or indeed that their outcomes were a foregone conclusion; on the contrary, it will be argued that these battles have a much richer, more complex and more nuanced history than has been recognised hitherto by the mainstream narratives. The old 'U-boat vs merchant ship and escort' narrative is no longer sufficient to describe these events.

Why the Arctic convoys were attempted at all, and why they were continued until the end of the war, is a political question that has exercised numerous historians. Similar questions can be asked of their actual economic and military benefit, or otherwise, to the Soviet Union. However, those questions lie outside the scope of this account, which concentrates on the SIGINT developed during the campaign, and the operational and tactical usefulness of that intelligence. This is the story of Bletchley Park's dealings with the Admiralty, and in turn with ships at sea. The political dimension is left to other scholars. Indeed, the codebreakers of GC&CS had remarkably little to do with British–Soviet relations in this period. Such was the impermeability of Soviet diplomatic ciphers that there was little Bletchley Park could add to Churchill's knowledge of Stalin's changing moods and fancies. It is on the war at sea, therefore, that we shall fix our focus.

THE RIVAL FORCES

The supply of raw materials and military equipment to the Soviet Union began in August 1941. Some supply was possible overland into the southern USSR via Persia, but the sea route to the Persian Gulf was very long, and the capacity of the Persian railways would be a limiting factor. A more direct route to the USSR was via the Arctic Ocean around the northern tip of Norway to the Russian ports of Murmansk and Archangel. The latter port was only available in the summer months, as the sea ice closed the White Sea for part of the year. Murmansk was accessible year-round, but with Norway occupied by the Germans, and the Finnish border only about 50km away to the west (Finland was at war with the USSR alongside Germany), this harbour lay dangerously close to enemy forces. Both ports were linked to the heart of Russia by rail, but neither was provided with a very well-equipped harbour, so as convoy destinations neither port was ideal, nor were the facilities for arriving seamen particularly welcoming; however, there was little alternative.

Unlike the convoys which crossed the Atlantic, those sailing to Russia were forced to sail in a confined area of the ocean. The stretch of sea which provided the battlefield for the Arctic convoys can be viewed as a roughly rectangular box, approximately 2,000km (1,200 miles) long, from the coast of Iceland in the west to the islands of Novaya Zemlya in the east. The southern and eastern edges were defined by the coast of Norway and Russia, while the major land masses to the north and west were the islands of Svalbard (Spitzbergen) and the coast of Greenland. A more significant northern boundary, however, was the southern limit of the polar ice cap. Only two landmarks occur in this area: the island of Jan Mayen, 580km (360 miles) east of Iceland, and Bear Island, 1,500km (950 miles) east of Iceland. In winter these two islands also mark the southern limit of the ice, but in summer the ice retreats north, making passage north of the two islands possible. While a route north of Iceland, Jan Mayen and Bear Islands was longer (roughly fifteen days rather than ten), it allowed the ships to sail further from the Norwegian coast, and thus further from the German airfields in northern Norway. In winter the navigable passage was relatively narrow, being only 430km (270 miles) wide between Bear Island and the North Cape of Norway.

Even in summer, the weather in this region was hostile, with significant storms and wildly varying visibility. On some days, crystal-clear air could be replaced by dense fog within a few minutes, and sea mist was a perennial problem where cold air met warmer water. The proximity of the magnetic north pole also made navigation by compass both difficult and unreliable, as compasses tended to point downwards through the earth in this region. Added to this was the problem that for part of the year it was almost perpetually dark, while in summer almost twenty-four-hour daylight meant that ships were constantly vulnerable to air attack. All in all it was a difficult and dangerous place to take a ship, and sea temperatures meant that in the event of a disaster survival was unlikely.

By the summer of 1941 the *Kriegsmarine* had been at war with the Royal Navy for nearly two years. Conflict in the North Sea and the Arctic had taken place sporadically since 1939, but on 9 April 1940 the Germans began Operation *WESERÜBUNG*, the invasion of Denmark and Norway. This brought the waters around those two countries into focus as a naval battlefield for both sides. The occupation of Norway was part of Hitler's long-term plan for the domination of Europe, but, more specifically, it would secure the flow of Swedish iron ore via Norway's railways and ports to Germany's war factories. The invasion stretched the resources of the German navy. Not only did the invading forces have to be protected on their journey to Norway, but in many cases the need for speed meant that German warships had to act as the actual transports for the troops, particularly those travelling to northern ports such as Trondheim and Narvik. Two thousand soldiers of the *3. Gebirgs-Division* (3rd Mountain Division) were carried to Narvik on a fleet of ten destroyers protected by the battleships *Scharnhorst* and *Gneisenau*, while the heavy cruiser *Admiral Hipper* and four destroyers took a further seventeen hundred troops to Trondheim. What is more, the campaign was extremely costly in warships. The heavy cruiser *Blucher*, one of only three ships in its class (along with *Admiral Hipper* and *Prinz Eugen*), was sunk in Oslo Fjord in the opening hours of the invasion. Two of the six available light cruisers, *Königsberg* and *Karlsruhe*, were also lost. Perhaps more significantly, of the twenty-two destroyers available to the German navy in April 1940, ten were sunk during the invasion campaign. Eight of these were lost in a single day during the Second Battle of Narvik on 13 April. Although a further nineteen destroyers would be completed before 1945, the loss of ten vessels from a class of ship of which only just over forty were ever built was a massive blow. This would have a knock-on effect on the German campaign against the Arctic convoys, as the shortage of destroyers not only was a hindrance to their independent operations against the convoys, but also restricted the escort ships available for sorties by the larger capital ships, which as a result often had to sail unescorted.

The successes of the invasion of Norway and the following conquests of France and the Low Countries were a double-edged sword for the German navy. On the one hand, the occupation of the French Atlantic ports gave the *Kriegsmarine* ideal bases for operations in the North Atlantic, and for commerce raiders and blockade runners to come and go from further afield. The Norwegian fjords were also useful staging posts for ships and submarines heading into the Atlantic from Germany via the northern route. On the other hand, having previously had to concern themselves only with coastal defence in the Baltic and a short stretch on the North Sea coast, the navy now had to protect ports and coastal shipping from Spain to north of the Arctic Circle. This placed a significant strain on their resources, and on their fleet of smaller patrol craft in particular. Nor were the French ports ideal as bases for larger ships. *Scharnhorst*, *Gneisenau* and *Prinz Eugen* spent much of 1941 in the French ports and attacks on these vessels by the RAF demonstrated that the proximity of these ports to British bomber airfields made them impractical as bases for capital ships. The U-boats would continue to operate out of French ports but only at the cost of building massive bomb-proof shelters for them at huge expense of labour and scarce materials.

The result of this was a progressive migration of the German surface fleet to bases in the Norwegian fjords. Here they were out of range of all but the most far-reaching bombing attacks from the UK, and at the same time constituted an ever-present threat to the UK and to Atlantic commerce. This in turn tied up a large proportion of the British navy in the Home Fleet at Scapa Flow. However, despite the presence of much of their fleet in the region, the commencement of the Arctic convoys can only have represented yet another unwelcome headache for the already overstretched German Naval High Command.

In the spring of 1942 German defences were improved as more naval and air resources were moved to Norway. In part, this was a response by Hitler to fears for the security of Norway, which he regarded as a vital and 'decisive' part of his empire. This was fuelled by British raids on the Norwegian coast in 1941, on the Lofoten Islands in March and December 1941 and on Vaagso, also in December 1941, which raised German fears of a more long-term attack on this northern flank. However, once there, the German defensive forces were ideally placed not only to defend Norway from attack but also to interdict convoy traffic around the North Cape. As the war progressed, more and more of the surviving German surface fleet would be positioned in Norway, along with ever larger numbers of U-boats and aircraft.[20]

After the fall of France in 1940, Germany had moved a number of its larger surface ships to ports on the coast of France with a view to raiding out into the Atlantic. However, after the sinking of the *Bismarck* in 1941 and increasingly heavy air raids on the French ports, a decision was taken to withdraw the surface fleet back to Germany and ultimately to Norway. By the spring of 1942 most of the *Kriegsmarine's* larger vessels were in Norwegian ports. This included the formidable battleship *Tirpitz* (the sister ship to *Bismarck*), the smaller 'pocket' battleships *Admiral Scheer* and *Lützow*, the heavy cruisers *Admiral Hipper* and *Prinz Eugen* and a (somewhat diminished) fleet of escorting destroyers, torpedo boats (which in German service were equivalent to small destroyers) and smaller vessels.[21] It was intended that the two sister battleships *Scharnhorst* and *Gneisenau* would also be redeployed to Norway, but both were damaged during their passage north from France (the famous 'Channel dash' of February 1942). *Scharnhorst* would not reach Norway until January 1943 (as discussed in a later chapter), while *Gneisenau* was damaged in dock after returning to

Germany and would play no further active part in the war. Against the defensive escorts of a typical Arctic convoy, an attack by any one of these larger ships, let alone a battlegroup of several, would be disastrous. The risk also existed that such a battlegroup might make a break through the UK–Greenland gap into the wider Atlantic, where it could cause equal havoc with the Atlantic convoys.

Submarines were moved north to Norway shortly after the invasion in 1940, but in the first instance no formal facilities or command structures were established for these boats. It was not until August 1941 that Bergen was officially declared as a base, followed by Trondheim in October 1941.[22] Substantial concrete protective pens were built at both of these bases to protect the submarines when they were not on patrol. In the spring of 1942, basing of submarines was extended northwards, with boats based in Narvik from March of that year, and in nearby Skjomenfjord in May. Boats were also stationed in the extreme north, at Kirkenes from July 1941 to August 1942 and Hammerfest from January 1943. Local command of these submarines was established in May 1942 with the creation of *11. Unterseebootsflottille* (11th Submarine Flotilla) headquartered at Bergen. In April 1943 the additional *13. Unterseebootsflottille* was created, headquartered in Trondheim.

The U-boats themselves which operated in the Arctic were almost exclusively the most common type, the Type VIIC. Over five hundred of this type were built. Each had a crew of around fifty and carried a dozen torpedoes, fired from four forward tubes and one astern. They also carried an 88mm deck gun for use when surfaced. What has to be remembered is that these vessels were not true submarines in the modern sense. A modern submarine operates almost exclusively under water, surfacing only occasionally. U-boats, on the other hand, are better viewed as small submersible ships. The Type VIIC could cruise on the surface at around 17 knots (32km/h), but when dived switched to electric power, using which it could achieve only about 7 knots (14km/h). It could remain dived for up to twenty hours running on minimum power, but in order to do so it would have to reduce its speed to around 4 knots (7km/h). The boats carried enough fuel for a range of around 8,500 nautical miles (15,000km). This was a concern for U-boats operating in the Atlantic, as the outward and return journeys to the convoy routes consumed much of their endurance; however, this was much less of a factor in the Arctic, where the boats were operating only a few hundred miles from their bases. Although small and cramped in their interior, the Type VII boats were popular with their crews, possibly because their lack of range meant that patrols were typically quite short. They were also reputed to dive very quickly versus a larger boat (such as the Type IX), which could be an asset when under attack.[23]

Given that an average convoy made a speed of around 8 knots, in order to manoeuvre effectively against a convoy a U-boat would have to do so on the surface, and even then it was only twice as fast as its prey. Once dived in the vicinity of the enemy, the U-boat was, if anything, slower than its target. This made bringing U-boats into contact with convoys very difficult. There was little point in trying to chase a convoy; instead, its course and timing had to be predicted and the U-boats positioned in advance across its path, where they could lie submerged, more or less stationary, and let the convoy steam over them. This made SIGINT and other forms of prior intelligence about convoy movements vital to U-boat operations, as the submarines had to be deployed in advance in order to be effective. Surface ships, by contrast, were typically capable of 25–30 knots, which made manoeuvring in reaction to events in the course of a battle much more of an option.

Finally, there was the German air force: the *Luftwaffe*. Unlike the British or American navies, the *Kriegsmarine* had little or no autonomous air capability. All aircraft used in maritime operations were controlled by the German air force. This even extended to aircraft actually carried on larger German battleships. (The *Kriegsmarine* never brought any fully-fledged aircraft carriers into service.) Command of the *Luftwaffe* was divided into *Luftflotte* (air fleets), of which there were originally four, covering different geographical parts of Germany itself. A fifth, *Luftflotte 5*, was created in 1940 to cover Norway and Denmark. Operations within Norway were controlled by a *Fliegerführer-Nord*, whose command in the summer of 1942 was divided into three separate commands. Of these, *Fliegerführer-Lofoten* had particular responsibility for attacking Arctic convoys.

In addition to fighter and transport aircraft, *Luftflotte 5* had a number of bombers under its control. Two formations in particular were concerned with operations against the convoys. The first was *Kampfgeschwader 30 (KG30)*, which mostly flew Junkers Ju 88 twin-engined aircraft. The second was *Kampfgeschwader 26 (KG26)*, equipped with Heinkel He 111 bombers. The aircraft were mostly armed with conventional bombs, although some were converted to carry torpedoes. The German air force had been slow to develop an air-dropped torpedo capability due to separation and rivalry between the air force and the navy; however, in 1942 this situation changed with the development of new specialist equipment and a training school, established jointly with the Italians in the Mediterranean. In March 1942, Goering, as head of the *Luftwaffe*, also took an interest in the problem and specifically tasked *Luftflotte 5* with attacking Arctic convoys with torpedoes. For this, a series of He 111 H-6 bombers were converted to carry two torpedoes each, and crews were specially trained in techniques of torpedo attack.[24]

Each *Geschwader* was divided into three *Gruppe* of around thirty aircraft each. Not all of these *Gruppe* were available in Norway, as some, particularly those of *KG26*, served in other theatres at various times. However, in the summer of 1942 all three *Gruppe* of *KG30* and two of *KG26* were typically present, based in the extreme north of Norway on airfields at Bardufoss, Banak and Petsamo (near the Finnish border). This gave the Germans over one hundred anti-ship aircraft. The Ju 88 had a range of around 1,800km and the He 111 2,300km, meaning that from these bases a significant proportion of the convoy route was within easy range for air attack.

These attack units were supported by reconnaissance aircraft. *Luftflotte 5* included several *Küstenfliegergruppe* (coastal patrol groups). These units flew the BV 138 and He 115 float-planes. Both these types could carry torpedoes and were capable of attacking surface vessels, but their real strength lay in long endurance (both aircraft had a range of over 4,000km), which allowed them to stay in the air for long periods, shadowing convoys and vectoring other aircraft or submarines onto their position. These were supported by dedicated reconnaissance units (*Aufklärungsgruppe*), flying aircraft including the Fokker-Wolff FW 200 Condor. This was a four-engine aircraft originally designed as a civil airliner. In 1938 a specially adapted version of the FW 200 was the first heavier-than-air aircraft to fly non-stop from Berlin to New York, a flight that took over twenty-four hours.[25] The military version had an endurance of fourteen hours, making it a very capable long-range maritime patrol aircraft. In December 1941, FW 200s of *KG40* moved from Bordeaux to Trondheim for reconnaissance work on the convoy routes.[26]

With these assets available, the *Luftwaffe* presented a significant threat to Arctic convoys as well as to the naval groups protecting them. German aircraft could find, follow and attack surface ships throughout the relevant areas of the Arctic Ocean. Only two factors mitigated against their effectiveness. One was weather, which could be as hostile to aircraft as it was to ships. The other was latitude, as in winter convoys could operate largely under the cover of darkness. In the summer, on the other hand, convoys could be found and attacked around the clock.

On the other side of the North Sea, ultimate responsibility for the safe passage of the convoys to Russia rested with the Royal Navy. As the Western Approaches tactical policy stated: 'The safe and timely arrival of the convoy at its destination is the primary object of the escort.'[27] In overall command of all UK naval operations was the First Sea Lord, a position held from June 1939 until September 1943 by Admiral of the Fleet Sir Dudley Pound. Having joined the navy at fourteen years old, Pound had fought at the Battle of Jutland in 1916 in command of the battleship HMS *Colossus* (where he was joined as a midshipman by the young Jack Broome, as described earlier). In 1941 he was sixty-four years old and was widely considered to be 'worn out'. His health was poor and he had a reputation for dozing off in meetings; indeed, he would die from a brain tumour in October 1943. He was, however, a close confidant of the Prime Minister, Winston Churchill, and the two would confer at length on naval matters, with Churchill often deferring to Pound's superior knowledge. Unfortunately, one area in which Pound was not able to shake the Prime Minister's views was on the Russian convoys. Despite the First Lord's arguments that, especially in the permanent daylight of summer, the whole project was 'fundamentally unsound', Churchill tried to enforce a punishing year-round schedule of a convoy every ten days (although this was never achieved in practice).[28]

Although his was a land-based position, Pound was able to communicate directly with forces at sea, and as such he could issue tactical instructions to his subordinates in a way that his Army or Royal Air Force (RAF) equivalents would have been unable to do. His rank also gave him access to intelligence, including 'Special Intelligence' from Bletchley Park, which informed his decision-making and often gave him insights not shared with his subordinate commanders at sea. Pound's ability to deliver direct instructions to the convoys and their escorts would have profound implications for convoy operations, and most notoriously for PQ 17. This 'remote control', or, as others have termed it, 'back-seat driving', will be assessed in later chapters, but it forms a crucial part of the intelligence picture.

Subordinate to Pound was the Commander-in-Chief (C-in-C) of the Home Fleet (acting) Admiral John Tovey, and latterly Sir Bruce Fraser and Sir Henry Moore. As C-in-C Home Fleet, Tovey was based aboard ship. At first he 'flew his flag' from HMS *King George V*, but after it was damaged in a collision he moved to its sister ship HMS *Duke of York*. Tovey had also served at Jutland, in his case as captain of a destroyer, but had ascended the ladder to command a cruiser squadron in the Mediterranean in 1940 before taking over as C-in-C Home Fleet in November of that year. He was a man of deep religious conviction, and his strength of character inspired loyalty and affection in many who served under him.[29] To his superiors, he was often seen as more difficult, happy to stand his ground if he knew he was right. When Tovey was in command of HMS *Rodney* in the early 1930s, his confidential report was written by one of his predecessors as C-in-C, Admiral John Kelly. Of Tovey Kelly wrote: 'A man of strong and forceful personality. A strict disciplinarian. A particularly straight and honest character. He shares with me a peculiarity of temperament which, in myself, I describe as tenacity of purpose, but, in him, obstinacy.' He went on to add: 'Would he but cultivate the sense of humour which I am convinced is latent in him, he would be the ideal leader and commander of men.'[30] Tovey shared Pound's scepticism of the whole Arctic convoy project and took a dim view of the Prime Minister's command of naval affairs, commenting: 'As a strategist and tactician [the Prime Minister] is liable to be most dangerous.'[31] Nonetheless, given the task, however unappetising, he would carry it out with his characteristic vigour and skill.

Tovey's specific role as Commander of the Home Fleet was to draw from his forces available at Scapa Flow a 'distant covering force' for the Arctic convoys. The purpose of this force was to patrol in the western Arctic Ocean and deter the larger German surface vessels from venturing out of the Norwegian fjords to attack the convoys, or to intercept the Germans if they tried to break out into the Atlantic. This covering force was composed of one British battleship (initially HMS *King George V*, and later HMS *Duke of York*) and later one American battleship (USS *Washington*), an aircraft carrier (HMS *Victorious*), several cruisers and an escort of destroyers. HMS *Victorious* was a key asset in this force, as its aircraft gave Tovey both an air reconnaissance capability and a striking force against surface ships which could reach many miles from his task force's position. Finding the location of the carrier would become a major preoccupation for the German naval commanders, and surface-ship sorties by them were rarely undertaken unless it had first been located. In turn, monitoring the *Luftwaffe's* search for the carrier group via SIGINT became a key tool in understanding German decision-making, as we shall see.

The difficulty for Tovey was that this force could not sail into the confined waters of the Barents Sea as, even with an aircraft carrier as part of the group, the large ships were vulnerable to air and submarine attack and could only be risked in exchange for a certain encounter with the German capital ships such as *Tirpitz* or *Scharnhorst*. The carrier, in particular, was a precious and hard-to-replace asset. Their role was therefore to stay to the west, close enough to intervene, but also evading as far as possible location by the Germans and providing a threat which it was hoped would curtail the ambitions of heavy units of the German surface fleet against the convoys.

Nearer to the convoys, and sailing further east into the Arctic, a second covering force was typically provided, composed of heavy cruisers with an escort of destroyers. These ships were intended to defend the convoy from attack by smaller German surface ships (destroyers and torpedo boats) and were risked further along the convoy route than the battleships. This was to prove a costly duty, as two cruisers would be lost from these forces, which latterly led to a degree of nervousness about this force and a reluctance to let it venture too far east beyond Bear Island. More covertly, the British and Russian navies also maintained a submarine patrol barrage off the coast of northern Norway. This was intended to, if not attack, then at least report the presence of any German surface vessels leaving the northern fjords. By the summer of 1942 there were around a dozen submarines involved in this cover.[32]

Finally, the convoys themselves were also provided with a close escort, a group of warships which sailed in company with the convoy, providing a protective ring around it throughout its journey. These escort vessels were typically small, the largest being destroyers, but were more usually corvettes, a class of ship specifically designed for this purpose, along with anti-submarine trawlers (purpose built for the navy, but based on a fishing-boat design) and minesweepers. These ships were equipped with ASDIC (an anti-submarine sonar system) and also later in the war with surface-search radar systems. With their ASDIC and depth charges, these ships were a genuine threat to any attacking U-boat but could do little about air attack, and would be sitting ducks for any larger German surface warships. These ships were organised into 'escort groups' commanded by an Escort Leader, typically on a destroyer. The size of these small escort vessels meant that their range was limited, and so they would often hand off convoys at a mid-point on the journey, and some were based long-term at the Russian end of the route. Often convoys were also accompanied by a fleet oiler to supply the escort with fuel, but this of course provided the enemy with another target.

Attempts were also made to provide air cover from within the convoys themselves. The first iteration of this was the so-called CAM ships, CAM ship being an acronym for 'catapult aircraft merchant ship'. These vessels were merchantmen equipped with a steam catapult capable of launching a Hurricane fighter. The project was abandoned in August 1942 and replaced by the use of 'escort carriers'. These were aircraft carriers built on merchant ship hulls. They were smaller than fleet carriers and typically carried only around twenty aircraft. They also lacked the speed of their larger cousins so could not keep up with warship groups, but they were ideal to sit within a slower-moving convoy and provide intrinsic air support. These ships and the aircraft they carried would play an increasingly important role in the defence of the convoys.

This brief outline has shown the range of offensive and defensive assets the two sides had in the Arctic. It can be seen that, in comparison to the North Atlantic, at least in its early years, both combatants had a wider range of tools available to them, and that these were in many ways quite symmetrical: both had capital ships at their disposal, as well as smaller surface vessels, aircraft and submarines. It was only in their strategic intent that they differed – one aiming to fight the convoys through to Russia, the other to prevent their safe arrival. Given that balance of forces, it would be intelligence which would provide the crucial direction to those forces and make the difference between success and failure on each side. It is to the acquisition of that intelligence, the role of SIGINT and the GC&CS in particular that we must now turn our attention.

CHAPTER TWO

DOLPHIN AND OTHER ENIGMAS

THE WIDOW TWANKY

In 1938 a comic crime caper hit British cinemas entitled *The Villiers Diamond*. In it, an ex-convict, Silas Wade, is trying to 'go straight' while in possession of a stolen jewel. The reappearance from prison of one of his co-conspirators throws Silas' life into confusion and ultimately results in the return of the diamond to its rightful owners. The film was not a huge hit, nor has it stood the test of time, with more recent reviews describing it as 'vapid' or only 'modestly enjoyable'.[1] Its historical significance lies in a fact completely unknown to contemporary (and most modern) audiences. The actor playing Silas Wade, Frank Birch, was actually one of Britain's most significant naval codebreakers.

Francis (Frank) Lyall Birch was the third son of John Arden Birch, a banker. He was born in London on 5 December 1889 and educated at Eton College before going to King's College, Cambridge, to study history and modern languages. In 1912 he obtained a double First in the History Tripos. When the First World War broke out two years later, the young Birch was eager to do his bit, and as a keen yachtsman he enlisted as an Able Seaman in the Royal Navy. He would see action against the Turks in the Dardanelles in 1915.

Meanwhile, the navy was looking for new talent to support its codebreaking effort against the Germans. This work was based in the Admiralty's cryptological department, 'Room 40'. Its head, Alfred

Ewing, had also been at King's College before the war as a professor before going on to be Director of Naval Education. Ewing went back to King's to find suitable recruits, and this led him to Frank Birch.[2] Birch was to spend the remainder of the war decrypting and interpreting German and other enemy wireless and cable communications in Room 40. He was appointed OBE in 1919 for his work as an intelligence analyst.[3]

After the war Birch returned to Cambridge University and to King's College, where he was a Fellow between 1916 and 1934. He also lectured in history from 1921 to 1928. His lectures were said to be spectacular in their histrionics, and he was one of the outstanding Directors of Studies of his time. This was followed by a spell as a theatre producer and actor. He took to producing and acting at Cambridge for undergraduate societies, and then in 1927 he moved to the London stage for some thirty-five productions. He also worked at the BBC, delivering radio talks. In particular, he delivered a series of talks considering the values of freedom and democracy, which were especially pertinent in the late 1930s. This series was subsequently published in book form in 1937 by Cambridge University Press as *This Freedom of Ours*.[4]

Between 1937 and 1939 Frank Birch appeared in seventeen films and fifteen shorter television dramas. These included portraying a British officer involved in a scheme to escape from a German prisoner-of-war camp during the First World War (*Who Goes Next*, 1938), as well as his appearance as Silas Wade.[5] Birch's stage performances included 'Widow Twanky' in pantomime, and this would be a source of one of the common nicknames by which he was known during the next stage of his career.

As war looked likely in August 1939, Britain's codebreaking organisation, the GC&CS, moved from London to Bletchley Park. The Head of GC&CS Naval Section was Birch's old Room 40 colleague from the First World War, William 'Nobby' Clarke. Clarke was keen to expand his team and identified Birch as just the man to head his German sub-section, which at that time consisted of only two staff. Clarke, referring to himself in the third person as 'H.N.S.' (Head of Naval Section), recalled:

> The scheme which had been worked out contemplated a strength of at least 40 but it was a long time before this was reached. However

one part of the scheme worked according to plan and this was probably the most important in the early stages. Cdr. F.L. Birch had been selected by H.N.S. as the head of the subsection if he was available. He at once offered to come and although he was at first put off by the Head of G.C.&C.S., H.N.S. got his way and he took over on the 5th (September). Steps were gradually taken to provide him with a staff.[6]

A more informal account of Birch's recruitment survives in a letter he wrote to Clarke on the outbreak of war on 3 September 1939.[7] 'Dear Nobby,' he wrote, 'got in touch with Dilly [Dillwyn Knox, another Room 40 veteran,] who told me to get in touch with Denniston [Head of GC&CS] [. . .] reception less than lukewarm.' Despite this rebuff, Birch offered his services to Clarke, suggesting that while he did not want simply to be 'an old bugger who might fill in a card index', if there was a more responsible role available, he had 'perhaps smugly and sentimentally thought myself bound for the old firm'. He was right, and Clarke was able to overturn Denniston's objections. Birch described how on his arrival the German staff 'swelled to five', including two 'university girls', with two tables and four chairs at their disposal – meaning that if all were present, one had to stand.[8] At that point, partly due to the difficulties faced in reading German Enigma messages, 'No German naval signals had been broken for 20 years.'[9]

However, over the next six years all of that would change. Birch would rise to become Head of Naval Section in place of Clarke in August 1941, and Naval Section would grow to a staff of over nine hundred people by 1945. Not all of these worked on German codes – others were concerned with the other Axis powers, as well as neutral nations – but the teams working on German naval Enigma would by 1945 have delivered to the Admiralty decrypts and translations of over half a million messages.

According to an account provided by GCHQ – the Government Communications Headquarters, as GC&CS became known after the war – Frank Birch was 'a short, balding man with a complex character; on the one hand he was a great man for a party, being an excellent raconteur; on the other hand, his abrasive style led to his making few friends. But Birch was constantly demanding greater commitment of resources for his team and encouraged co-operation with the US naval code-breakers.'[10]

At Cambridge, Birch had developed a reputation as an actor, comic and mimic. Once he moved to Room 40 he took rooms at 14 Edith Grove in Chelsea. Here, Birch would hold weekly musical parties. His more sober roommate and fellow codebreaker Dilly Knox would absent himself, taking the opportunity to spend all night at work.[11] Birch's party spirit was maintained on his arrival at Bletchley. According to Denniston's assistant Barbara Abernethy: 'He was billeted in the Duncombe Arms at Great Brickhill. They had a lot of dons there, Gordon Welchman, Patrick Wilkinson. It was full of dons all the time. All of them having such a jolly time that they called it the Drunken Arms.'[12]

He also had a certain reputation for eccentricity. Barbara knitted him a blue balaclava helmet, which he wore more or less constantly for the remainder of the war, the hat becoming one of his trademarks. Molly Darby, a Wren (a member of the Women's Royal Naval Service, WRNS) who was appointed as one of Birch's secretaries, had a some-what surprising first encounter with him: 'when I did meet Frank I was told to go in – I went in with my book and I went into his office and there he was standing on his head. So I said, "Well I'm ready if you are." He said, "Well I'm ready," and I said, "Well you don't look it." And anyway that was usual with him.'[13]

Penelope Fitzgerald described him as 'a many-sided human being – a rather dull historian, an acceptable drinking companion, a mysterious private personality, a brilliant talker and a born actor'.[14] Phyllis Drinkwater, a civilian in Naval Section, put it more simply: 'he was a nice man, he made me laugh'.[15] Above all, however, Birch was a brilliant intelligence officer, and he would preside over one of Britain's most successful codebreaking efforts of the war.

THE BIRTH OF NAVAL SECTION

During the First World War, naval SIGINT had been entirely the domain of the Admiralty, who controlled both the intercepting

Y stations and the cryptanalysts who, like Frank Birch, worked in the famous Room 40 of the Old Admiralty Building. This situation changed in 1919 when British codebreaking for both the navy and the army was civilianised in a new agency, the GC&CS. Initially, this organisation remained funded by, and under the management of, the Admiralty, but in 1921 responsibility and funding passed to the Foreign Office and, more specifically, the Secret Intelligence Service, whose head (informally known as 'C' or 'Chief') Sir Hugh Sinclair, became Director of GC&CS.[16] When GC&CS was established in 1919, it contained no specific naval department. This was despite the fact that the organisation was directly descended from Room 40 (NID 25). The GC&CS Naval Section was created in 1924 by William F. ('Nobby') Clarke (whom we met earlier), a trained lawyer who had served as a naval officer and codebreaker in Room 40 during the First World War. Initially, the section consisted of just two staff (Clarke and one other). They were supported by wireless interception carried out at the Royal Navy operated Y stations at Flowerdown (near Winchester) and Scarborough, but no direction finding (D/F) capability existed at that time.

By the later 1930s, inspired in part by the use of air power in the Spanish Civil War, a prevailing opinion formed in government circles that the organs of government and the Civil Service based in London would be critically vulnerable in the event of war. It was believed that heavy air raids by enemy air forces would be sufficiently destructive that nations could be effectively defeated from the air within days, or even hours, of the opening of hostilities. This led to the development of a series of evacuation plans for government departments to safer locations in the suburbs and the home counties. There was concern that GC&CS would be vulnerable to bombing if it remained in London, so it was argued that the cryptographers should be placed remotely all together in 'the country', but with 'first-class communications' to the Admiralty, which would – initially, at least – stay put.

In 1938 Hugh Sinclair purchased the mansion and a small portion of the estate at Bletchley Park, a country seat in Buckinghamshire which had recently been auctioned by its former owners and was in the process of redevelopment. This was to be a wartime base, or 'War Station', for GC&CS. During the Munich Crisis of September to October 1938, a

Naval Section of twenty-eight staff was part of the GC&CS group which travelled to Bletchley Park to prepare for what seemed like an imminent European war. Many of them were concerned with Italian traffic, as Italy posed a substantial threat to the UK in the Mediterranean and might be drawn into a conflict with Germany. In the event, however, thanks to Chamberlain's negotiations with Hitler, war did not break out, and the Naval Section party which had gone to Bletchley returned to London.

When Naval Section returned to Bletchley Park in 1939, it consisted of twenty-five people. Frank Birch provided a list of the tasks of these staff on arrival. It is clear from this list that Italian traffic was a key preoccupation of the section, with eleven staff devoted to that nation, while Germany had only two, equal to Spain, and outnumbered by the Japanese sub-section of five, despite the fact that neither of the latter powers were currently at war with the UK. Naval Section was housed in the library of the mansion. It contained equipment, tables and chairs, as well as a direct telephone line to the Admiralty and a card index for secret call-sign identifications. This room soon became too small: 'files were increasing and the numbers of staff were slowly mounting.' According to early German sub-section recruit Phoebe Senyard: 'A colleague and I were working together on a small kitchen table and getting very much in one another's way. Even the floor was used to sort signals into dates and frequencies and it must have been amusing to see us on all fours doing this job. It needs no great effort of the imagination to realise how delighted we were to hear that we were to move into Hut 4.'[17]

In early 1940, Naval Section moved into Hut 4 on the south side of the mansion. GC&CS had been aware from the outset that in the event of war the mansion at Bletchley Park would not be large enough, so through the summer of 1939 a number of timber huts were constructed to absorb the overflow staff. By the summer of 1940 the section had grown to a staff of seventy-six of all ranks, both service and civilian. Hut 4 housed the section from early 1940 until mid-1942, when it outgrew its accommodation again and was moved into a new large purpose-built brick and concrete home in Blocks A and B on the north side of Bletchley Park's ornamental lake.[18]

The German sub-section had been expanded from its previous two members by the addition of Frank Birch and others in September 1939. After complaints from Birch, the team was expanded again in March 1940 by seven recent graduates, plus one cryptanalyst: Wilfred Bodsworth, a more experienced pre-war GC&CS staff member. By August 1940 the German Naval sub-section consisted of thirty-seven people, of whom three (including Birch) were naval officers[19] This at last made it the largest team within Naval Section. This was despite the fact that little meaningful cryptanalysis had been achieved. In the absence of any cryptanalytical success, the sub-section concentrated on external analysis of German signals procedure and structures. This work was spearheaded by RNVR (Royal Naval Volunteer Reserve) Sub-Lieutenant Geoffrey Tandy, who joined in November 1939 from the Natural History Museum on the recommendation of Edward Travis. Tandy was also a pre-war colleague of Frank Birch at the BBC. The two had recorded a radio show, *Men Talking*, broadcast in the late 1930s.[20] Through this work, a good picture of German procedures was developed, and it was discovered that, while much of the smaller ship traffic using hand codes, which had been a fruitful source of intelligence in the First World War, was now replaced by voice, or 'radio telephone' (R/T), communications, almost all of the longer-range wireless Morse traffic (95 per cent) was sent after being enciphered using Enigma.[21]

NAVAL ENIGMA

Given that 95 per cent of *Kriegsmarine* wireless traffic was encrypted using the Enigma cipher system, the success or failure of Bletchley Park's German Naval Section, and indeed the degree to which SIGINT could influence the battle for the Arctic (or any other theatre), hung almost entirely on the ability of Bletchley Park to break this traffic. It is helpful, therefore, to outline how the various Enigma cipher machines worked, how the German armed forces, and the *Kriegsmarine* in particular, used them, and how Bletchley Park began to read those messages.

In 1918 Arthur Scherbius, a German electrical engineer, submitted a design to the German navy for a rotor-based encryption machine. The navy was not particularly interested in his design, nor was the

German Foreign Office, neither of whom felt that they generated enough radio traffic to justify the expense.[22] Undeterred, Scherbius continued to develop his ideas and in 1923 founded a company to market them commercially, in particular in the postal and banking sectors, where secret communications were potentially useful. By 1925 he finally persuaded the *Reichsmarine* (the inter-war German navy) to adopt a version of the device, and in 1927 the system was also adopted by the *Reichswehr* (the inter-war German army).

More than twenty different variants of the Enigma machine were produced, but only two of those had any bearing on the operations against the Arctic convoys. These machines were functionally more or less identical. They were the *Reichswehr* Enigma I, developed in 1927 and introduced into service with the army and air force in 1932; and the Enigma M1 and its successors the M2 and M3, adopted by the German navy in 1934.[23] These models were the principal machines used by the German armed forces through the Second World War.

The basic three-rotor military and naval Enigma types (known as 'I' and 'M1-3') had a simple keyboard of twenty-six letters (no numerals or punctuation keys were provided), connected to a twenty-six-letter output lamp-board. When a key was pressed, the chosen letter was encrypted by passing a current through three interchangeable encryption rotors, before being reversed by a fourth, static *Umkehrwalze*, or 'reflector wheel', which sent the current back through the encryption rotors and on to the lamp-board, where a different letter would light up, representing an enciphered version of the input letter. The clever part of the device was that if the same letter was pressed on the keyboard again, the rotors would change position one place before the encryption took effect, resulting in a different encryption path through the rotors, and a different cipher-letter being illuminated. With three rotors, around seventeen thousand encryption pathways through the rotors were created before the machine repeated itself, resulting in a sophisticated version of a poly-alphabetic substitution cipher. In effect, any letter of the alphabet in a message might be represented by any other letter, and these pairings constantly changed through the message, meaning that, unless the reader of the message knew exactly which position the rotors in the enciphering machine occupied at the start of the message, the message was unreadable, even if the reader had access to their own Enigma machine. There is a myth, perpetuated by Hollywood, that in order to read German Enigma messages, it was necessary simply to capture a machine. In fact, that was only the beginning of the problem, as knowing the exact starting set-up, or 'key', for each message was essential, which presented GC&CS with a much larger problem than that of simply acquiring the physical device.

Critically, these machines also had a *Steckerbrett*, or plugboard, on their front face. Here letters could be linked by a series of double-ended plug cables and the current passed across the board in both directions between keyboard and lamp-board, vastly increasing the complexity of the encryption.[24] The choice of keys was also expanded by the fact that, by 1939, five encryption rotors were available for the machine, of which three, in varying order, were used each day. The *Kriegsmarine* adopted the same three, and then five, rotors as their land-based colleagues, which allowed intercommunication between the services. However, in 1939 they introduced three more rotors, VI, VII and VIII, exclusively for naval use. This would have increased the range of rotor-order options from 60 (5 x 4 x 3) to 336 (8 x 7 x 6), but the selection was reduced by the insistence that one rotor out of any three chosen had always to be one of rotors VI–VIII. This would prevent decryption using a non-naval rotor set but limited the overall number of variations to 276.

By late 1941 the *Kriegsmarine* was sufficiently concerned about U-boat cipher security to introduce a separate key network for Atlantic U-boats only. This network had the German codename *Triton*, and its intercepts became known at Bletchley Park as SHARK. In February 1942 a new 'four-rotor' Enigma machine was introduced on this network. This machine is widely known as the 'M4'. Although in the later part of the war M4 Enigmas were issued to U-boats as well as other vessels, the machine had the advantage that if the fourth rotor were set to a specific 'neutral' position then it encrypted and decrypted in exactly the same way as a normal M3 machine. This allowed M4-equipped vessels to communicate with those equipped only with M3. When the four-rotor M4 machines became fully operational for U-boats operating in the Atlantic in February 1942, the result for GC&CS was catastrophic. Bletchley Park was unable to read Atlantic

U-boat traffic for much of 1942, until a solution (aided by captured materials from a submarine) was found. However, when these boats operated in Arctic waters they continued to use their M4 machines as if they were M3s with the fourth rotor in the neutral position. The story of the so-called 'SHARK blackout' and how Bletchley Park overcame it is a fascinating one, but as it had little or no impact in the Arctic it will not be pursued here.

In 1939, GC&CS was already familiar with the Enigma I and M3 machines. They were not, in that sense, much of a secret. However, the security of the machines lay not in their physical construction but in the variety of ciphers that they could create. Each individual message was sent using a different key. This key was created by rearranging the various components of the machine, which in turn would produce a different encipherment. Some of these settings formed part of a key retained for twenty-four or forty-eight hours, while others were changed before each message was sent. The number of options available is known as the 'keyspace' and is often used as a measure of the security of a cipher system, as it is the number of possibilities an opponent would have to try in order to find the individual key used for any one message.

As has been described, a *Kriegsmarine* signaller had the choice of eight rotors, from which he would select three (including one from numbers VI–VIII) in any order to fit in the machine. The outer ring on each of these rotors was then moved to one of twenty-six positions. These were known as the 'inner settings' of the machine. The operator would then plug in the ten plugboard cables on the front of the machine and finally set the rotors to a starting position chosen for the message he was about to send. The last two choices were known as the 'outer settings'. There is some dispute about the possible number of available settings which would produce a different encryption, but the keyspace of M3 has been recently calculated as 103,325,660,891,587,134,000,000, or 103 thousand million million million.[25] Clearly a 'brute force attack', whereby keys would be tried one after another, would be impractical.

Each group of wireless users in the German armed forces would be issued with a different key to use to communicate with others on their radio network, and these were typically changed on a twenty-four-hour cycle. Settings for each key were typically issued on sheets providing settings for a month at a time, allowing users in different locations to set their machines to corresponding settings. At GC&CS the discovery of the settings behind each key, each day, was vital to the ability to read any messages sent during that twenty-four-hour period, and this was the task to which a huge proportion of Bletchley Park's resources were set.

Unlike the German army, who used Enigma only at divisional level and above, and the German air force, who similarly used a series of 'low-grade' encryption systems (i.e. worked by hand rather than machine), the German navy issued Enigma machines to all but its smallest vessels. However, again unlike the German army and air force, where Enigma keys proliferated, the German navy used a relatively small number of keys for most of their traffic for much of the war, only introducing larger numbers of keys in the second half of 1943.

In the first part of the war, the *Kriegsmarine* had only two Enigma keys in regular use. These were *Heimische Gewässer*, or 'Home Waters' (also codenamed '*Hydra*' by the Germans), used by vessels in the North Sea, Atlantic and Mediterranean, and *Ausserheimisch*, used by surface raiders and blockade runners further afield. The former, codenamed DOLPHIN at Bletchley Park, was a high-priority target for GC&CS. *Ausserheimisch* represented a lower priority and carried much less traffic, and as such it was never broken. A third key for use in the Mediterranean, known by the Germans as *Sued* and at Bletchley as PORPOISE, was introduced in April 1941. Famously, as has been described above, a fourth key, *Triton* (SHARK at Bletchley Park), was also introduced for Atlantic U-boat use, which switched to using four rotors in February 1942. In the last two years of the war, the German navy introduced a series of around a dozen additional local Enigma keys, but these were either rapidly broken or carried so little traffic as to not be worth attacking.

From May 1941 a second key was identified, used alongside *Hydra* (DOLPHIN) in home waters – *NEPTUN* (BARRACUDA), used for high-level fleet communications. Similarly, for important messages, the German navy used a procedure where messages would be enciphered on the normal daily key and then re-enciphered using a separate key known only to senior commanders. This system, known as *Offizier* ('officer-only'), presented a significantly more complex decryption challenge for Bletchley Park. As they were harder to break, these keys were given Bletchley Park codenames based on shellfish. The *Offizier* key of DOLPHIN was codenamed OYSTER.

The German navy typically changed its Enigma key settings every twenty-four hours, with the change taking place at midday. However, daily keys were 'paired': all machine settings were changed on the first day, but on the second day the inner settings (the rotor choices and *Ringstellung*, the settings of the outer tyres on the rotors) remained the same, and only the outer settings (the plugboard and the *Grunstellung*, or rotor start position) were altered.[26] This meant that if it were possible to break into a key at Bletchley Park on the first day, on the second day this could be achieved much more quickly. As we shall see, once reading of naval Enigma at GC&CS was eventually achieved, these periods of blindness followed by light, and delays on the first of each pair of days, were to have profound effects on the intelligence available to fight the battle at sea.

BREAKING DOLPHIN IN HUT 8

Given the extent to which the *Kriegsmarine* used Enigma, it was clear from the outset that being able to read traffic enciphered using this system would give the Royal Navy a decisive advantage in the conflict at sea. However, in 1939, as was described earlier, no German naval Enigma message traffic had ever been read at GC&CS. The situation with army and air force Enigma improved quite rapidly. These systems had been attacked by Polish codebreakers pre-war with significant success, and, using a technique based on Polish methods, GC&CS was able to start reading *Luftwaffe* traffic as early as January 1940. Simultaneously with the breaks achieved using these manual methods, a team at Bletchley Park was working on a partially mechanised approach. This 'Enigma Research Team' was headed by Dillwyn 'Dilly' Knox (Frank Birch's former flatmate from the First World War) and included Alan Turing, Peter Twinn and others. They were based in a cottage in Bletchley Park's former stable yard. The method derived by the team, and developed by Alan Turing in particular, was embodied in a series of machines known as 'Bombes'. Each of these was about the size of a large wardrobe, and by the end of the war over two hundred would be built for Bletchley Park in the UK. Another one hundred similar devices would be constructed in the US. These machines were the backbone of the Enigma-breaking effort for the remainder of the war. Given their importance, some explanation of their working process is required here.

In simple summary, the process was as follows. A message would be identified of which the deciphered content, the so-called plain text, could be guessed with reasonable certainty. The German armed forces sent any number of routine messages every day which often took stereo-typed forms. Once the senders and recipients had been identified, the likely contents of these messages could be guessed by the team at Bletchley Park with some reliability. A short section of one such message, often around twelve characters (a 'crib') was then compared in both enciphered and (guessed) plain-text forms. From this, a sequence of letter relationships could be postulated between the two texts. These relationships were then expressed in special notation, known as a 'menu'.

The menu then allowed a Bombe machine to be configured using wires and plugs to reflect the letter pairings previously identified. The machine itself was equipped with sets of three drums, each of which mimicked the enciphering effect of the rotors in an Enigma machine. Each set of drums on the Bombe was equivalent to the possible rotor positions in an Enigma at the point when each letter in the crib was enciphered. Starting with the input of one letter from the 'crib' and a postulated *Stecker* (plugboard) partner (reflecting one of the settings of the encrypting machine), the logical implications of this pairing and the series of other postulated letter pairs in the menu were tested electro-mechanically for each of the 17,576 possible rotor positions. One or more 'stops' might occur. This was when a combination of rotor order and positions arose on the machine which allowed an electrical current to pass along a path which obeyed all the logical relationships implied by the starting menu. This could occur when a correct setting was iden-tified but could also occur by chance. Each 'stop' was then tested for its logical consistency on a separate checking machine.

When a correct stop was encountered, the complete key settings of that particular message could be deduced. This allowed the daily rotor selection and order, plugboard and ring settings to be identified – the 'daily key'. These could then be applied to other messages sent using the same daily key. For army and air force traffic, this was all that was needed, as the individual message settings (the starting positions of each rotor for each message) were sent effectively *en clair* as part of the message text.

The process was still rather laborious. Each 'Bombe run' took about twelve minutes, but the plugging up of the machine to reflect the menu was a complex task, and each machine could typically test only three different rotor combinations in any one run. With sixty possible rotor combinations available to the Germans, this meant running the machine multiple times, or, in extremis, plugging up a series of machines with the same menu. Also, with multiple Enigma keys in play on any one day, there were multiple menus to test, all competing in priority. Although the Allies would end the war with over three hundred machines, there were never enough to test all keys, especially in the early years of the war. Only sixteen Bombes were in operation at the end of 1941, and by the end of 1942 the figure stood at fewer than fifty.[27]

Despite the complexities of the decryption process, Bletchley Park was able to break German air force Enigma to some degree every day from January 1940 until the end of the war. The naval Enigma, however, was another matter. There were three main added difficulties. The first was the larger number of rotors, meaning that instead of the sixty possible rotor combinations used by the army and air force, there were 276. This would require an impractical number of Bombes to test all the possibilities, so a method was needed for reducing the number of rotor orders to be tested.

The second problem was that, once the daily parts of any key had been determined (the rotor order, rotor ring settings and plugboard pairings), the starting positions of the individual rotors for each individual message still had to be worked out. As has been described, the army and air force signallers included this information in the preamble of the message, using only a basic encryption which was easily broken when the remainder of the daily key was known. The German navy, on the other hand, used a much more complex method of hiding these message settings. A procedure was used whereby the two three-character settings required for each message were first obtained from a pair of codebooks. This prevented the use of obvious or predictable settings which happened quite often during the army and air force procedure, where the operator himself could choose these settings. These characters were then divided into pairs and enciphered using a 'Bi-gram Table', where each pair of letters was substituted for a random pair of letters prescribed by the table. This meant that unless Bletchley Park could understand the workings of the Bi-gram Tables, obtaining a set of daily key settings using the Bombes would still leave the code-breakers blind to which one of 17,576 message settings (rotor starting positions) had been used for all messages apart from the single one used as a crib for the Bombe.

The third problem was that the German navy was acutely aware that D/F could be used to locate a ship if it transmitted a wireless message, so the shorter the message, the better, as this reduced the likelihood of a successful D/F fix. To shorten their messages, a series of codebooks were introduced which allowed a message which would be very long if written out fully to be compressed using a series of code letters and abbreviations into only a short stream of twenty or so characters. This had the disadvantage that, if Bletchley Park could obtain the short-signal codebooks, the compression would create ideal stereotyped message texts which could be used as cribs, but in the absence of the codebooks, cribs would be difficult, if not impossible, to create.

In order to confront these challenges, work on naval Enigma was taken over in early 1940 by a new section, the German Navy Enigma Processing and Decryption Section. The team were placed in a large newly built timber hut on the north side of the lake at Bletchley Park. This was the eighth hut built in the grounds of the park and was known as a consequence as 'Hut 8'. It was by this title that the section was almost universally known for the remainder of the war, while their original, longer title fell rapidly into disuse. The team in Hut 8 at the outset consisted of Alan Turing, Peter Twinn and two female assistants.[28] By August of that year, Hut 8 was employing thirty-two staff, making it almost as large as the German sub-section itself. At its peak in September

1944, Hut 8 would employ 147 staff.[29] Initially, its head was Alan Turing. Turing handed over to C.H.O'D. ('Hugh') Alexander in 1941, who in turn was replaced by A.P. Mahon in December 1944.[30] The Hut 8 organisation moved out of its hut and into Block D in February 1943 but retained its original wooden hut number as a permanent section title. To avoid confusion, the original Hut 8 was then re-numbered 18 and allocated for use by other sections.

The challenge faced by Hut 8 in the early days seemed enormous. However, Alan Turing remained optimistic. By the spring of 1940, the first Bombe machine had been delivered (in March), and although much work remained to make it effective, a solution to a large part of the Enigma problem was clearly in sight. This gave him both the background and the opportunity to attack the specific problem of naval Enigma. A.P. Mahon in the post-war 'History of Hut Eight', describes how, 'When Turing joined the organization [GC&CS] in 1939 no work was being done on Naval Enigma and he himself became interested in it "because no one else was doing anything about it and I could have it to myself".'[31]

The first of Turing's achievements was to develop a method for reducing the number of rotor choices which had to be tested for each key. This was solved by a process known as 'Banburismus', carried out initially on long sheets of stiff paper, acquired in Banbury (hence the name), printed with repeated vertical columns of alphabets. Turing had observed that if two random strings of letters are compared, the chances of the same letter appearing in the same position in each string is 1 in 26. However, because in real language some letters occur more frequently than others, if the same exercise is carried out with two stretches of real language, the repeat rate increases. He found that for naval German the rate was about 1 in 17. He postulated that if two messages were encrypted using the same Enigma settings, the cipher text would also have this 1 in 17 repeat, since if the same letter appeared at the same point in both messages, it would be encrypted as the same cipher letter. In Banburismus, the text of a message was punched into one of the special sheets by making holes in the alphabets corresponding to the letters of the cipher text. This allowed messages to be compared by overlaying them over a dark background and counting the matching holes. By applying a great deal of tedious statistical analysis to the results of this process, some of the rotors used for the messages could be determined, reducing the choices from 276 down to 90 or even 30. This allowed for a massive saving in the required Bombe runs to identify any one particular key, as only the rotor choices identified by Banburismus need be carried out.

The second technique Turing devised was for determining the starting positions of the rotors for individual messages if the rest of the daily key settings were known. As has been described, once the daily parts of a key were established, there still remained 17,576 possible rotor start positions for each message. Turing took advantage of the facilities of Hut 7 at Bletchley Park. This hut contained a suite of Hollerith tabulating machines. These were devices invented at the end of the nineteenth century which used holes punched in cards to perform a variety of data manipulation tasks very rapidly. The potential of Hollerith punch-card machines for codebreaking had been established during the First World War, and Bletchley Park would use the technology for a wide range of cryptanalytical tasks in the Second World War. In this case, Turing set them to a particular job. He knew that, since the Enigma machine had no numerical keys, numbers had to be written longhand in messages. Further, he hypothesised that the number 'one' – 'eins' in German – would occur frequently in naval traffic; he reckoned about 40 per cent of messages would contain the word.

The process for finding the message settings required using the daily key settings to create all 17,576 possible four-letter encipherments of 'eins'. The next step was to punch the cipher texts of the required messages onto punch-cards, in itself a long and tedious process for the women working the punches. A search could then be made using Hollerith machines of all the cipher texts to look for occurrences of any 1 of the 17,576 possible encrypted versions of 'eins'. This was clearly a task that was beyond the power of humans to do by hand but was relatively simple using the machines. If one of the four-letter groups forming one of the encryptions of 'eins' occurred in a message, the rotor position when that encryption occurred could be identified, and a count-back to the start of the message would give the starting rotor setting for the message. There was a degree of error, as letter combinations could occur by chance which did not represent '*eins*', but again, weeding these out was a task which could be accomplished in reasonable time. Thus, what was a hopeless task for a human could be carried out more quickly using Hollerith punch-card machines. 'Quickly' is a relative term here, as thousands of characters of cipher text had to be manually punched into cards, but it was a workable, if tedious, solution.

'PINCHING' AND CAPTURED DOCUMENTS

The real breakthrough with German naval Enigma came about, however, not via these ingenious intellectual solutions, but by a more old-fashioned method: the 'pinch'. It is a common misconception that the codebreaking achievements of Bletchley Park were the result of the application of mathematical and linguistic genius, without the assistance of outside factors. In fact this was far from the case, and many of the successful breaks of enemy code and cipher systems were achieved at least in part through the physical acquisition of cipher equipment, codebooks, key sheets and other cryptographic materials. Christopher Morris, a civilian codebreaker who worked on German hand-ciphers, made the point that 'most cryptographers were in fact ordinary if moderately intelligent people and, further, that a good deal of deciphering owed something to the fortuitous capture of some document such as a codebook or a set of tables, not to mention cribs. In other words [. . .] there was hardly such a thing as "pure" cryptography.'[32]

This was not a new idea. Such captures, or 'pinches', as they were colloquially known, had been an important feature of historic codebreaking, including the vital capture of German naval codebooks at the beginning of the First World War. Thus, Naval Section would have been alive to the potential of such captures. In the course of 1940 and 1941, a series of pinches occurred; some were accidental, others were the result of naval operations specifically designed to capture documents. For example, on 12 February 1940, the U-boat *U-33* was sunk in the Firth of Clyde by the minesweeper HMS *Gleaner*. When the surviving crew were brought aboard the British ship, one was found to have three out of the eight rotors for the naval Enigma machine in his pockets, having forgotten to dispose of them once he was in the water.

This was an important find for Bletchley Park, as the wiring of the three rotors specific to the navy was not yet known at Bletchley Park, and it turned out that, of the three recovered from the German sailor, two were the as yet unknown numbers VI and VII.[33] Rotor VIII was also acquired subsequently in August 1940.[34]

Similarly, on 26 April 1940, during the ill-fated British campaign in Norway, the Royal Navy destroyer HMS *Griffin* captured an armed trawler off the Norwegian coast. The vessel was flying Dutch colours and claimed to be the trawler *Polares*, but it became apparent that it was actually the Hamburg-built German trawler *Julius Pickenpack*, which had been taken into *Kriegsmarine* service and equipped with both guns and torpedoes. The crew of the trawler had thrown overboard a canvas bag with all their confidential papers, but this was successfully recovered and returned with the ship to the UK.[35] A number of documents were passed to Bletchley Park from *Polares*. These included Enigma settings for 23 and 24 April and plain-text of several messages from 25 and 26 of that month. Using these, Bletchley Park was able to break a few naval Enigma messages from 22 to 27 April. Unfortunately, the significance of the capture of *Polares* was not fully appreciated, and the ship was not systematically searched until after it had been thoroughly looted by its captors. Nor was the capture kept secret (which would have been vital if cryptological material had been recovered), and it was soon widely known in the Royal Navy.

A month later, on 31 May 1940, the U-boat *U-13* was sunk off Lowestoft by the sloop HMS *Weston*. As the wreck lay in relatively shallow water, a salvage dive was conducted, and a large box of documents was recovered and sent to Bletchley Park. The arrival of this material in Naval Section prompted Geoffrey Tandy, who was responsible for captured documents, to establish a formal library and catalogue for these items. The task was given to Valerie Travis (daughter of the Deputy Head of Bletchley Park, Edward Travis), and she would remain in charge of what would become the Naval Section Library (later renamed as Naval Section VI) for the remainder of the war. Inspired by the *U-13* materials, Tandy asked for any other captured documents in Naval Section to be handed over to him; however, he discovered that the cryptographers were reluctant to part with them, and so a physical search of the huts had to be made. This produced a number of documents, including those acquired from *Polares*. One of these, the *Allgemeines Funkspruch Buch* (a German codebook sometimes used to encrypt messages prior to Enigma encryption) had been recovered wet and had been stored with blotting paper between the pages. This had resulted in a thick growth of mould, which had to be washed off using surgical spirit. A total of 106 separate documents were catalogued initially, a figure which had risen to 130 by the end of 1940.[36]

Unfortunately, the initial captures of naval Enigma materials did not lead to sustained success against the traffic, and no further breaks were achieved during 1940. This led to several proposals to deliberately capture cipher documents rather than waiting for them to be found by chance. These proposals included the rather far-fetched Operation RUTHLESS, proposed by Ian Fleming in the NID, whereby a captured bomber would be deliberately crashed in the Channel in order to attract a German rescue vessel, which could then be boarded by the bomber crew, its crew killed and its codebooks stolen. A similar plan was developed to capture one of these *Flugsicherungsschiff* (air-rescue ships), the *Bernhard von Tschirschky*, which was known to carry both naval and air Enigma, using surface vessels. Neither project was ever carried out. The Channel proved to be a very poor place for such operations as it was under too close German observation both from shore and air.[37]

In early 1941, to assist with coordination between Naval Section at Bletchley Park and the NID at the Admiralty, a position was created for a liaison officer between the Admiralty and GC&CS. This post was held by Captain Jasper Haines, who would become a key player in later pinching operations. The next batch of captured documents to arrive at Bletchley Park were acquired on 4 March 1941, when, during a commando raid on the fish oil processing plants in the Lofoten Islands in northern Norway, another German armed trawler, the *Krebs*, was boarded and then sunk by the destroyer HMS *Somali*. Although the crew of the ship managed to burn or jettison much of their signals equipment and paperwork, a thorough search of the vessel produced additional documents including current bi-gram tables used for disguising the settings communicated in Enigma messages, and key tables for the month of February 1941.[38] This material arrived at

Bletchley Park on 12 March and allowed all traffic from February to be directly deciphered, and extrapolations from the captured keys allowed some unknown keys for April and May to be constructed and traffic from those months read as well.

The success of this work led members of Naval Section, including Harry Hinsley (of whom we will hear more later), to the idea that a deliberate pinch of further key sheets might be possible, targeting the German Enigma-equipped weather ships, which were stationed in the Norwegian Sea east of Iceland. This idea was discussed with Jasper Haines at the Admiralty, and he arranged for just such an operation to be carried out. On 7 May 1941, HMS *Somali*, with Haines on board, captured the weather ship *München*, recovering both the Enigma keys for June and a vital Weather Short Signal Book (*Wetterkurzschlüssel*) used in formatting messages prior to encryption. Just two days later, on 9 May 1941, further materials were captured by chance when the destroyer HMS *Bulldog* captured the surfaced German submarine *U-110* south of Iceland. On this occasion, the boarding party was able to completely strip the submarine of its signal books and equipment, including its Enigma machine. Some of the items collected duplicated those found on the *München*, but others, including the U-Boat Short Signal Book (*U-bootskurzsignalheft*), had not been seen before at Bletchley Park.[39] It was these short signal books, captured from the *München* and *U-110*, which would allow Hut 8 to understand the third decipherment problem described above, which was the system of message compression. With the books in hand, new cribs could be created which would allow further naval Enigma keys to be broken. A second weather ship was also attacked at the end of June. On 28 June 1941, HMS *Tartar* successfully captured and boarded the weather ship *Lauenburg*. This time, a member of Naval Section from Bletchley Park, Allon Bacon, was on board to assist with the search, a role he had adopted after being sent to Scapa Flow to collect the Enigma captured by HMS *Bulldog* back in May. Further Enigma keys, this time for the month of July, were recovered.[40]

The result of all these various captures was that by the middle of 1941 Hut 8 was able to develop a pretty complete understanding of naval Enigma. The capture of bi-gram tables, in particular, was vital, as these stayed in circulation for longer than the monthly key sheets, and while the key sheets had provided a quick route into the messages sent during the month to which they applied, a more permanent solution was required. Having the short signal books and the bi-gram tables in hand, combined with other techniques, meant that the capture of the monthly key sheets was no longer required, as the daily keys could be recovered by other methods. As a result, the Home Waters key (DOLPHIN at Bletchley Park) was broken continuously and more or less currently (that is, within a few hours or days of the message being intercepted) from mid-1941 until the end of the war. A.P. Mahon, who would later be Head of Hut 8, recorded in his history of the ID8G (the section at the Admiralty which dealt with Enigma traffic) that 'Operational Breaking of Dolphin (which at that time included Shark) started in earnest in August 1941 – at a time when not only had the previous two months' keys been captured and decoded, but also all Short Signal code books and indicator tables were in our hands.'[41]

The last active participation by Naval Section in pinching was as part of the simultaneous commando raids on the island of Vågsøy, in southern Norway near Trondheim (Operation ARCHERY) and on the Lofoten Islands in the north (Operation ANKLET) on 27 December 1941. On this occasion, pinches from German patrol vessels were considered a real possibility and plans were laid accordingly. Allon Bacon from Naval Section again joined the southern operation to supervise the collection of secret material. Both operations were equally successful from a cryptographic point of view. At Vågsøy, the armed trawler *Föhn* was forced ashore and boarded by a party from HMS *Onslow* including Bacon. He returned with two sacks of material, including a set of Enigma bi-gram tables found folded among the captain's clean shirts, and a set of Enigma rotors. HMS *Offa* was also able to chase down and capture another trawler, the *Donner*, and recover further cipher materials. Meanwhile, in the north, at Lofoten, the destroyer HMS *Ashanti* successfully captured the trawler *Geier*, collecting further bi-gram tables as well as other cipher material. All of this bounty was delivered to Naval Section and Hut 8 on 1 January 1942.

As a consequence of this success, attitudes towards pinching of cipher material became less enthusiastic in Naval Section, as it was feared that if the Germans identified that a pinch had taken place they would change their codes and ciphers as a consequence. The mood was now changing. As Birch put it: 'Indeed, as time went by, the desire for pinches gave place to apprehension lest even fortuitous capture should compromise the steadily favourable and self-perfecting sigint situation.'[42]

It was perhaps unfortunate that while Naval Section was becoming increasingly wary of further pinches, the NID was moving in the opposite direction. In October 1941, Commodore Lord Louis Mountbatten took over as Director of Combined Operations HQ, tasked by Churchill with carrying out commando raids of the western coast of Europe. Mountbatten was an enthusiastic advocate of this policy. The head of Naval Intelligence Admiral Godfrey and his assistant Commander Ian Fleming were equally keen to participate in these operations and saw in them an ideal opportunity for further pinches of cipher material. A meeting was held on 21 January 1942 between Naval Section at Bletchley Park, represented by Frank Birch, and Admiral Godfrey and the NID.[43] Unfortunately, this meeting did not lead to agreement, and as a result, the NID continued to plan pinch operations despite objections from Bletchley Park. It was during this period that the first steps were taken by combined operations to create (at the behest of Fleming) a specialist unit of commandos who could be used for pinch operations. This force would evolve into 30 Assault Unit in later 1942 and was slated to take part in the Dieppe landings (Operation JUBILEE) in August 1942, but, perhaps fortunately, never made it ashore during that operation.

The potential for disaster from ill-advised pinches was demonstrated in the raid carried out on Casquets lighthouse, near Alderney, on 2 September 1942. The raid was a complete success and the seven-man garrison of the lighthouse was taken prisoner with no loss to either side. However, several codebooks were stolen by the raiders, including the 'ABC' code used for communications between lighthouses. This led to the Germans changing that particular code, a minor setback in this case but evidence that a pinch of more significant material might lead to wholesale changes which Bletchley Park might not overcome.[44]

OTHER CODES AND CIPHERS

While Hut 8 broke naval Enigma, responsibility for non-Enigma German naval codebreaking remained with Naval Section. In this they were quite successful. The *Kriegsmarine* used a number of hand-ciphers and codes for lower-level communications or in situations when Enigma encryption was not suitable. The German navy used as many as twenty-seven hand-ciphers, the majority of which were read regularly by Bletchley Park. Important among these was the *Werftschlüssel*, a dock-yard hand-cipher used for communication with vessels in harbour. This was identified in April 1940 and was broken currently from May 1941, after capture of a copy of the codebook. The cipher was based on bi-gram substitution tables. Thirty-three thousand signals were read, equivalent to twenty-three per day right up to the end of the war.

Additional hand-ciphers attacked by Bletchley Park included *Schlüssel H*. This was used by merchant ships, but its complexity was not often balanced by the interest of the signal contents. *Reservehandverfahren* (*RHV*) was used when Enigma machines were broken or not trusted. It used a transposition 'cage'. It was broken through the capture of a code-book in June 1941 and continuously thereafter. Traffic amounted to 1,400 signals in total. As well as the information contained in the traffic itself, messages were often sent using dockyard cipher, while also being sent to other recipients encrypted with Enigma (for example, this was common with weather forecasts). These messages were therefore vital as 'cribs' – examples of known plain-text used in the Enigma decryption process.[45]

It was a coincidence, but probably a fortunate one, that Hut 8 became master of the *Kriegsmarine*'s Enigma systems in the summer of 1941 at the same time that the first Russian convoys were sailing into the Arctic. As a result, Naval Section at Bletchley Park was supplied with a steady flow of message decryptions on the Home Waters or DOLPHIN key for the remainder of the war. It was equally fortunate that when, in February 1942, the U-boats operating in the Atlantic switched to four-rotor SHARK, those in the Arctic persisted with the old three-rotor keys. This meant that GC&CS had good access to German naval messages throughout the Arctic campaign. Typically, the only messages which were not readable were those sent in other rarely used keys, or using the *Offizier* system of double-encryption.

This wealth of knowledge was also supported by reading of the *Luftwaffe* message traffic used in the Arctic. *Luftwaffe* signals fell into two types. Firstly, there were high-level communications between ground units and airfields. Much of this communication travelled by landline, but the German air force also made heavy use of wireless, and much of this traffic was encrypted with Enigma. For aircraft in the air and for lower-grade communications, the *Luftwaffe* also used a number of non-machine-based 'pencil-and-paper' codes and ciphers. These had also been identified and in many cases broken by Bletchley Park; however, these messages were often sent using relatively short-ranged VH/F (very high frequency) radio systems, which, while audible when the Germans were over the UK during the Battle of Britain, were harder to detect in the waters of the Arctic, far from UK listening stations. A system was developed whereby trained operators with suitable receivers would be placed aboard British warships specifically to intercept and interpret these signals. In the case of the Arctic convoys, these operators were placed on the ship carrying the Flag Officer commanding the shadowing cruiser force, the first sailing with PQ 16 in May 1942 (described in a later chapter). Kept abreast of the latest changes to German coding systems and communications procedures, these operators could give advanced warning of air attacks, sometimes when these attacks were as much as twenty minutes out. However, there was little a convoy could do to enhance its defensive readiness, anyway, so this information was not decisive in the protection of the convoys.[46]

The breaking of the ciphers was not the end of the story. Successful exploitation of this intelligence required the contents of these messages to be organised, digested and passed on to those best placed to make use of them. In turn, the information gained by SIGINT had to be combined with knowledge gathered from all the other sources of intelligence available to the Allied navies and applied to the current picture of friendly forces at sea. It is to this next phase of the intelligence process which we must now turn.

CHAPTER THREE

THE BIG PICTURE

HARRY HINSLEY

In the early hours of 1 September 1939, a young Cambridge undergraduate made his way towards the bridge over the river Rhine in the German city of Kehl. On the other side of the bridge was France, in the form of the city of Strasbourg. At the frontier check, the young man, Francis 'Harry' Hinsley, was relieved of all his remaining Reichsmarks and was given no Francs in return, leaving him penniless. As a result, Harry was forced to spend his first night in France sleeping on a park bench, before hitch-hiking to Switzerland and arranging travel home. Importantly, however, he had succeeded in escaping Nazi Germany on the very eve of the war, as the first *Panzers* crossed the border into Poland.

Harry was born in Birchills, Walsall. His father worked in the coal department of the Walsall Co-op. His mother, Emma, was a school caretaker. Despite these modest beginnings, Harry went to grammar school at Queen Mary's in Walsall and in 1937 won a scholarship to read history at St John's College, Cambridge. After two years he was awarded a First in part one of the History Tripos, and in the summer of 1939, as he had done the summer before, he went to stay with his girlfriend and her family in Koblenz. The difference was that during that second summer he was required to report weekly to the local police, although they seemed friendly, and particularly in August the tension seemed to ease and war seemed far away. However, at the end of the month the police visited the house and warned Hinsley to leave the country immediately. He left for France that night. This timely warning was to have a massive impact on Britain's SIGINT effort in the coming war.[1]

Hinsley returned to Cambridge as usual in October 1939 to complete his studies, but almost immediately he was asked to call on Martin Charlesworth, a Fellow of St John's but also a key Cambridge recruiter for GC&CS. The result was that in October 1939 Hinsley was, as he put it, 'pitchforked into Bletchley Park' and into the world of naval codebreaking and intelligence.[2] In the absence of any deciphered German naval messages, he was forced to study the patterns of the traffic and the external characteristics of the messages. However, this was not a hopeless task, and as Hinsley put it himself:

> By the end of 1939 I was the leading expert outside Germany on the wireless organisation of the German Navy. This may sound like an arrogant claim, but it does not amount to much. Nobody had known anything about that organisation at the outbreak of war, and on the other hand, until it expanded in preparation for the invasion of Norway in the spring of 1940, it remained so simple that little could be learnt from studying it. But its behaviour was one of the few sources of information about the German Navy.[3]

Hinsley's early efforts to communicate his new-found insights to the Admiralty were, as we shall see later, not entirely successful, but as the war progressed he would rise, despite his youth, to be a central figure in Bletchley Park's Naval Section, and indeed in all UK naval SIGINT. By 1941 he was Head of the German and Italian 'W/T Intelligence' sub-section of Naval Section (explained in more detail below), and by 1943 had acquired the somewhat nebulous title of Intelligence Staff Officer. The title reflected his involvement in, and importance to, all aspects of intelligence in the war at sea. His significance is characterised by messages sent between the Admiralty and the Home Fleet in late 1940. The latter queried some information, asking: 'What is your source?' The Admiralty sent a one-word reply: 'Hinsley'.[4]

OTHER KINDS OF SIGINT

As Harry Hinsley's early work demonstrated, it is a common misconception that if a coded message cannot be read it is otherwise useless. In fact, a significant amount of information can be gained from intercepting traffic, even if the ciphers used are impenetrable. The simple fact that two parties are communicating with each other is significant – rather like the use of telephone call logs in criminal investigations. In addition, the volume of 'calls' can also be monitored. Increases in message traffic are often a good indicator that operations of some kind are coming up, even if it is not known exactly what is going to happen. It was on these scraps of information that Naval Section at Bletchley Park was mostly forced to feed for nearly two years from the start of the war until the regular breaking of naval Enigma in summer 1941. Nor did the work stop then: external analysis of message traffic continued to provide vital information even after the majority of the message contents could be deciphered.

The process of analysing wireless messages was known as 'Wireless Telegraphy Intelligence', or 'W/TI'. It consisted of the analysis of the external characteristics of intercepted messages and the derivation of intelligence without recourse to reading the contents of the messages themselves. This included the frequencies used, times of day, call-signs, signal characteristics such as operator and transmitter identification, and importantly, of course, D/F, of which more is explained below. Collectively, the examination of these features of messages is commonly known today as 'traffic analysis', although this term was not widely used in Naval Section during the war. The purpose of this was two-fold. Firstly, it provided a rich source of intelligence in its own right, but secondly, once ciphers were being broken, it also allowed messages to be identified according to the particular key used, and helped in identifying 'cribs' – guesses at the likely content of the messages, which could in turn be used to assist the decryption process. Along with the rest of Naval Section, work on W/TI would grow as the war progressed, becoming the preserve of Naval Section V. This sub-section would eventually employ over one hundred staff, with teams involved with traffic analysis, decryption of call-signs and 'Communications

Intelligence', which concerned the understanding of enemy radio procedures and communications organisation.

A fundamental component of W/TI was D/F. Bletchley Park had access to a series of D/F stations around the UK and overseas. D/F stations in the UK extended from Wick in Scotland to Land's End and were supported by stations at Gibraltar, and latterly Iceland, the Azores, Freetown and Simonstown in South Africa. These stations would listen to wireless transmissions originating from enemy vessels and use specialist equipment to identify the direction, in the form of a compass bearing, from which the signal emanated. When several of these bearings had been established from different locations (ideally spaced far apart), the bearings could be plotted on a map to reveal the approximate location of the transmitting vessel. This technique was not new, having been used successfully in the First World War to locate both ships and German zeppelins (airships), but it was further developed after 1939.

Accurate D/F was a skilled art. It required the use of specialist gnomonic projection charts, which differed from normal Admiralty charts which used a Mercator projection to represent the curvature of the earth. The bearings could also be affected by atmospheric conditions and the nature of the equipment in use. Typically, an angular accuracy of plus or minus 3 degrees was achieved for each bearing, which meant that more than two were needed for a really good fix, as each would reduce the overall margin of error. It was estimated that with six good bearings a submarine could be located in the Atlantic to within around 25 miles. The D/F expert at the Admiralty was Lt Commander Peter Kemp. He was a former submariner who had lost a leg in a submarine accident in the 1920s. Kemp devised a plotting system whereby he fixed a suitable gnomonic chart to a board. He then drilled holes in the board at the location of each D/F station and marked the bearings from each station on scales around the edge of the board. A weighted string was threaded through each hole, allowing him to draw out the string to the edge of the board to indicate the line of each reported D/F bearing. Where the strings crossed on the chart gave him the position of the target vessel.[5]

A similar method was used in Naval Section at Bletchley Park. This was recalled by Wren Caroline Rowett:

> Standing on one side of the room not far from the wall chart was a small and rather ramshackle looking table on the surface of which was a projection of the same area as that on the wall chart. Round the edge were cuts calibrated to represent degrees and hanging round from the edge were strings to which were attached plumb weights at either end. Everybody took a hand at 'laying off' these reports which you did by hauling on an appropriate string and lodging it in the opposite appropriate edging slot, repeating the process for as many bearings as the transmission in hand had engendered. Ideally you needed at least three bearings to arrive at what was known as 'a fix', an area on the chart which was cross-hatched by the strings and within which your signal originator might lurk.[6]

In addition to D/F revealing where a target at sea might be, techniques were also available for identifying who it might be. Vessels at sea typically included call-signs in their messages as a means of identification of sender and recipient, but these were often encrypted. As well as Naval Section trying to understand the encryption of the call-signs, intelligence could also be gained from the characteristics of the wireless signal itself. Two key techniques were used. The first of these was known as 'TINA'. Any wireless operator using a Morse key to transmit a message will have a particular style, known as his or her 'fist', using different lengths for dots and dashes, gaps between words, etc. This is analogous to an accent when speaking. A skilled listener can quickly spot transmissions from a familiar operator. As well as being listened to directly, a Morse transmission can also be recorded on paper tape using a device known as an 'undulator'. This would allow closer analysis of the sender's fist by physically measuring the lengths of the letters on the tape. Thus, TINA would allow individual wireless operators on particular enemy ships to be identified and tracked.

A similar technique was known as 'Radio Fingerprinting'. This exploited the fact that all radio transmitters are slightly different due to tiny variations in their manufactured components. This means that the signal from each transmitter was slightly different, and, again, if the signal were recorded it could be analysed using an oscilloscope and the individual radio set identified. Even if the individual vessel could not be identified, the differences between signals from a U-boat, as opposed to a battleship or merchant vessel, could be discerned, allowing the type of target to be known, if not exactly which ship. These two technical methods were used to identify particular ships at sea, even when their messages were otherwise unreadable, and combined with D/F to provide a significant insight into the movements of hostile ships and submarines.

The difficulty with W/TI, even when it could be combined with some decryption, was that it relied heavily on inference. Someone who studied enemy messages from a particular group of stations would become familiar with their routines and 'patterns of life'. Changes in this were often subtle, and while the analyst might be concerned that something was happening, it was often a difficult task to persuade those in command of the fleets at sea that these feelings, or disturbances of the norm, could be used as the basis for operational decision-making. Equally, the absence of traffic – negative evidence which a Bletchley Park expert might find compelling – could be difficult to explain to those in charge. The effects of these problems will become apparent as the story of the Arctic convoys unfolds.

OTHER SOURCES OF INTELLIGENCE

Information derived from signals was not the only form of intelligence available to the Admiralty. Old-fashioned spying also played its part in completing the picture of German naval activity. This came via two routes. The first was through diplomatic connections, especially in neutral Sweden. The British naval attaché in Stockholm, Henry Denham, made it his business to maintain close contacts with his Swedish opposite numbers and with the Norwegian military attaché, Roscher Lund. These channels were able to provide information garnered from the Germans themselves, who had diplomatic and commercial links with neutral Sweden, and by more clandestine means. German landline communications between their various headquarters in Norway and their higher commanders in Germany passed through

Swedish territory. The Swedish intelligence service were not only tapping these lines but had also made significant progress in reading the various ciphers used for these messages, including the German navy Siemens T52 teleprinter cipher system. The Swedish government had to be extremely circumspect in sharing this information, as if it became public it would be a clear violation of their neutrality, but, nonetheless, naval intelligence was shared with Denham. Onward transmission of this intelligence from Sweden to London often took some time, but the material was nonetheless extremely useful on a strategic level.[7]

The second source of information was provided by coast-watching stations in Norway managed from the UK by the Secret Intelligence Service (SIS/MI6). These were small teams of Norwegians equipped with wireless sets, who braved not only the risk of capture by the Germans but also frequently extreme physical hardships from weather and isolation in order to keep watch at the entrances to harbours and fjords and report what they saw. In the summer of 1941, SIS had only one station in operation, 'Skylark B' in Trondheim, but this station was able, for example, in May 1941, to report on German destroyers which turned out to be escorts for the battleship *Bismarck*.[8] Further stations were established later in the year and were able, as we shall see later, to report on the movements of *Tirpitz* and other large surface units up and down the Norwegian coast. Around one hundred coast-watching stations were in operation at one time or another. Some lasted only a few weeks before they were withdrawn or compromised, while others lasted much longer; Station 'BETA' in Oslo remained in operation from 14 January 1942 to the end of the war. A historian of the intelligence war in Norway, Tony Insall, summed up their contribution: 'The reporting of SIS coast-watching stations was a very important supplement to Ultra, and regularly provided the first intelligence about German naval movements to be received in London. Its value cannot be overestimated.'[9]

Another source of direct observation of German activity was via air reconnaissance, and much information was acquired by the efforts of RAF photo-reconnaissance pilots in long-range Spitfires and Mosquitos flying over the fjords to establish the presence, or often, crucially, the absence, of German warships. Unfortunately, this source was dependent on good weather over the target, and many sorties were frustrated by poor visibility. As we shall see, often it was the job of analysts at Bletchley Park or the OIC to piece together fragmentary and often outdated information from all these sources as well as SIGINT in order to try and create a joined-up picture of what was happening in the Arctic.

SORTING THE DATA

Although, by the time the Arctic convoys began, Naval Section at Bletchley Park had begun to read German naval Enigma with some regularity, this created its own problems. Messages flooded in every day from a multitude of stations, referring to a multitude of different subjects. Gaining the maximum intelligence value from them, indeed in some cases making sense of them at all, required a prodigious effort of organisation and data capture. It was vital that all of the intelligence information contained within them be collated and stored in a fashion which made it available for future use. This is where the indexes and their compilers came in. All intelligence derived from messages – places, individuals, ships, items of equipment, etc. – would be logged in a series of card indexes in order that the information could be recovered and rapidly collated with data from other subsequent messages. Card indexes were compiled in a variety of sub-sections throughout Naval Section according to their various needs.

A wide variety of information was retained on the German navy and its activities. One example that survives in Bletchley Park archives is the index of torpedo stocks of German U-boats. This contains a card for each individual submarine, and a record of every reported torpedo firing, its effectiveness (target hit or missed) and the relevant intercept serial numbers. This provides striking evidence of the detail and granularity of information which Naval Section was able to assemble on the U-boat force. Margaret 'Peggy' Senior, a Foreign Office civilian in Naval Section, recalled compiling a very similar record:

> The thing that I look back on with pleasure is my U-boat log. I had the job of recording which U-boats were in action and I had a log

book, each boat had its own page with its number, its type (you wouldn't think that there were so many U-boats but there were), and the name of its Commandant. You then had to record what torpedoes or mines it had fired, did they hit the target and did they sink it and what stocks they had got left. So I knew quite a bit about the submarine war. You got quite interested in individual U-boats, for no reason at all, a particular number took your fancy and you sort of wanted to know how that got on, as far as I know the U-boat I followed, I can't remember its number now, survived, at least it may have been sunk after I left.[10]

Wren Gwen Acason was responsible for a similar task, in her case recording the signals sent by individual U-boats. Perhaps surprisingly, Gwen learned not only operational information but also snippets about the personal lives of the crews.

I was sent to Block A, the Naval Section, and discovered I was indexing signals from U-boats. We had to copy these signals onto little cards under the correct U-boat Number so that the intelligence people could come down and find out where these U-boats were. [. . .] I do remember one or two personal signals came in; maybe the commander of the U-boat was told that his wife had had a son, or the homes of members of the crew had been bombed. But mostly it was to do with positions, sightings and possible attacks.[11]

It is an interesting feature of U-boat Enigma traffic that the land headquarters of the fleet was keen to maintain morale by sending large quantities of personal messages and other news out to the submarines at sea. Reports of medal awards, promotions, births and the safety of crews' family members after air raids were all transmitted. No doubt it was felt that these outgoing messages, even if deciphered, offered no intelligence to the Allies, but in fact even reporting the birth of a son to the engineer of a U-boat revealed the simple fact that his boat was at sea – a piece of information which would be duly recorded in the Bletchley Park system.

A further problem also presented itself. Many deciphered messages referred to technical matters. Submarines would report defective parts, or on other occasions report the effectiveness of trials of new equipment. Many of the messages decrypted in Naval Section and elsewhere contained abbreviations and technical jargon. These terms were often incomprehensible to the Bletchley Park translators unless their specific meaning could be derived by looking at enemy technical manuals. It was therefore desirable to capture as many enemy instruction books, technical manuals, training aids, etc., as possible in order to be able to interpret this information. Many such manuals were captured during the pinch operations described earlier, in addition to the specifically cryptographical materials also recovered.

In addition, these terms then needed to be translated consistently into the equivalent English-language terms which would be understood by Naval Section's customers in the Admiralty. The Royal Navy had its own wide variety of abbreviations, acronyms and jargon which in many cases corresponded with those of the Axis forces. It was no use for a translator at Bletchley Park to understand a particular technical description if they did not in turn express it in the equivalent Royal Navy jargon. Therefore, Naval Section also needed to collect as many of the equivalent Allied manuals as possible to match the terms. This dual requirement for the collection and management of both captured documents and their Allied equivalents became the responsibility of Naval Section VI Technical Intelligence.

The function of Naval Section VI was to produce translations and equivalents of technical terms encountered in enemy messages and captured documents. Work began on this in earnest in May 1941, when a consistent flow of naval Enigma messages started to arrive in Naval Section. We heard in the last chapter how Geoffrey Tandy had established a captured documents library under the management of the daughter of the Deputy Head of Bletchley Park, Valerie Travis. In addition to the purely library function established the year before (storing German documents and making them available for consultation), it was decided by Tandy that an attempt should be made to index the documents which had been collected and to create a catalogue of technical terms and abbreviations and their English equivalents. Tandy expressed what was actually an extremely complex task in relatively simple terms:

> It was reasonably clear that a prime requirement was stability of translation; right if possible, but stable at all costs. The solution of the problem of stability was easy: continuous record in a properly referenced card index of the equivalents actually used. [. . .] It only remained to devise the means of persuading the translator to call attention to such words as held him up in any way [. . .]. This was achieved by the simple device of providing the translator with a green pencil and saying to him: If you will underline all tiresome words, they will be picked up and recorded for you.[12]

He went on to demonstrate the nature of the problem by reference to a cartoon in *Punch* which depicted an army instructor with a metal plate with a circular hole, and the caption '. . . and here we have a hole, which we call the aperture'.[13] A similar example was given of the fact that the German abbreviation 'Lw.' could either mean *Luftwaffe* (the German air force) or *Leberwurst* (liver sausage), depending on context.[14] Clearly, a rigorous system for dealing with these issues was required.

A second member of staff, Hazel Williams, was found to assist Valerie Travis in this task, but they were nonetheless almost immediately overwhelmed by the amount of material arising from Enigma intercepts. Each difficult term underlined by the message translators was written onto a 5 x 3-inch index card, with details of where it had occurred and likely suitable English equivalents. Initially, they were assisted by a captured book – a dictionary of useful terms in other languages issued to German officers for use in foreign ports.[15] A similar Royal Navy book, *General Signalling Instructions*, was also acquired. Subsequently, the project was given a boost when the capture of the submarine *U-570* in September 1941 provided the team with a complete set of U-boat technical manuals, explaining many of the more obscure parts of the submarine and its equipment.[16] As the war progressed, the team was expanded, and the indexing and translation task was separated into a sub-section apart from Miss Travis and her library cataloguing. In the end, however, it was not possible to keep up with the influx of both queries from translators and the indexing of captured documents, so it was decided that only the most important documents would be fully indexed.

The work of indexing captured documents and finding equivalents was time-consuming and, like so many tasks at Bletchley Park, potentially unrewarding to those carrying it out. This was captured by Dr Forster in his report on the history of the section, in which he singled out one of the translators, Dione Clementi, for his particular praise: 'Miss Clementi's remarkable qualities of character enabled her to continue for three years doing work she did not like, of whose ultimate value she was extremely doubtful, with admirable competence and tireless industry. Her upbringing as the daughter of a senior colonial civilian in the best traditions of that service was undoubtedly a factor in this achievement.'[17]

Much of the information collated in the indexes of Naval Section was of longer-term value, but there was also a requirement to monitor the state of the war at sea in as close to real time as possible. Often the contents of a message were rendered urgent or otherwise by the sender's position in relation to Allied forces. This could only be done by maintaining up-to-date maps, or 'plots', of the current situation at sea. This work was carried out both at the Admiralty and, later, in Naval Section at Bletchley Park itself, as it was found that it was impossible to decide which intelligence gained by Naval Section needed to be passed to the Admiralty urgently, without Bletchley Park's own understanding of current events.

Prior to the war, most of this information was gathered by the Admiralty from 'open source' (non-secret) material, such as the reports of the insurers Lloyd's of London, as well as lists published by shipping companies, news reports and watches kept on harbours by diplomats and attachés. After war broke out, it became necessary to use more clandestine means to obtain this information. They needed to know not only which ports ships had sailed from but exactly where they were (as far as possible) on the oceans of the world. This information was often derived, as described above, from D/F and W/TI, as well as from decrypts of naval messages.

The information was recorded on constantly updated 'plots' in the form of wall maps which were annotated with pins or markers to indicate the position of different vessels. A series of plots were maintained by the Admiralty, as well as at local commands including the Western Approaches Command in Liverpool, which managed convoy operations across the Atlantic. Once information on enemy shipping became available via ULTRA, the Admiralty created an additional set of 'secret plots' which recorded information from decrypts which could not be shared with the wider staff who were not indoctrinated into the work of Bletchley Park.

Naval Section itself rapidly established its own series of plots. It was found that by doing their own plotting, the teams in the section could better understand the situation out at sea, and this helped in the interpretation of the incoming messages. It also helped in the decryption process, as cribs could be developed from knowledge of the situation an enemy vessel might find itself in. This work was carried out in what became Naval Section IV. Initially, there were a series of separate plots for different functions. The 'submarine tracking room' had its own plot dedicated to the position of U-boats, and separate plots existed for enemy surface warships and Allied and neutral merchant ships. The plots of friendly shipping did not rely on intercepts; rather, they were updated based on a daily briefing message sent from the Admiralty at 8 a.m. which described the locations of all Allied vessels. Later in the war these plots were amalgamated onto one large master plot, as it was found to be easier to see all of the information in one place rather than tracking convoys on one plot and U-boats on another. Specific local plots were also created for particular operations. Prior to D-Day, Naval Section IV built a large-scale plot of the English Channel which allowed them to follow the thousands of Allied ships supporting the invasion, as well as any German ships which might be a threat to them.[18]

Both the plots at Bletchley Park and those in other naval establishments were updated and maintained by teams of Wrens. The Bletchley Park Oral History Project has recorded a number of these individuals, and collectively they give a detailed account of the work of the plotters. Wren Jean Tocher recalled:

> The whole wall was papered all round with the Plot, there was a chart of the world and we plotted all the British and Allied ships,

then the German and Italian ships and the Japanese ships in the Far East. We got Secret, Top Secret and Top Secret U – meaning Ultra – messages and every day we were hastily plotting all the convoys. We had a colour code, blue for cruisers, green for destroyers, purple for frigates and pink for corvettes and there were other pins which had a piece of white cardboard in the middle and on that we would put the number of the convoy and it had to be absolutely accurate and quick so that we could see, for instance, when a German code had been cracked, and you could see U-boats moving towards a convoy and would then send urgent messages to the RAF and Coastal Command. [. . .] We had a little tag for each vessel on to which we put the name – that's where Jane's Fighting Ships came in – the colour codes were used because the signals didn't mention whether a ship was a destroyer or sloop, so we used coloured pens to differentiate so that we knew exactly which ships had been sunk. There were little pins along the way, for each position as we got the signals through, with cotton threaded around them so we could see the pattern.[19]

As these Wrens were plotting the war at sea as it happened, they had a much clearer idea of the purpose and importance of their work than many of the staff at Bletchley Park involved in more obscure crypto-graphic tasks. Jean Tocher made this precise point: 'unlike some of the people on the machines, we did know exactly what we were doing and why we were doing it. Some at Bletchley Park didn't quite understand where what they were doing fitted into the big picture, but it was quite clear to us where it fitted in and we had to be fast and accurate. What we did mattered very much because people's lives were at stake.'[20]

Inevitably, this confronted the plotters with the harsh realities of the battle, as Wren Sheila Willson recalled:

The bit that I remember being the most worrying or difficult was plotting the British convoys leaving to take supplies to Russia in the most appalling weather. They went fortnightly in the most dreadful conditions and they never came back intact. I did have a very strong feeling attached to moving that convoy towards Murmansk. Added to this was that the people in the neighbouring room would be plotting U-boats. Also there were very often fatalities which made quite an impact on me. It means that if I ever see the Marines [*sic*] in their white hats parading at the Cenotaph I always think of their bravery and how courageous they were.[21]

We will hear more of the events the WRNS plotters of Naval Section were party to in later chapters.

DELIVERING TO CUSTOMERS

The perennial question for any intelligence agency is how the information it has accrued can be passed to those able to take advantage of it, while at the same time preserving the secrecy of the sources. There is a further problem with specialist intelligence (such as SIGINT) of making it intelligible to the recipients and, where large volumes of material are concerned, separating the wheat from the chaff and passing on only what is useful and relevant. These problems dogged GC&CS throughout the war, and Naval Section was no exception. In order to understand the role played by SIGINT in the Arctic, it is also necessary to understand the relationship between Bletchley Park and the Admiralty, a relationship which was not without its problems.

The underlying issue was the perception of the role of GC&CS. In the eyes of the Admiralty, at least early in the war, GC&CS existed only for the purposes of cryptanalysis. Their job was to break codes and provide plain-text copies of enemy signals, and that was it. On the other hand, it was quickly apparent to the members of Naval Section that their role was much wider, encompassing all aspects of communications intelligence. Solving this division of responsibility was at times a painful process. By 1941 the question had in large part been resolved, but the resulting arrangements would impact on the flow of naval intelligence from 1941 onwards and so are important to an understanding of the convoy battles.

The Admiralty had its own intelligence section in the form of the NID, created in 1912. It was run by the Director of Naval Intelligence, who was typically a rear admiral. In 1939 the job was in the hands of

Rear Admiral John Godfrey, who was in turn replaced in 1942 by Edmund Rushbrooke. During the First World War, naval codebreaking had taken place within the NID in the famous Room 40, but that organisation had been moved out of the Admiralty to become part of GC&CS in 1919. The Admiralty had always assumed that this was a temporary measure, as naval SIGINT should only be the concern of GC&CS during peacetime, and that in the event of war all Naval Section's activities would revert to the Admiralty and be continued 'in house'. This approach was formally agreed in 1927, but in 1932 was once more relaxed so that the transfer away from GC&CS would not necessarily be automatic.[22] From 1934, study of Italian naval communications grew in importance and occupied eighteen staff in Naval Section. During the Italian–Abyssinian crisis of 1935, GC&CS was able to follow Italian naval movements almost completely using a mix of D/F, traffic analysis and cryptanalysis.[23] Perhaps in light of this experience, in 1936 Admiral Sir William James, Deputy Chief of Naval Staff, advocated the creation at the Admiralty of a joined-up intelligence section which, unlike Room 40 in the First World War, would not just do cryptography but would also have access to D/F, human intelligence (HUMINT, i.e. spies), friendly ship reports, etc., and thus could work as well with no decryption of enemy messages as with 100 per cent decryption.[24]

This was the genesis of NID 8, which was created in June 1937 and had as one of its founder members Paymaster Commander Norman Denning. This organisation, joined in November 1937 by DSD 9, the 'Enemy Wireless Section' run by Commander Humphrey Sandwith (and three clerks), would become the OIC.[25] We will have cause to hear much more of the OIC later. A tension thus existed between GC&CS and NID 8 over areas of responsibility and who would do what in the event of a war. During the Munich crisis, effective operations at the Admiralty's newly established OIC broke down due to lack of staff and suitable teleprinter links to the Y stations responsible for intercepting traffic, and thus it had to rely entirely on intelligence generated by Naval Section at Bletchley Park.[26]

Due to the apparent impenetrability of Enigma, German naval codes were not studied in any quantity until May 1938, when, as was outlined earlier, a section of two staff was established in GC&CS Naval Section for that purpose.[27] In addition to the cryptographers, there was a team of three Royal Navy personnel and two civilians doing 'W/T operational intelligence' (i.e. D/F, traffic analysis (T/A), etc.). This team were successful in following all German movements in Spanish waters during the Spanish Civil War. Unfortunately, the same desire in the Admiralty for these operations to be conducted at the OIC led to the creation in August 1938 of ID8G (not to be confused with the similarly named NID 8). This section was established in Room 13 of the Admiralty basement and absorbed all but two of the German sub-section staff from Naval Section at GC&CS.[28] This remained the situation when GC&CS moved to Bletchley in August–September 1939 – hence the German Naval sub-section consisting of only two souls when Frank Birch arrived on 5 September 1939.

Given that in the early part of the war German naval Enigma traffic was unreadable, W/TI and other external analyses of traffic provided the only source of intelligence on German naval activity. This was the work that occupied Harry Hinsley in the autumn of 1939. However, he was not the only one engaged in this task. While Naval Section was carrying out its own analysis of enemy traffic, often focused on longer-term intelligence such as identifying enemy orders-of-battle and communications networks, the team at the Admiralty in ID8G were responsible for what was known as 'current W/TI'. This was the short-term identification of where enemy ships and submarines actually were at any time. Since this work was not considered to be 'cryptological', the Admiralty saw it as the preserve of the NID rather than of GC&CS, and so work on this was reserved for the OIC in London rather than Bletchley Park.

The consequences of this became painfully apparent in June 1940. As the unsuccessful Allied defence of Norway was coming to an end, the *Kriegsmarine* redeployed the battleships *Scharnhorst* and *Gneisenau* from Kiel to the Norwegian coast. This movement was hinted at in message traffic, and W/TI analysis was carried out at Bletchley Park by Harry Hinsley. Unfortunately, at that time his relationship with the OIC at the Admiralty was tentative at best, as he later described: 'In keeping with the scarcity of intelligence, communication with the Admiralty was distinctly primitive. I used a direct telephone line which

I had to activate by turning a handle energetically before speaking. On this I spoke, a disembodied voice, to people who had never met me [. . .] They rarely took the initiative in turning the handle to speak to me, and they showed little interest in what I said to them.'[29] Hinsley passed his conclusions about the German battleships to the OIC, and their reception was recorded by Patrick Beesly of the OIC: 'Hinsley's study of German W/T traffic had persuaded him that heavy ships were probably at sea. He spoke direct to Clayton and Denning [the heads of the OIC] but his studies were still very tentative and his conclusions could not be confirmed from other sources. W/T intelligence on its own was no more than a straw in the wind [. . .] and in the end it was again decided to take no action.'[30]

The fleet at sea was not informed of the possible presence of two German battleships in the North Sea. As a result, the aircraft carrier HMS *Glorious* and its two destroyer escorts were surprised and sunk by the German ships on 8 June, at a cost of 1,519 British lives. So fast was the sinking that the first the Admiralty knew of the battle was when it was reported in a German news broadcast.[31]

Hinsley was sanguine about the whole affair. 'Looking back, I sympathise with the OIC. It must have seemed to them that GC&CS was intruding by watching enemy wireless traffic which was an Admiralty responsibility. I was a young civilian who, as they correctly assumed, knew nothing about navies.'[32]

The Admiralty was quick to rectify matters. Hinsley was immediately invited to spend a month with the Home Fleet at Scapa, including spending time with the C-in-C Admiral Tovey. His wind-up telephone was also replaced with a proper scrambler system. By the end of 1940, it was appreciated at the Admiralty that this divided system was not effective, and on 15 November current W/TI was returned to the control of Naval Section at Bletchley Park. Bletchley Park continued to share its results with its main customer, the OIC, in the form of twice daily 'Y reports', which provided W/TI intelligence. It had, however, taken a disaster at sea to resolve the relationship between Bletchley Park and the OIC.

The relationship would change again as Hut 8 at Bletchley Park began to read naval Enigma regularly in the second half of 1941. After a relatively slow start, much of German naval Enigma was read currently from the start of June 1941. By the end of 1942 four-rotor Enigma was under attack, and it would be readily readable by mid-1943. The separate key used by the *Kriegsmarine* in the Mediterranean was also broken in the summer of 1942. This led Frank Birch to observe in his history of Naval SIGINT: 'Thereafter, in spite of the multiplication of keys and intensification of other enemy security measures, the cream of operational Italian, and virtually the whole of German, naval W/T traffic remained continuously and currently – or near-currently – available to the Allies until the respective defeats of the enemy.'[33] The only gaps in this coverage were caused by the famous 'SHARK blackout' during 1942, when four-rotor U-boat Enigma was introduced in the Atlantic.

After they had been deciphered by Hut 8, naval Enigma messages were passed to Naval Section for translation and forwarding to the Admiralty. This traffic was handled by a team initially known as the 'Z Watch'. The term 'Z Watch' probably originates with the use of the letter Z to distinguish decrypts passed to the Admiralty. Unlike in Hut 3, where army and air force messages forwarded to customers were routinely known as 'ULTRA', this term was used more narrowly by Naval Section, and forwarded messages were more often known as 'Z traffic'. Patrick Beesly in the OIC described this:

> The word Ultra has now come to be used in a generic sense for all information available to the British in the last war derived from cryptanalysis, whatever the nation or service of origin and whatever form it took. This usage is incorrect and in the Navy, at least, it was only applied to outgoing signals and documents as a security grading and the actual information itself was always referred to as 'special Intelligence' or 'Z' because this letter was used as a prefix in the telex messages from B.P.[34]

Thus, messages sent from Bletchley Park to the OIC were 'Z traffic', while messages re-enciphered and sent to commanders at sea became 'ULTRA'. Alec Dakin was a member of the Z Watch, after being recruited from Oxford University, where he was studying Egyptology, in April 1940. He described a twenty-four-hour watch system staffed by three shifts of three people. His own consisted of himself, Charles Leech, a former business 'troubleshooter', and Gordon Priest, a young German scholar. The second consisted of Eric Turner, a Greek papyrologist, Anne Toulmin, a German-speaking Wren, and Leonard Forster, formerly a professor of German at Cambridge. The last was formed of Walter Ettinghausen, a German Jew who had lectured in medieval German at Oxford, his younger brother Ernest, and Thelma Ziman, a Wren from South Africa.[35] We will hear more from these individuals later in our story.

In the early days, Dakin described messages arriving in bundles from Hut 8 in a wire basket. These consisted of the raw decrypt, pasted in paper strips on the back of the original intercept. The messages would be sorted for urgency by the 'sorter' (No. 2 of the watch), who would then pass them to the No. 3, who would carry out a process known as 'emendation'. This involved expanding abbreviations, removing garbled sections and producing a clean plain-text of the message in the original language, with the words separated from the four-letter groups of the intercept into normal word-lengths. This text would be stapled to the message form and passed to the No. 1 of the watch, who was responsible for producing a formal English translation. The message might also be further edited to make it more readable to the customer, or more often to disguise the original text and mask the source of the message. The message would then be given a serial number, prefixed 'ZTP' ('Z Teleprint'), or latterly 'ZTPG' (German) or 'ZTPI' (Italian), and passed to teleprinter operators provided by the Womens' Auxiliary Air Force (WAAF), who would forward it to the Admiralty with the initials of the No. 1 of the watch appended at the bottom. Dakin recalled that while a steady flow of decrypts did not start until May 1941, the first teleprint to the Admiralty 'ZTP/1' was sent at 11.31 a.m. GMT on 12 March 1941 and carried the initials of C.T. Carr, who would go on to be Professor of German at St Andrews University.[36] By the beginning of June 1941, the first thousand ZTPs had been sent and the team had expanded. By 1944 each shift of the watch had nine members, and they were supported by twenty-one teleprinter operators (seven on each watch).

For the remainder of the war, in theory all decryptions of German messages were sent verbatim from Naval Section to the OIC at the Admiralty. However, Birch pointed out that this was largely a 'pious fiction', as actually Naval Section sent only about 50 per cent of high-grade and 1 per cent of low-grade traffic, and translations were 'anything but literal'. This was because much of the traffic was either dummy, of very low intelligence value or so garbled during transmission and interception as to be unreadable.[37] Birch recognised the impossibility of separating cryptanalysis and SIGINT. Not only would the crypt-analysts be hindered by being denied the vital context of the traffic they were examining, but the raw decrypts, if passed on without explana-tion, would be incomprehensible to their recipients at the Admiralty. Birch explained how the supply of raw data straight from the cryptog-raphers would often be useless. As he put it, the Admiralty 'would have been overwhelmed with ullage and stumped by the apparent gibberish of enemy signalese'.[38]

Birch's assessment was based on the view that raw data could not be used for intelligence analysis in any operational environment unless it made sense. To that end, 'emendation' of text as well as translation was required to fill in gaps, along with the coordination of other relevant data obtained from other sources being deciphered at the Park. Birch also recognised the problem that traffic was intercepted from multiple sources, and that no single mind oversaw the nature of the material that was being sent to the Admiralty; therefore, it could arrive from different sections in different forms. He made it his goal to make sure that all the material emanating from Naval Section was consistent in form and quality. In this regard, his vision and oversight were crucial to the success of Naval Section. As a result, part of the role of the watch was to filter out those messages which would essentially only waste the OIC's time, and only forward the material which was of operational importance. There were also messages which would serve to improve Naval Section's background knowledge of the German navy, and so would be passed to the indexers, but had nothing to offer of immediate tactical importance so were not passed on as Z messages.

In terms of the volume of traffic handled by Naval Section, Birch suggests that on average the section was handling over 1,000 decrypted messages per day.[39] His history also provides an overall count of messages forwarded to customers either at the Admiralty or elsewhere. These numbers are also reproduced (with minor differences) in a separate document, 'Notes for Naval Section Output', available in The National Archives.[40] Nearly 750,000 decrypts were forwarded by Naval Section during the war. Of these, 632,821 (85 per cent) were sent as 'T/P' or teleprint messages in various series. The remainder formed part of type-script reports sent by bag. The total number of German messages for the whole war was 530,138 'machine' (i.e., Enigma) messages and 20,752 hand-cipher messages. The 'Notes' record that the peak of production was April to June 1944, when an average of 18,100 German Enigma messages were issued each month. Birch also provided an esti-mated breakdown of the proportion of decrypted messages which were actually issued, as opposed to those which were deemed too corrupt or too uninteresting to send on. In addition to the roughly 750,000 issued messages, a further 400,000 were emended but never issued. On top of that, around 1 million messages were found on decryption either to be dummy traffic or weather information and were not emended. As a result, Birch estimated that the total number of messages handled by Naval Section between 1939 and 1945 'was probably well over 2,000,000'.[41]

For some messages, however, this was not the end of the journey. We have seen in an earlier chapter how the OIC and the Admiralty were in a position to communicate with ships at sea to intervene directly in ongoing operations; indeed, this was common Admiralty practice. A system therefore existed to pass on SIGINT to commanders at sea as ULTRA. The messages would be re-enciphered, typically using a highly secure 'one-time-pad' system, and forwarded by wireless. However, only officers of Flag rank were permitted to be indoctrinated into the ULTRA secret. This meant that the source intelligence could be shared with Admiral Tovey as C-in-C Home Fleet, and sometimes with the commanders of smaller forces such as the leaders of the shadowing cruiser forces in the Arctic. For example, at the time of PQ 17, Rear Admiral Louis Hamilton aboard HMS *London* commanded 1st Cruiser Squadron. As a Flag Officer, Hamilton was also indoctrinated into ULTRA and could receive material from Bletchley Park while at sea.

Those of more junior rank, however, such as close escort commanders and convoy commodores, were not permitted to see this material; they had to receive the information in a veiled or generalised form, or be simply told what to do by direct orders without any explanation.

This partial information-sharing was a recipe for miscommunication and confusion. As the next chapters will reveal, the lengthy chain from intercepted message to action at sea was not always effective. A variety of situations might result: the Admiralty might share intelligence with the C-in-C Home Fleet and allow him discretion on how to act, they might share the intelligence but accompany it with instructions, or they might simply instruct him to act. In the worst case, they might expect him to use his own judgement, assuming he understood a situation for which the relevant intelligence had not in fact been shared. All of these situations would arise in the Arctic, and the outcome for the convoys was not always rosy.

THE OTHER SIDE OF THE HILL

Before leaving the question of codebreaking and the delivery of SIGINT, it would be remiss not to consider what was happening, in the words of the Duke of Wellington, 'on the other side of the hill', or, in this case, the other side of the North Sea. A number of symmetries in the assets and capabilities of the two sides in the Arctic have already been described. Another lay in the mutual SIGINT capabilities of the belligerents. Not only were the British reading German signals, but the Germans were also reading British ones, at least for the first part of the campaign.

In 1978, historian David Kahn observed: 'If one man in German intelligence ever held the keys to victory in World War II, it was Wilhelm Tranow.'[42] In 1914, as a twenty-three-year-old radio operator, Tranow was on duty in the radio room of the German battleship SMS *Pommern* when an encrypted signal was received from the cruiser *Breslau*. Tranow re-transmitted the message, still enciphered, to fleet command as per routine, only to receive the reply that the message was incomprehensible. As he was interested in codes but not otherwise occupied, Tranow set about trying to break the message without access to the original codebooks. After two hours he had succeeded, and he forwarded a plain-text version to his superiors. Their response was perhaps predictable for the navies of the early twentieth century; he was reprimanded and told not to poke his nose into matters which did not concern him. No changes were made to *Kaiserliche Marine* codes as a result.[43]

Soon, however, Tranow had the opportunity to transfer to the cryptographic department of the *Nachrichten-Abteilung* (German Naval Intelligence Service) at Neumünster, north of Hamburg. There he spent the remainder of the First World War solving the British Royal Navy three-letter code. At the end of the First World War, the German navy scuttled most of its modern ships to avoid them falling into Allied hands. The subsequent Treaty of Versailles limited Germany to a tiny navy of 15,000 men and only eight antiquated battleships. Despite the treaty restrictions, on 28 April 1919 a new Radio Monitoring Service (*Funkhorchdienst*) was created for the *Reichsmarine* in Berlin. To avoid the manpower restrictions on naval personnel, this was staffed by civilians, of whom there were a grand total of eight. Tranow had not yet been demobbed when he was asked to stay on as one of the staff of this new codebreaking unit. There were only three cryptographers: Tranow, dealing with English systems, Lothar Franke, dealing with French, and Paul August, dealing with Italian.[44]

Tranow immediately set about attacking British codes and ciphers, and within a year he was able to read messages in the UK Government Telegraph Code which dealt with Royal Navy activity in China. He also attacked several French navy systems. In 1929 the unit acquired a naval officer as its head, but at the same time, in order to save money on staff allowances, the team was moved from Berlin to Kiel. Around this time, also, the unit was identified by the name it would carry through the Second World War: the 'Observation Service', or *Beobachtungsdienst*, typically abbreviated to *B-Dienst*. After the rise of the Nazi Party in the 1930s, the *B-Dienst* returned to Berlin as part of the new *Kriegsmarine*, and while still only twenty-strong, plans were made to expand the staff to 200.[45]

In 1935 Hitler forbade further attacks on British codes and ciphers, believing naively that he could achieve a rapprochement with the UK, and ordered codebreaking efforts to be focused on France. Tranow thought this a rash decision, arguing: 'I don't want to delve into high policy, but I want to say one thing: You know the English report their worldwide ship movements through these codes. Suppose their Mediterranean Fleet pours through the Straits of Gibraltar, and moves in to the Atlantic, or the Channel or even into the North Sea. Don't you want to know this in advance?'[46] The *Kriegsmarine* relented, and Tranow was allowed to continue his work.

The 1930s were a particularly fruitful period for him. In 1932 he had broken enough of a Royal Navy four-digit code then in use to follow a convoy exercise in the Atlantic, tracking the location of each individual ship.

In 1934 the Royal Navy introduced two new systems. These were:

Naval Cypher No. 1

This consisted of a code group book, providing the required words and phrases for naval communication as four-digit numbers. Once a message had been created using the four-digit groups, this was re-enciphered (or in the language of the day 'super-enciphered') by adding a series of random four-digit numbers taken from a second book to the individual number groups in the message. These 'additives' were selected from tables of 5,000 number groups. Different parts of the navy re-enciphered their messages using different additive tables. Five were in use: the Commander-in-Chief's Table, a Flag Officers' Table, a General Table held by all ships below destroyers, Small Ships' Tables and China Gunboats' Tables.

Naval Code (Administrative Code)

This had a five-digit code group book and was used for communications to merchant shipping, i.e., convoys. This was often used without any re-encipherment for messages considered of low security.

Tranow began his attack on the Naval Code, as its lack of re-encipherment made it vulnerable. This was assisted by the fact that merchant ships frequently used it to report movements which could be compared with publicly available information such as Lloyd's List, or reported by Germany's network of spies and attachés in ports around the world. By late 1935 the *B-Dienst* had a fairly complete command of the Naval Code, but the Naval Cypher was proving difficult. Fortunately for Tranow's team, the Royal Navy then made a significant cryptographic blunder. Messages began to be sent in the five-digit Naval Code, but re-enciphered using the four-digit additive books of the Naval Cypher. Armed with the meanings of all the five-digit code groups, it was a relatively simple task for the *B-Dienst* to strip off the additive groups from these messages and reconstruct the additive books themselves, before applying these to the messages sent using the other four-digit Naval Cypher. By 1937 the Germans could read a significant proportion of the Royal Navy's messages with some ease.[47]

Progress was interrupted in August 1939, when the Royal Navy introduced new additive tables for both Commander-in-Chief and Flag Officer traffic on the Naval Cypher; however, around 30 per cent of Naval Code traffic was still accessible. Some Naval Cypher was also read using the additive tables used by submarines. On the day the war started, the *B-Dienst* were well aware of British merchant ship movements in the seas off Germany. On 11 September 1939, they read a message that informed them of a convoy assembling off the coast of the Bristol Channel and despatched U-boat *U-31*, which sank the SS *Aviemore* south-west of Ireland.

In August 1940, Naval Cypher No. 1 was replaced by Naval Cypher No. 2, along with new additive books. The Naval Code was also revised to use four-digit groups. One result of this was that it made all messages externally identical, as all now used four-digit groups. The *B-Dienst* attacked the new systems, and, by the start of 1941, over 700 ship names and 1,200 other vocabulary words had been identified for Naval Cypher No. 2. Despite various changes in additives and procedures, the Germans were able to develop their understanding of Naval Cypher No. 2 to levels equal to that of its predecessor. This continued until Naval Cypher No. 2 was replaced by Naval Cypher No. 4 on 1 January 1942. Within the *B-Dienst*, these different systems were given codenames based on German cities. The Naval Cyphers were *COLOGNE* and Naval code was *MUNICH*.

Of particular relevance to the Arctic convoys was the German breaking of Naval Cypher No. 3 (codenamed 'Frankfurt'). This was a four-digit codebook with additive tables introduced in June 1941 for intercommunication between the Royal, US and Canadian navies when on convoy duty. The *B-Dienst* had reconstructed this codebook by February 1942. Apart from a brief hiatus in winter 1942–1943, they read large volumes of traffic up to June 1943. At times, up to 80 per cent of intercepted traffic was successfully broken, including the daily Admiralty estimates of known U-boat positions. By unfortunate coincidence, this was the same period when GC&CS was unable to read four-rotor U-boat Enigma messages in the Atlantic, the contents of which, when broken at the end of 1942, were found to reveal information pointing to the compromise of the Allied code. In addition to the systems used by naval vessels, the merchant ships in the convoys also used two codes: the Merchant Navy Code, introduced in January 1940, and its successor, the Merchant Ships Code, introduced in April 1942. Both of these were read without much difficulty by the *B-Dienst*. The latter code was compromised before it began by the capture of a codebook from an Allied merchant ship four weeks before the code even came into operation.[48]

The *B-Dienst* made its discoveries available to senior commands within the German navy and air force, including those in Norway dealing with Arctic convoys. The information was disseminated in a weekly report. This included 'B-reports', which were based on unencrypted information such as D/F, traffic analysis and the reading of unenciphered messages, and 'X-B-reports', which contained material specifically derived from high-grade decrypts. A combination of traffic analysis and D/F, as well as the regular routine adopted by the Allies for the frequency and routing of convoys, meant that the *B-Dienst* had a thorough understanding of the convoy system and was confident at any time of which convoys were at sea and their rough positions. This extended to a familiarity with the numbering and route coding of individual convoys. This allowed U-boat groups to be directed into the path of a convoy.[49] It was this kind of knowledge which also allowed the German navy to plan in advance deliberate operations against Arctic convoys.

German success against Allied codes would diminish in 1943 after the introduction on 1 June of Naval Cypher No. 5, which included a number of security improvements. The work of the *B-Dienst* was also significantly interrupted when their offices on the Tirpitzufer in Berlin were bombed in December 1943. The bombing destroyed large parts of *B-Dienst* records, markedly reducing their operational efficiency and forcing them to move to the town of Sengwarden, located about 50km north-east of Berlin. Tranow would continue to attack Allied ciphers until January 1945, but his early successes would not be repeated. Nonetheless, it should be remembered that for at least the first two years of the Arctic convoys, the codebreaking was not all one way.

Unfortunately for the Germans, all of Tranow's and the *B-Dienst*'s efforts were undermined by a much larger cryptological failure on the part of the *Kriegsmarine*. This was their failure to appreciate the extent of the Allied penetration of their own systems, and of course naval Enigma in particular. Faith in Enigma was not always universal. Admiral Dönitz himself was concerned that the system used too few keys and was too widely distributed to be fully secure. As early as April 1941 (before GC&CS had achieved regular breaks) he pressed for a separate key for his Atlantic U-boats, separate from the wider run of Home Waters traffic. His suspicions were heightened in September 1941 when the British submarine HMS *Clyde* appeared unexpectedly to disrupt a U-boat rendezvous off the Cape Verde islands. The U-boat command *Befehlshaber der Unterseeboote* (*BdU*) war diary reported these suspicions: 'Either our ciphers have been compromised or it is a case of leakage. A British submarine does not appear by chance in such a remote part of the ocean. The Naval staff is requested to take the necessary measures to safeguard the cipher system.'[50]

Dönitz was right, in that *Clyde* had indeed been guided by Enigma decrypts, but the subsequent enquiry by Rear Admiral Maertens, head of the signals service, concluded:

In the last few weeks there has been no evidence of leakage either through cipher material which we previously lost, or through espionage. But for operational security it seems important to make every effort to restrict the circle of personnel having access to secret material, and thereby reduce the chances of betrayal. The more important ciphers do not seem to have been compromised, despite their heavy use and occasional loss.[51]

Atlantic U-boats were provided with their own key in October 1941, and this moved to the infamous *Triton* four-rotor system (SHARK at Bletchley Park) in February 1942. However, even this was not impervious to Allied attack, and the Arctic U-boats remained on the Home Waters key for much of the remainder of the war.

The fundamental failure on the part of the German navy was an appreciation that Enigma itself was vulnerable to mathematical and statistical attack. Any concerns that arose were focused on breaches of security around distribution of keys, espionage or betrayal, all of which by their nature could be overcome by frequent key changes and renewal of associated signal books. The underlying cipher was always believed to be bullet-proof. It was not until 1974 that Admiral Dönitz would learn of the ULTRA secret and the widespread compromise of his ciphers. His reaction was recorded by the German historian Jürgen Rohwer:

> So that's what happened! [. . .] I have been afraid of this time and again. Although the experts continually proved – with conviction it seemed – that there were other reasons for the suspect observations, they were never able to dispel my doubts completely. [. . .] Only after the war did I feel reasonably reassured by the lack of any reports from the Allied side. [. . .] Well, now you historians will have to start right back at the beginning again![52]

This book is in many ways an attempt to do exactly that.

PART II
DEFENCE
The PQ–QP Convoys, 1941–1942

CHAPTER FOUR

TIRPITZ: THE BATTLE THAT NEVER WAS

CONVOYS PQ 1–PQ 12, AUGUST 1941–MARCH 1942

ATTACK OF THE ALBACORES

At 7.30 a.m. on 9 March 1942, a force of twelve Albacore torpedo bombers took off from the Royal Navy aircraft carrier HMS *Victorious* in the North Sea and headed south-east towards the Norwegian coast and the entrance to Westfjord, the channel providing access to the port of Narvik. Five of the aircraft were from 817 Squadron Fleet Air Arm and the remainder from 832 Squadron, led by their recently appointed commander Lt Commander W.J. Lucas. Despite only entering service in 1940, the Albacore was already an outdated aircraft. A bi-plane with fixed undercarriage, it improved on its predecessor the Swordfish only in having an enclosed and heated cockpit, but at a price of being heavier to control and less manoeuvrable in a crisis. This led pilots to prefer the earlier aircraft – better to be cold than dead.

Flying at 500 feet above the sea to avoid enemy radar, Commander Lucas spotted his target in the clear air from 20 miles out. At 8.42 a.m. he identified the pride of the *Kriegsmarine*, the battleship *Tirpitz*, with only one surface escort and with no air cover beyond its two reconnaissance float-planes launched earlier. It was steaming as fast as it could go almost due east towards the safety of the fjord and was thus heading way from Lucas' aircraft in an approximately 'ten o-clock' direction. The battleship was making nearly 30 knots, while the pursuers were flying at around 130 knots but into the teeth of a 35-knot wind. This made them only about three times faster than their target. Fleet Air Arm doctrine dictated that torpedo attacks should be made from ahead of the target towards the front quarter, ideally from both sides at once so that if the target turned to 'comb the tracks' of one set of torpedoes it would expose its broadside to the other set from the other side. However, to overtake *Tirpitz* from behind and execute a textbook attack with such slow aircraft would be nigh on impossible. Lucas ordered his force to climb to 4,000 feet into the base of the clouds. He hoped he could hide for long enough to drop onto his target at the last minute and surprise it at close range.[1]

This torpedo-bomber attack on *Tirpitz* was the only opportunity so far the Royal Navy had managed to orchestrate to take on the largest warship of the enemy fleet in open sea. If successful, it would prove a point which was becoming painfully clear to the world's navies in the Second World War: the era of the big-gun capital ship was coming to an end. The sinking of *Tirpitz*'s sister ship *Bismarck* in 1941 as a result of damage caused by torpedoes delivered by Swordfish from the carrier HMS *Ark Royal*, and the swift destruction of HMS *Prince of Wales* and *Repulse* by Japanese dive bombers only three months earlier in December 1941, demonstrated that large warships were hopelessly vulnerable to air attack unless well protected by their own air cover. By 1945 the battle-fleets of 1916 would have been replaced by carrier battlegroups, and the big-gun ships relegated to shore bombardment duties and ultimately the scrap yard.

However, to launch a successful attack from a carrier on an enemy that was out of sight over the horizon, and potentially many miles away in an empty ocean, required one thing above all: good intelligence. Unless the likely position of the enemy could be pinpointed and its likely movements predicted, time and aircraft could easily be lost searching in vain for a small needle in a large haystack. This information could be provided by air reconnaissance but was also increasingly the province of SIGINT. The story of how Lt Commander Lucas and his force were successfully directed to the same piece of sea as their quarry is one in which the Naval Section of GC&CS and the OIC played a central role. At the same time, the battle (or lack of one) to protect convoy PQ 12 demonstrates the limitations of even the most timely intelligence, and how difficult it was even with plentiful SIGINT for both the Royal Navy and the *Kriegsmarine* to bring each other to battle to attack or defend the Arctic convoys.

THE CONVOYS BEGIN

The first convoy taking supplies to Russia left Hvalfjordur in Iceland on 21 August 1941. Codenamed DERVISH, the small fleet of seven merchant ships arrived in Archangel ten days later, undisturbed by any German interference.[2] It carried principally wool, rubber and tin, but it also contained fifteen crated Hurricane fighter aircraft. These were complemented by a further twenty-four Hurricanes delivered simultaneously by the aircraft carrier HMS *Argus*.[3] The first 'PQ' convoy followed the same route, sailing on 29 September 1941 and arriving on 11 October. A further five numbered convoys (PQ 2 to PQ 6) would follow before the end of 1941. For the remainder of the year, these runs were made, along with their return trips (QP 1 to QP 4) 'without interference from the enemy'.[4] By the end of December, 800 fighter aircraft, 750 tanks, 1,400 trucks and about 100,000 tons of ammunition and other supplies had been delivered to the Russians without loss from the enemy (although some ships had been damaged by bad weather).[5] This run of success would continue in the first months of 1942. By the end of February, 157 merchant ships had made the run to and from Russia with the loss of only 1 merchant ship and 1 destroyer to enemy action (described in more detail below).[6]

These halcyon days were not to last, however, as from the outset of the war with Russia the Germans had taken steps to reinforce their fleet and air forces in Norway and to interdict the convoys. As has been described earlier, Hitler was keen both to attack the supply route to Russia and also to protect what he considered one of the jewels of his empire, Norway, from potential Allied invasion. On a practical level, it was also vital to prevent interruption to the iron-ore trade from Sweden to Germany via the port of Narvik (the shorter Baltic supply routes being ice-bound for much of the year). As the *Führer* put it in January 1942: 'Every ship which is not stationed in Norway is in the wrong place.'[7]

U-boat operations in the far north began in July 1941 with patrols by two boats in the Kola Bay area targeting Russian coastal traffic. Two further boats were added in September, but little was achieved. High-level discussions were begun in October over the establishment of a permanent U-boat force in the Arctic. Admiral Dönitz as commander of the U-boat force *BdU* was opposed to such a move and was supported by the Naval War Staff. Firstly, he felt that redeployment of U-boats to the Arctic would severely weaken his efforts in the Atlantic, which he considered to be the vital theatre of the naval war; secondly, he considered that the conditions of weather and ice in the Barents Sea would significantly inhibit submarine operations there. He was overruled by Hitler, who on 15 October determined that a permanent force of U-boats should be stationed in northern Norway for Arctic operations. To manage these operations, a new headquarters was established under *Admiral Nordmeer* (Admiral Northern Waters).[8] The first incumbent of this post was Admiral Hubert Schmundt, who was in command until August 1942.[9]

Given that much of the SIGINT work of Naval Section at Bletchley Park which is the focus of this study involved the analysis of messages between German naval commands, some account of the German command structure is useful. The German navy (*Kriegsmarine*) was nominally commanded by Hitler as C-in-C of all German armed forces. Under him, the navy was commanded by the Naval High Command, the *Oberkommando der Marine*, or *OKM*, with a Commander-in-Chief (*Oberbefehlshaber der Kriegsmarine*), *Großadmiral* (Admiral) Erich Raeder. At the next level, the navy was divided into four regional *Gruppe*: *Nord*, *Ost*, *Süd* and *West*. Norway fell under *Gruppe Nord*, which was commanded from Kiel by *Generaladmiral* Rolf Carls until February 1943, and later by *Vizeadmiral* Otto Schniewind. Within *Gruppe Nord* were further separate regional commands, of which Norway was one, commanded until May 1943 by *Generaladmiral* Hermann Boehm (as *Kommandierender Admiral Norwegen*). In turn, Norway was divided between three Flag Officers, *West*, *Nord* and *Polarküste* (Polar Coast), who were responsible for minor defensive operations, minesweeping and patrolling. Confusingly, this structure did not control major surface vessels or U-boats, the main attacking arms of the navy, which were commanded directly from *Gruppe Nord* or *OKM* and in turn by a Flag Officer Battle Group, who actually took the ships to sea.[10] The fact that his command did not extend to the control of major naval operations was not lost on Admiral Boehm, who described the limits of his command as 'a case of over-organisation which was bound to have a bad effect'.[11] If this were not enough, each ship type, battleships and cruisers, destroyers, torpedo boats, etc., had its own Type Commander responsible for the administration of those vessels. One particularly powerful member of this group was *Vizeadmiral* Karl Dönitz, who as *BdU* held command of all German submarines. He would go on to succeed Raeder in 1943 as commander of the *Kriegsmarine* and would ultimately be nominated by Hitler as his successor as *Führer* in 1945.

It was onto this already bloated command structure that the post of Admiral Northern Waters was appended. Schmundt's immediate request was for nine U-boats, which he considered the minimum required to keep three at sea, which he believed was the minimum number that would have an appreciable effect on the convoys. He also, perhaps optimistically, argued that, given the difficulties of northern operations, these boats should be permanently and not temporarily attached, and that they should consist only of experienced crews. By February 1942 he had been allocated six U-boats for convoy work. A further fourteen were sent to more southerly ports for reconnaissance and coastal defence and for operations towards Iceland and Scotland.

The first problem the Admiral faced in conducting effective operations was to understand the size, routing and schedule of the convoys. In order to place his U-boats in a position to attack a convoy, he would need to be able to predict in advance their dates of sailing and their probable routes and pre-deploy his submarines, as to try and respond only after one had been sighted at sea would be extremely difficult. He was also hampered by the fact that effective German air force reconnaissance aircraft did not become available until the FW 200 Condors of *7/KG40* were deployed north from Bordeaux in January 1942. On the other hand, the conditions worked to his advantage, as during the winter the navigable corridor between the Arctic coast and the limit of the sea ice was only just over 250 miles wide. What is more, the convoys could be expected to sail as far away from the coast as possible, in the northern half of the available seaway.

On Christmas Day 1941, Schmundt despatched his three available U-boats to patrol the likely convoy route 'to comb and identify the probable convoy route which the United Kingdom-Russia might use and to determine the rhythm of the convoys'.[12] This was more of a fact-finding trip than an attempt to sink ships directly. Ironically, the U-boats were successful in sinking Allied shipping but were not able to gather useful information about the habits of the convoys. On New Year's Day 1942, U-boat *U-134* found, mostly by accident, the MV *Waziristan* 11 miles south of Bear Island, and sank it with torpedoes. This ship was actually part of convoy PQ 7, but the convoy had been broken into two parts, A and B, and *Waziristan* was sailing with only one other ship as PQ 7A and had become separated from its escorts.[13] As a result, the Germans concluded that it was sailing independently and did not infer from its position and course the broader information about convoy routings that they were looking for. SIGINT information had been provided to Admiral Northern Waters from the *B-Dienst* that convoy PQ 7 was at sea at that time, but the two ships identified were not recognised as the convoy, which it was assumed would be a larger group of vessels.

Similarly, another German success achieved during this period (two U-boats stayed at sea until 20 January) was the sinking of the Tribal-class destroyer HMS *Matabele*, which blew up with the loss of all but two hands after being torpedoed by *U-454* on 17 January 1942. It had been escorting PQ 8 and was almost within sight of Russia when lost.[14] Again, its position was such that it was not clear whether it was escorting a convoy from the UK or merely covering local coastal operations around Murmansk. Another patrol of three U-boats was sent to Bear Island, sailing between 24 January and 4 February, but they found nothing, returning to port on 20 February. Meanwhile, on 21 February, Admiral Northern Waters was again informed by the *B-Dienst* that convoy PQ 11 had sailed on 10 February. The depressing conclusion drawn from this information was that not only had the U-boats missed PQ 11, but PQ 8, 9, and 10 had probably also sailed previously without discovery.[15] It was clear to Schmundt and his colleagues even at this early stage that, as Dönitz had predicted, using U-boats effectively against convoys in the Arctic, especially in winter, would be no simple matter.

GERMANY'S BIG SHIPS

German surface reinforcements were slow to arrive in Norwegian waters until after the plan for invasion of the UK was finally abandoned in the winter of 1941–1942. The first and the most potent of the surface-ship reinforcements for the *Kriegsmarine* in Norway, and one which was to preoccupy British Admiralty thinking for much of the remainder of the war, was the battleship *Tirpitz*, which sailed for Norway in January 1942. *Tirpitz*, or 'Schlachtschiff G', as it was known in the German pre-war fleet construction programme, was laid down in 1936. *Tirpitz* and its sister ship *Bismarck* were the largest warships operated during the war outside the Pacific. *Tirpitz* measured over 250m in length and carried eight 38cm (15-inch) guns, as well as powerful secondary and anti-aircraft armament. After the war, Admiralty specialists studied the plans of the ship and were rather dismissive of its design, claiming there was 'nothing very sensational about the design of the *Tirpitz*. It was merely a very large battleship.'[16] However, even if conventionally designed, it was more than a match in a one-to-one fight with anything the Royal Navy had available, including the newest King George V-class battleships. Its mere existence, especially after it was commissioned operationally in February 1941, forced the Royal Navy to maintain a substantial counterforce in the Home Fleet, including several of those new battleships. The British had been lucky to catch *Bismarck* before it could wreak too much havoc in the Atlantic convoy routes, and they did not relish the prospect of a repeat performance. As historian John Winton put it, 'All *Tirpitz* had to do, like Mount Everest, to be there.'[17]

As a result, *Tirpitz* had been a target for attack from the outset. Plans for bombing of its construction yard were made as early as January 1939, and repeated efforts were made by the RAF to damage it prior to launch and whenever it returned to Kiel during its working up in the Baltic. None of these attacks caused significant damage.[18] Both photographic reconnaissance and SIGINT efforts were also made to follow it and monitor its location. In December 1941 the decision was taken in Germany to redeploy *Tirpitz* to Trondheim in Norway. This decision was confirmed by the *Führer* on 29 December, and 10 January 1942 was set as a departure date. Meanwhile, for the British, Enigma intercepts in the first week of January confirmed its presence in the Baltic.

On 14 January, a few days later than planned, the battleship sailed via the Kiel Canal into the North Sea. Several Enigma messages from *Gruppe Nord* to *Tirpitz* were intercepted on 15 January relating to the weather for a possible passage through Skaggerak and providing information that poor weather in the UK was likely to hamper hostile air reconnaissance.[19] Messages were also sent to U-boats operating in the North Sea warning of the transit of friendly vessels 'on passage to Trondheim'.[20] Unfortunately for the British, these messages were not deciphered and passed to the OIC until the morning of 17 January, by which time *Tirpitz* was safely moored in Foettenfjord, a finger of water surrounded by mountains deep within Trondheim Fjord, having arrived the previous evening. Undeterred, an air raid was arranged by Bomber Command for the night of 30 January, but a combination of bad weather, cloud cover and the extreme range of the target from the UK meant that this was unsuccessful, and no bombs were dropped.[21]

The presence of *Tirpitz* in Norwegian waters was a serious concern to the British, as it presented a dual threat – to the Arctic convoys, and to those in the Atlantic should it break out past Iceland. This concern was only heightened in February when the battlecruisers *Scharnhorst* and *Gneisenau* made their successful 'Channel Dash' from Brest back to Germany. In fact, both ships were sufficiently damaged by mines laid in their path to be out of action for the remainder of the year (*Gneisenau* permanently), but this was little comfort to the Admiralty, who perceived a surface fleet of growing strength being formed in Norway, which if it sailed as a combined force would be more than a match for the British Home Fleet.

The Germans were thinking along the same lines and developed plans to attack the Arctic convoys using their surface fleet. In order to carry out this operation, C-in-C Battleships, *Vizeadmiral* Otto Ciliax, embarked on the heavy cruiser *Prinz Eugen*, which had recently accompanied *Scharnhorst* and *Gneisenau* in their run back to Germany. On 21 February 1942, *Prinz Eugen*, in company with the heavy cruiser *Admiral Scheer* and five destroyers (*Richard Beitzen, Paul Jakobi, Z25, Hermann Schoemann* and *Friedrich Ihn*) departed Brunsbüttel at the mouth of the Elbe and headed north. After stopping briefly in Grimstadfjord, near Bergen, on 22 February, the ships proceeded on to Trondheim.[22] These moves were followed closely by GC&CS. Due to the forty-eight-hour key-change cycle used by German naval Enigma (described earlier), Naval Section at Bletchley Park were able to pass on decryptions of traffic on the afternoon of 21 February within a few hours. Not all of these messages were readable, as some were re-enciphered using *Offizier*, but many were. A particularly telling example is a message from *Gruppe Nord* to Admiral Commanding Battleships (Otto Ciliax aboard *Prinz Eugen*), sent at 15.44 GMT and passed on to the Admiralty less than four hours later at 7.32 p.m. on 21 February. In part, it read: 'Put into Skerries at Dawn. Onward passage through the Skerries until you are off Bergen. [. . .] Destroyers are to refuel at Bergen during the day. Leave the Skerries at nightfall and carry out passage to Trondheim.'[23]

Forewarned by earlier intercepts that *Tirpitz* was exercising in Trondheim Fjord,[24] Tovey and the Home Fleet had sailed on 19 February, and, acting on this new intelligence, the carrier HMS *Victorious*, with suitable escort, was detached to try to launch an air attack on the new arrivals; however, the weather was so poor that no attack was possible. Fortunately for the British, four submarines had also been despatched to the Norwegian coast at the same time. As *Prinz Eugen, Admiral Scheer* and their escorts were nearing Trondheim Fjord, they were sighted by HM Submarine *Trident*. *Trident* was able to loose three torpedoes at the enemy group, scoring one hit on *Prinz Eugen*. The torpedo struck the ship in the stern, killing fifty men, causing serious damage and rendering the ship un-manoeuvrable. However, on its own power it managed to reach Trondheim and from there was towed to Lofjord. Over the next few months, jury rudders were fitted and the ship was able to limp back to Kiel in May 1942, but for the present it was out of the battle.[25]

This left Ciliax with a rather diminished force. Instead of the planned fleet of *Tirpitz, Scharnhorst, Gneisenau, Prinz Eugen* and *Admiral Scheer*, he was reduced to one battleship, *Tirpitz*, one 'pocket battleship' (heavy cruiser), *Admiral Scheer*, and the half-dozen destroyers which had provided their escorts. He was also faced with a severe lack of fuel oil, which limited the number of ships he could put to sea. This was a concern not only for operations but also for training. His ships were unused to operating as a battlegroup with destroyers escorting heavy units, and such operations needed practice if they were to run smoothly. Without fuel for group training, any multi-ship sortie risked confusion and accidents. Nonetheless, he was determined to carry on his mission of attacking the convoys.

OPERATION *SPORTPALAST*

With the help of the *B-Dienst*, Admiral Ciliax drew up his plans for an attack on the next available convoy. The Admiral transferred his flag to *Tirpitz* and developed Operation *SPORTPALAST*: an attack on the Allied convoys PQ 12 and the returning QP 8. He was aware that a covering force from the Home Fleet was likely to be at sea but calculated that his ships could intercept the two convoys as their courses converged and then crossed south-west of Bear Island, destroy them and return to Norwegian waters before the Royal Navy could intervene. *Tirpitz* and three destroyers, *Friedrich Ihn*, *Hermann Schoemann* and *Z25*, were prepared for the mission. Four U-boats from Schmundt's Northern Waters group were also to participate as a patrol line across the assumed route of the convoys.

Convoys PQ 12 and QP 8 sailed simultaneously on 1 March, a fact which is likely to have been known to the Germans via their own SIGINT. The outbound convoy consisted of eighteen merchantmen, and the returning QP 8 of fifteen ships. In addition to their smaller close escorts, Admiral Tovey had ordered that, given the range of threats in the Arctic, each convoy should additionally be escorted by a cruiser and two destroyers. In practice, this meant two cruiser/destroyer groups, one westerly working from Iceland to Bear Island and a second in the Barents Sea, passing over responsibility for the inbound and outbound convoys as they crossed over. Covering PQ 12 outbound was HMS *Kenya*, acting as a seagoing sheepdog, directing the convoy route, investigating threats and rounding up stragglers. To the east in the Barents Sea, HMS *Nigeria* performed the same role with the returning ships.[26]

Luftwaffe air patrols located the outbound convoy on 5 March. This was the first successful PQ convoy sighting achieved by the *Luftwaffe*, and there was some delay in the passing of the intelligence. Despite the convoy being sighted early in the afternoon, this information did not reach Admiral Northern Waters until after 8 p.m. Schmundt was extremely unhappy about this but rapidly communicated the news to his U-boats. Meanwhile, Ciliax requested permission to act with his surface group, a request which went first to *Gruppe Nord* and *Generaladmiral* Rolf Carls. He escalated it to *Kriegsmarine* Commander *Großadmiral* Erich Raeder, who in turn consulted Hitler, who agreed on the basis that no risks be taken and the operation be abandoned if heavy enemy forces were likely to be encountered. This was rather typical of the *Führer's* contradictory position that the fleet should be as active as possible against the convoys, but without risking his precious, and rapidly diminishing, number of capital ships. With his orders confirmed, Ciliax and *Tirpitz* sailed from Trondheim Fjord at 11 a.m. on 6 March.[27]

Given the new threat to the convoys from the German heavy units, the Home Fleet had for the first time provided a distant covering force for the passage of the two groups of merchantmen. In fact, this was initially two forces: the Home Fleet's deputy commander Vice Admiral Alban Curteis departed Iceland with his flag in the battleship HMS *Duke of York*, accompanied by the battlecruiser HMS *Renown* and six destroyers. Meanwhile, the C-in-C Home Fleet, Admiral Tovey, was based on board HMS *King George V* at the fleet's main base at Scapa Flow. He was of the opinion that he was better off remaining at Scapa in case *Tirpitz* attempted to break out into the Atlantic and remaining in contact by telephone with his sources of intelligence. The Admiralty took a different view, and so he also put to sea on 3 March, with HMS *King George V*, his fleet carrier HMS *Victorious* and an escort consisting of the heavy cruiser HMS *Berwick* and six destroyers. The two elements of the Home Fleet met at a rendezvous to the east of Jan Mayen island at 10.30 a.m. on 6 June.[28] Tovey's orders required that he give precedence to protecting the convoys over destroying *Tirpitz*. He was unhappy with this and regarded the sinking of the battleship as being of 'incomparably greater importance to the conduct of the war than the safety of any convoy',[29] but he was obliged to observe the detailed instructions he received from the Admiralty.

On departing Trondheim Fjord, *Tirpitz* sailed parallel to the Norwegian coast for several hours before turning due north on a course which it was assumed would bring it into contact with the two convoys. At about 6 p.m. that evening (6 March) it was sighted by the Royal Navy submarine *Trident* just north of Trondheim. Its captain, Lt R.P. Raikes, made an immediate but conservative report stating that he had sighted an enemy battleship or heavy cruiser; in his own view, however, 'I was certain in my own mind that it was the *Tirpitz*.'[30] Despite this report being sent at 6.02 p.m., its contents were not forwarded to Admiral Tovey and the Home Fleet until midnight on 6/7 March. He had spent the morning of 6 March sailing north-east towards the convoys, and at 2 p.m., on reaching their approximate track, he had turned south-west on a reciprocal course. Now, at midnight, on receipt of the new information, he reversed course again back towards the north-east. At 8 a.m. on the morning of 7 March he altered course slightly to the east and ordered *Victorious* to prepare an air reconnaissance to look for *Tirpitz*. Unfortunately, the weather was so bad as to prohibit flying all day. This was unlucky, as such a search 'would almost certainly have located the *Tirpitz*'. Shortly after Tovey's change of course at 8 a.m., *Tirpitz* had also moved onto a north-westerly heading, which left it converging with the Home Fleet and less than 100 miles away.[31]

Had Ciliax and Tovey continued on their respective courses in the afternoon of 7 March, it is possible that they would have directly encountered each other. Also, by this point *Tirpitz* was sailing unescorted, as its three destroyers had been sent to sweep north on parallel courses to the east of its own track in order to increase the likelihood of spotting one of the convoys. However, this possibly decisive engagement failed to materialise, as at 11.22 a.m. Tovey, frustrated by the weather, turned south again to try and find clearer air to launch *Victorious*' aircraft, and later in the afternoon Ciliax, knowing that he had probably crossed the convoys' likely tracks, turned north-east towards Bear Island in a further attempt to locate them, before turning to the south again to link back up with his destroyers. Having almost met, the two forces were once again sailing away from each other.

In fact, *Tirpitz* had only narrowly missed the convoys. Its destroyers were to have more luck when the *Friedrich Ihn* sighted a Russian straggler from QP 8, the *Ijora*. The German ship made short work of the *Ijora*, sinking it with its guns, but before it sank, the *Ijora* made a desperate distress call reporting that it was being attacked by a warship. This call seems to have been heard by everyone in the vicinity – telegraphists on both convoys, *Tirpitz* and in the Home Fleet – at about 4.30 p.m., and Ciliax was able to determine that this was the work of his destroyers, while to Tovey this warship might equally be *Tirpitz*. However, the location of the origin of the call was not clear.[32] Shortly after, at 4.40 p.m., Tovey's telegraphists picked up an encrypted message which D/F suggested was on a similar bearing. This was actually from a U-boat in the patrol line looking for the convoy, but Tovey took it to be *Tirpitz*. His hunch was supported by a series of Enigma messages forwarded to him in the course of the afternoon and evening of 7 March. These included a general warning to all vessels issued by *Gruppe Nord* as *Tirpitz* was sailing on the afternoon of 6 March, intercepted at 3 p.m. on that day. This message read: 'Admiral Commanding Battleships [Ciliax] with "Tirpitz" and three destroyers will leave Square 6717 at 1700/6/3 northbound at 25 knots to operate against enemy convoy.'[33]

It had taken GC&CS almost twenty-four hours to read this message, it having been forwarded to the OIC at 2.12 p.m. on 7 March. It was then repeated to the Home Fleet by the Admiralty at 3.18 p.m. Despite the delay, it confirmed to Tovey that the German battleship was heading for the convoy, not out into the Atlantic or on some other mission. It also included the information that 'the enemy was apparently not [. . .] aware that the Home Fleet was at sea'.[34] Accordingly, at 5.50 p.m. the Home Fleet swung 90 degrees to port, onto a south-easterly heading, before turning again at 8 p.m. onto a north-easterly course back once again towards the convoys.

Shortly after this course change, another signal was D/F-ed on Tovey's flagship. It was assumed that this had originated from the same source as the previous signal (presumably *Tirpitz*), and the relative bearings 'showed that she was moving south at high speed'.[35] This supported the Admiral's view that *Tirpitz* was making a run for home to the south, so he detached his destroyers to head south-east towards the Norwegian coast to act as a blocking force, while he awaited confirmation of the origin of the signals he had intercepted. Unfortunately, these judgements by Tovey show the problems inherent in providing D/F equipment to commanders at sea who were not familiar with the nuances of SIGINT. Both signals had been intercepted on shore and passed to GC&CS, who were able to correctly establish that they were not from *Tirpitz*, and indeed were from two different vessels. However, having done so, they correctly dismissed them as not important, not realising the weight Tovey was erroneously placing upon them. At midnight, having heard no more from the Admiralty, Tovey changed course once again and headed south on the assumption that his target was returning to Norway. In fact, *Tirpitz* was far away to the north-east, on an easterly heading, south of Bear Island, and had detached its destroyers to Tromsø to refuel.

By 4 a.m. on 8 March, Admiral Tovey had heard no more of his opponent's whereabouts. He had received another forwarded Enigma message at 1 a.m., but this had informed him only that the Germans had not found the convoys and indeed had no knowledge that his own force was at sea.[36] His own wireless silence had kept his presence hidden from the Germans but at the same time left the Admiralty with little idea of his movements, or indeed his misconceptions. Concerned that he did not want to get too close to the Norwegian coast with *King George V* and his valuable carrier without destroyer escort, he turned back south-west towards Iceland to collect a new destroyer force. Two further Enigma messages were forwarded during the day, one describing the German search areas looking for the convoys between the North Cape and Bear Island, and a second reporting that British W/T traffic was still 'normal' (i.e., it contained no hint that the Home Fleet was at sea).[37] At face value, these did little to change Tovey's understanding of the situation. What the Admiralty had neglected to inform him was that both these messages were from *Gruppe Nord* to the Admiral Commanding Battleships – Ciliax, on board *Tirpitz.* This fact gave the messages a wholly different connotation, that the search by *Tirpitz* for the convoys was still on, and that, unaware that it was being stalked by the Home Fleet, it might yet still be in the waters south of Bear Island, which indeed it was at noon on 8 March.[38]

The situation resolved itself from the British perspective on the afternoon of 8 March. A message was sent from *Gruppe Nord* to Admiral Commanding Battleships at 10.34 a.m., repeated at 11.09 a.m. on 8 March. By this time, the point in the Enigma key-cycle reached by GC&CS meant that this message was decrypted in a little over three hours. It was in the hands of the OIC by 2.15 p.m. and was passed to the Home Fleet and Admiral Tovey at 3 p.m.[39] It read:

1) Estimate convoy's speed as 6 to 8 knots. Today at 0800 in the area Squares AB 5970, 5510, 6210, 6590. Tomorrow at 0800 in the area AB 6590, 6210, AC 1760, 4560.
2) I estimate the length of time devoted to the search should not extend beyond nightfall on 9/3. Then return to Trondheim.
3) U/boats have been detailed to operate against enemy ships in Square AW 2521 and the enemy cruiser in in Square AC 8988.[40]

For once, GC&CS had produced SIGINT gold: a message which gave the enemy's likely position only a few hours before and, more importantly, their intent and areas of operations for the next twenty-four hours. *Tirpitz* would continue to search for the convoys south of Bear Island until the end of the following day before returning home. Intelligence of this quality was a rare thing in the war at sea, despite the enormous efforts devoted to its production.

Admiral Tovey put his helm hard over and set off once again back towards Bear Island. Even as he did so, however, more information was arriving at the OIC on the teleprinters from GC&CS. A series of messages through the evening of 8 March showed that, rather than searching for another twenty-four hours, Ciliax had in fact broken off the search for the convoys, and *Tirpitz* was heading for a rendezvous with his re-fuelled destroyers and then heading back to Trondheim. Nonetheless, as late as 11.30 p.m. on 8 March, the Admiralty made the 'appreciation' that *Tirpitz* was likely to continue its search of the convoy south of Bear Island after the rendezvous with the destroyers, and signalled as much to Tovey.[41] Only an hour and a half later they revised their view, sending the simple instruction to Tovey, signalled at 1.37 a.m. on 9 March, 'Steer 120° Maximum speed'. This was followed by a further signal explaining that the *Tirpitz* had cancelled its search and was now heading to a rendezvous with its destroyers off the Lofoten Islands.[42] The course indicated by the Admiralty would take the Home Fleet on an intercepting course towards the *Tirpitz*. With luck, the Home Fleet could get into apposition by dawn to fly off *Victorious'* torpedo bombers and intercept the German battleship as it transited down the Norwegian coast. If they could slow it down, there might even be a chance for *King George V* to close with it and repeat the success over *Bismarck* the year before.[43] Further information on *Tirpitz*'s course and likely position was forwarded to the Home Fleet from the Admiralty at around 3 a.m.[44]

The Albacore crews of 817 and 832 Squadrons were roused at 5.30 a.m. on 9 March, and at 6.45 a.m. three search aircraft from each squadron, equipped with ASV (Air–Surface Vessel) radars, were despatched from *Victorious* towards the southern tip of the Lofoten island chain. Shortly after, they were followed at 7.21 a.m. by the twelve torpedo-carrying aircraft of Lt Commander Lucas' strike group. Unlike the appalling weather of the previous few days, visibility on 9 March was good, with 7/10ths cloud at 2,000 feet and occasional snow showers. Admiral Tovey signalled Captain Bovell of *Victorious*, expressing his delight and optimism at finally being able to strike at the German battleship: 'A wonderful chance which may achieve the most valuable results. God be with you.' Bovell himself observed: 'It was a chance they had dreamed and prayed for, and, they knew only too well, it was a chance that might not come again.'[45] Less than 200 miles away, Ciliax, on board *Tirpitz*, was finally informed by the *B-Dienst* radio intercept detachment aboard the battleship that traffic indicated that he was being hunted by a battlegroup including a carrier, and that carrier aircraft were inbound. It was, as the ship's gunnery officer

Kapitänleutnant Albrecht Schnarke ruefully observed, 'ideal weather for carrier aircraft'.[46]

The search Albacores located *Tirpitz* at just after 8 a.m. One of its float-planes made a brave but ultimately ineffective attack on the reconnaissance aircraft, wounding one of the British aircrew before heading for Norway, short of fuel. Meanwhile, *Tirpitz's* request for land-based air cover by the *Luftwaffe* went unanswered, ensnared in the complex chain of command ashore. Lucas' strike force of torpedo bombers dropped out of the cloud at 9.17 a.m., to find themselves more or less astride the target. Without space to plan his approach, Lucas ordered his aircraft to split up and make individual attacks. *Tirpitz* responded with a mighty barrage of *Flak* from its sixteen 104mm anti-aircraft guns, sixteen twin 37mm cannons and forty-eight smaller machine guns. It even fired several high angle broadsides from its 15-inch main armament while carrying out drastic evasive manoeuvring. There was no shortage of courage or aggression on either side. All the British aircraft launched their torpedoes, but none struck the swerving battleship. Two Albacores were shot down, while the remainder returned empty-handed to *Victorious*. Admiral Ciliax wrote thanking 'The good God's intervention' and awarded an Iron Cross to Captain Topp, commander of the battleship.[47]

Having revealed his hand, and lost, Tovey was now in an awkward position, relatively close to the Norwegian coast, without adequate destroyer escort and well within range of German land-based air attack, for which the few fighters on *Victorious* would be no match. He had little choice but to turn for home, and so he set course for Scapa. His fears were confirmed when a weak attack on his fleet was made during the afternoon of 9 March by three Ju 88 bombers. Fortunately, no bombs hit his carrier, and he was back in the Orkneys the following day.[48] *Tirpitz*, meanwhile, had taken shelter in Westfjord, but Ciliax was anxious to return to his secure anchorage at Trondheim. He sailed again with a large destroyer escort at dawn on 13 March, making his berth in Foettenfjord unscathed later that night. British destroyers and submarines were sent to intercept, but neither was able to make any impression. The submarines, in particular, picked up the German force but were kept at bay by vigorous patrolling and depth-charging by the escorting German destroyers.

THE BATTLE THAT NEVER WAS

The March 1942 sortie by *Tirpitz* is not an event on which much ink has been spilled. This is because it was in many ways the 'battle that never was'. Despite manoeuvring in close proximity to each other for four days, *Tirpitz* never came to blows with *King George V*, and although *Victorious* was able to launch an airstrike, it was ultimately ineffective. Similarly, the Germans were unable to inflict significant damage on the convoys, PQ 12 arriving in Murmansk unscathed and QP 8 losing only the straggler *Ijora*. And yet the circumstances of this incident were not hugely dissimilar to later moments of much greater consequence. Victory or defeat for either side were several times near at hand. It was only the intervention of weather, or the chances of the interception or otherwise of particular messages, both from friends and enemies, or indeed the correct interpretation of those messages, which prevented a decisive result. The episode therefore deserves detailed analysis, as it sheds interesting light on later encounters where significant (and historically better known) victories and defeats were the outcome.

The first factors to consider are the prevailing conditions in the Arctic Ocean in the second week of March 1942. Although at that time of year Bear Island got about twelve hours of daylight, the weather during *Tirpitz*'s sortie was almost uniformly awful. The primary influence this had was on air operations. The *Luftwaffe* was able to find the PQ 12 convoy on 5 March but despite subsequent efforts was not able to find it again for the remainder of the 6–10 March period. Similarly, had *Victorious* been able to launch an air search on the morning of 7 March, there is little doubt that it would have found *Tirpitz*, and at that point not only would an air strike have been possible but potentially also a surface engagement. The fact that *Victorious'* search aircraft were equipped with ASV radars mean that, had they been able to get off the deck, the fog which was shrouding the convoys would have been little protection for the battleship. Instead, the carrier was being thrown around like a top by massive seas, which would have made bringing an aircraft up on deck, let alone flying it, suicidal.

The same constraint applied to surface searches. In fact, when Tovey made his turn away to the south-west to find better visibility for his carrier, he comforted himself that the same weather that was hampering him in the air would provide protection for the convoys from discovery by the Germans both from the air and by surface ships.[49] *Tirpitz* was equipped with radar that could be used for surface search in bad weather or at night, as well as for gunnery control. But the ship's war diary records that this was not used, as its signal would be vulnerable to inter- ception by enemy vessels beyond the range at which it was likely to detect anything. It was only switched on very briefly on the afternoon of 7 March for calibration for gunnery.[50] Also, the German sweep looking for the convoys passed ahead of QP 8, at least in part because the convoy had been battling a force 10 gale and snow, and with lightly laden empty ships was able to make almost no headway, placing it further east than if it had kept to schedule. It is also worthy of note, even though it had no influence on events, that during this period station-keeping in the convoy became impossible, and many of the ships were dispersed on several occasions, only able to re-gather in breaks in the weather. Many of their masters would also have had only the vaguest idea of their posi- tion, as without a horizon, or stars or a stable platform for observations, accurate navigation was almost impossible.

The same factors which were making life difficult for the ships of the convoy were of course being experienced in equal measure by the German U-boats. In bad weather these boats were forced to submerge, which vastly reduced their ability to manoeuvre and rendered surface search almost impossible. Navigation into the search areas to which they were directed by their commanders ashore was also extremely diffi- cult. In these circumstances, it is little surprise that the 'Werwolf' patrol line, consisting as it did of only four U-boats, found no targets despite being correctly positioned across the course of both convoys.

In the absence of visual reconnaissance, either by air or sea search, the second factor influencing events was intelligence. SIGINT became increasingly the dominant method of calculating the enemy's where- abouts. In this area, the Germans seem to have had little success. Even though by this time the *B-Dienst* was reading both Naval Cypher No. 2 and the recently introduced Naval Cypher No. 3, they were not able to produce this material in a sufficiently timely fashion for it to be tactically useful. As a result, it would appear from the messages read by GC&CS

during the period in question that the Germans were relying on traffic analysis, and that, although they could detect transmissions from various stations in the UK, they were not able to detect any special activity. A typical example of their conclusions was sent by *Gruppe Nord* to Ciliax on 7 March: '18 Group: meagre aircraft W/T traffic without special characteristics. Rest of Home Area W/T service: nothing special.'[51]

RAF Coastal Command's '18 group' was the unit responsible for the northern North Sea, whom it was assumed would provide air cover for the Home Fleet if it were at sea. Similarly, the 'Home Area' referred to the Home Fleet base at Scapa. As a result, Ciliax sailed in blissful ignorance of the fact that Tovey was at sea with a powerful force including an aircraft carrier. Indeed, had he known that his enemy had sailed more or less simultaneously with his force on 6 March, it is likely that his sortie would have been immediately aborted in accordance with the *Führer*'s instructions not to risk his battleship. It must have come as something of a rude shock on the morning of 9 March to learn from his own W/T interceptors on board *Tirpitz* that enemy carrier-aircraft were in the air and heading towards him.

Interestingly, the writer of *Tirpitz*'s war diary expressed some concern over the whereabouts of the Home Fleet, and scepticism that the lack of diagnostic signals traffic was necessarily a guarantee that the enemy fleet was not at sea, especially after the sinking of the *Ijora* became public due to its widely heard distress call. The diary records (7 p.m., 7 March): 'After the warning report by the Ijora one must count on a change of course of the convoy and the putting out to sea of the English Home Fleet, because it is a plausible assumption that the departure of the formation from Trondheim during daylight has been reported to the opponent by the Norwegian spy service.'[52]

Actually, the sailing had been reported by a submarine, but the suggestion that the sinking of the *Ijora* had 'let the cat out of the bag' was a valid one. An hour later, the same author commented: 'The English surely had been prepared for the appearance of "Tirpitz" in the Arctic Ocean. The use of code words by the home operations office suffices for the execution of a well-thought-out operation; so that after delivery of the already mentioned "o.u." radio message, no other suspicious material needed to show up in the overall radio traffic.'[53]

The problem of the weight of evidence to be accorded to the *absence* of significant W/T traffic was one which would vex commanders on both sides throughout the Arctic campaign. It is not clear whether the diary writer was expressing the opinions of Admiral Ciliax, of Captain Topp, or indeed only his own. But it is possible that these reservations on board *Tirpitz* about the sailing of the Home Fleet, and the confidence with which *Gruppe Nord* could order the continuation of the operation, contributed to its earlier-than-ordered abandonment of the search for the convoys.

The British SIGINT effort was more productive. Enigma decrypts from both the German naval and air force networks were able to reveal useful information concerning the whereabouts of the enemy forces. Disappointment over the results of the operation led to a good deal of acrimony and scrutiny of the intelligence provided to the commander at sea, Admiral Tovey, and the decisions he made based upon it. Patrick Beesly in his history of the OIC was keen to exonerate the contribution of the OIC and GC&CS, claiming that the Admiralty 'had, however, been well served by O.I.C. and B.P., who fortunately had been able to provide cast-iron information and sound appreciations just when required. No awkward gaps in the flow of special Intelligence had intervened at a vital time.'[54]

This is somewhat of an overstatement. It is true that in the 'vital' period of 8–9 March when *Victorious* was moving to launch its air strike, Enigma messages were being broken and forwarded to the OIC within three hours of interception; however, this was not always the case. During the period of 6–7 March, the delay in decryption was in excess of twenty-four hours. It was fortunate that *Tirpitz* was spotted by a submarine when leaving Trondheim, as 'cast-iron' Enigma confirmation of this was only forwarded to Tovey at 3 p.m. on the afternoon of 7 March, twenty-eight hours after the enemy ships had departed from Foettenfjord. In the absence of this visual sighting, the German battleship would potentially have gained a day's sailing over its opponents. The impact of the German naval Enigma key-change cycle on GC&CS is manifested in a message sent by the Admiralty to the Home Fleet at 10.07 a.m. on 9 March (i.e., seven minutes after the German midday key-change): 'It is unlikely that further ULTRAs will be available for the present.'[55] It would not be until 6.40 the following morning (twenty hours later) that the flow of intelligence about *Tirpitz* would resume.[56] This intermittent flow of Enigma intelligence would dog Royal Navy operations in the Arctic for the rest of the campaign.

The third factor which hindered both sides' operations was divided command. The German operational command structure has already been discussed, but for this operation it was particularly labyrinthine. The surface task group was commanded by Admiral Ciliax. He was Type Commander for battleships, and thus *Tirpitz* fell under his remit wherever it might be (he had previously commanded *Scharnhorst, Gneisenau* and *Prinz Eugen* during the 'Channel dash'). The U-boats, meanwhile, were theoretically controlled by Admiral Schmundt as Admiral Northern Waters; however, both he and Ciliax were subject to instructions from *Gruppe Nord* and *Generaladmiral* Rolf Carls. Shortly after *Tirpitz* sailed on 6 March, *Gruppe Nord* signalled all the U-boats concerned in the Arctic (copying in Schmundt): 'With immediate effect all U-boats in the north Norwegian area will receive their orders from Gruppe Nord.'[57] It must have been doubly annoying only a couple of hours later for Schmundt to receive 'advice' from Admiral Dönitz, who despite being far away in Paris was *BdU* Type Commander of U-boats, and who thus had a measure of control over their operations. The (intercepted) Enigma message read:

> From: Admiral Commanding U-boats (From Admiral)
> To: Admiral Commanding Northern Waters (Personal for Admiral)
> Most Immediate:
> Judging from the evidence I have received I am of the opinion that the convoy will already have passed the position to which the U-boats have been ordered by 0400/8/3.
> I should shift the disposition further eastwards in order to catch the convoy by day, estimating the convoy's speed of advance at 7 to 8 knots.[58]

It would have been reasonable for the Admiral Northern Waters to reply: 'Don't tell me, tell *Gruppe Nord*, they're in charge now.' How he did respond is not recorded, although the GC&CS intercepts for the next few hours include a number of long message exchanges between *Gruppe Nord*, Admiral Northern Waters and even 'Supreme Command of the Navy' (Admiral Raeder), all in *Offizier* cipher and unreadable at Bletchley Park.[59]

Schmundt's opinion after the event was recorded in reports written on 13 and 16 March. He blamed *Gruppe Nord* for the lack of U-boat success and claimed that their assumption of command was 'without parallel' in previous combined surface and U-boat operations. He suggested two principles: either all U-boats remain under the command of *BdU* (Dönitz) at all times, wherever they may be in the world, or all assets in a single operation – air, surface and submarine – should be under a single commander. He was forced to admit, however, that gaining the cooperation of the *Luftwaffe* in the latter scheme would prove difficult. The result of his representations was an agreement that in future while pre-planning of operations would continue to rest with *Gruppe Nord*, Admiral Northern Waters would have a greater degree of control over operations once they were underway.[60] It remained to be seen, however, how this new compromise would work in practice.

The efforts of the Royal Navy were hampered by similar divisions of responsibility and difficulties of command. Admiral Tovey, as C-in-C Home Fleet, was the commander 'on the spot' and was empowered to make operational and tactical decisions for the vessels under his command. However, if he so chose, Dudley Pound as First Sea Lord at the Admiralty could overrule him by sending him direct orders (as indeed he did on 9 March). This situation was not one that was popular with fleet commanders, who looked back on the days when the Royal Navy at sea was out of reach of interference from its masters ashore. The Official Historian of the war at sea, Stephen Roskill, described how in the controversy which followed the failure to damage *Tirpitz*, Tovey 'criticised in forthright terms "the detailed instructions for the handling of his forces" which had been signalled from London'. However, Roskill sided with the Admiralty. Despite writing at a time when he could not discuss ULTRA intelligence directly, he argued:

In the first place the intelligence derived by the Admiralty and sent to the fleet flagship was, we now know, more accurate than the appreciations made afloat. Neither the signalling of the intelligence, nor the issue of orders when the intelligence available in London indicated that the assumptions on which our forces' movements had been based were wrong (as happened on the evening of the 8th of March), is open to criticism.[61]

Intervention by an (in its own mind at least) better-informed Admiralty was a price seagoing admirals would have to pay in the age of wireless communication.

Inevitably, while at sea Tovey relied on an intelligence picture that was inherently incomplete. Intercepted German naval wireless traffic was first decrypted and translated via GC&CS, who sent all that was relevant to the OIC (as has been described in an earlier chapter). However, this was not automatically shared with commanders at sea via ULTRA. Tovey only received those portions of the incoming information which the Admiralty thought would be useful to him, and often these were passed on without much of the surrounding context which would have made their nuances clear to the recipient. There was a distinct risk that the Admiralty might assume an understanding of the picture which Tovey did not actually have, and thus mislead him, if only by omission.

Faced with this lack of intelligence, Tovey also attempted to generate his own SIGINT, as was the case with the D/F bearings obtained by his on-board wireless teams on 7 March. Unfortunately, these teams lacked the expertise and background knowledge of their shore-based colleagues, and incorrect conclusions were drawn as to the origin of these signals – an assumption which was not corrected by the Admiralty, as their experts had already dismissed the transmissions as unimportant. Thus, the weight Tovey placed on them in his decision-making was not appreciated by his superiors. This can be compared with an incident in the hunt for the *Bismarck* a year earlier, when Tovey had been supplied with shore-based D/F bearings on the enemy ship but had his own on-board team plot the resultant position. An erroneous fix was derived from them, and the Home Fleet, at least for a short while, sailed away from its target.[62]

Frank Birch summed up this combination of lack of information from ashore and erroneous local information in his post-war analysis of the operation: 'The misadventures of C. in C. on that occasion are worth following in some detail. On the evidence, they were due to two causes. O.I.C. passed out to him too little special Intelligence rather than too much, and C. in C. himself was misled by misinterpretation of snippets of information picked up on the spot.'[63]

A significant contributor to these misunderstandings was the fact that the Admiralty to C-in-C Home Fleet conversation was essentially one-way. Tovey was obliged to maintain wireless silence, as otherwise his position would have been detectable by German D/F, and this would have compromised the operation. As a result, the Admiralty had to more or less guess what he was up to and send messages to him that they hoped would be helpful without really knowing what was going on. In fact, their knowledge of the German situation via SIGINT was probably only marginally worse than their understanding of the movements of their own ships. Tovey had access to 'Special Wireless Procedure', which was an arrangement whereby he could send messages on uncommon frequencies using disguised message formats which did not look like Royal Navy traffic. The hope was these could slip through unobserved by German Y operators. However, he struggled to make meaningful contact via this method.[64]

Tovey broke W/T silence only once, on the evening of 8 March. This was at the point when *Tirpitz* was believed to be searching for the convoy near Bear Island, and he reversed course in order to close with the enemy battleship. It would seem that he felt that a critical point had been reached and that it was worth the risk. Fortunately, his signal does not seem to have been intercepted by the Germans in a timeframe which affected events. At the same time, he asked the Admiralty to take over command of the cruisers and destroyers of his own fleet. The need for W/T silence was making even commanding his own force difficult. Ships sailing in close company could communicate securely via lamp and had the option of short-range VH/F voice channels, but if separated by any distance or in poor weather Morse W/T was the only option, and this was vulnerable to enemy interception.

Putting all these factors together, the operations of both fleets between 6 and 10 March 1942 can be compared to a huge seagoing game of blind man's buff. Neither the commanders at sea nor their shore-based superiors on either side had a complete picture of what was happening, and both were forced to act on guesswork. In the event, luck was against both the British, who found but failed to damage *Tirpitz*, and the Germans, who managed to sink only one ship from the two convoys. Many of the same circumstances would arise in future operations, but the outcomes, as will be described in subsequent chapters, were to be very different.

CHAPTER FIVE

THE SHIP THAT SANK ITSELF

CONVOYS PQ 13–PQ 15, MARCH–APRIL 1942

TREATIES AND CRUISERS

In 1922 the Washington Naval Treaty was signed by the governments of Great Britain, the US, France, Italy and Japan. These five nations, allies in the First World War, were concerned to prevent a peacetime naval arms race between them which no country could afford. It was agreed that all the signatories would suspend the building of 'capital ships' (battleships and battlecruisers), but no limit was placed on smaller vessels under 10,000 tons and armed with guns of 8-inch calibre or less. Earlier fleets had included multiple classes of 'cruisers' of varying size and armament, but the new treaty led to a standardisation around the world of cruiser-building close to, or at, the treaty limits. A second treaty, signed in London in 1930, limited the number of these 8-inch gun cruisers each navy could build but continued to allow unlimited construction of ships with 6-inch guns. This led to a distinction between 8-inch armed 'heavy cruisers' and 6-inch armed 'light cruisers'. Ships of these two classes became the backbone of the signatory navies. These ships were large enough to operate independently or support a force of destroyers and had the range to 'fly the flag' for their nations around the world.

In March 1936 the Second London Naval Treaty was signed. One of its clauses was to reduce the maximum permitted size of the 'light cruiser' class of warships from 10,000 tons to 8,000 tons. At the time, the Royal Navy had a force of ten 10,000-ton Town-class cruisers under construction, the most of famous of which is HMS *Belfast*, still afloat today on the Thames in London. In accordance with the terms of the treaty, the Admiralty ordered a further force of light cruisers which would be smaller than their Town-class cousins, to match the new treaty restrictions, but pack the same punch in terms of armament and equipment. This would make them cramped internally and difficult to upgrade or refit, but the result was a group of Colony-class light cruisers, named after Crown colonies of the British Empire.

The Royal Navy (and the fleets of its dominions) entered the Second World War with sixty-six cruisers in commission. A further thirty-five would be commissioned before 1945. Of these, thirty-four, or just over one-third, would be lost in action. This was the highest loss rate of any vessel type in the navy (followed closely by destroyers) and reflected the crucial and ubiquitous roles these vessels served in Allied operations.[1] The Arctic was no exception, with twenty-two cruisers of all classes serving in support of the convoys in the course of the war. These included the surviving *Belfast*, along with five other Town-class ships and seven of their larger County-class big sisters. Four of the smaller Colony class – HMS *Nigeria*, HMS *Jamaica*, HMS *Kenya* and HMS *Trinidad* – in spite of being named after warmer climes would also serve in the Arctic.[2] The crucial role these ships played in the battles in the Arctic, and the price they would pay, became apparent during 1942.

THE SPRING CONVOYS OF 1942

The period from March to May 1942 was marked by a regular cycle of convoys to Murmansk, the outbound PQ sailings 13, 14 and 15, and their corresponding westbound convoys QP 9, 10 and 11. These operations were not remarkable for catastrophic successes or failures by either side, and no large surface units put to sea from the German fleet in Norway. However, these months were not without incident, and it was during this period that both sides evolved their offensive and defensive tactics and committed new resources to the battle. Also, when the available signals traffic for the period is analysed, patterns begin to emerge which are very instructive in understanding the usefulness or otherwise of both sides' SIGINT efforts. The lessons of these spring convoy battles will be examined later, but first it is necessary to outline the events of the first part of 1942 in the Arctic.

Even as the Home Fleet was returning to its anchorages in Scapa after the unsuccessful hunt for *Tirpitz,* the relentless cycle of convoys to Russia was continuing. Convoy PQ 13 departed Loch Ewe in Scotland on 10 March 1942, sailing initially for Reykjavik in Iceland, where its numbers would be boosted by a rendezvous with ships arriving directly from the US. The convoy then departed Reykjavik for Murmansk with its close escort of warships on 20 March. It consisted of nineteen merchant vessels, escorted by an ocean escort of two destroyers and two trawlers, augmented by three whalers being transferred to the Soviet navy. Close cover to the convoy was provided by HMS *Trinidad,* commanded by Capt. L.S. Saunders, which rendezvoused with the merchant ships on the evening of 23 March.[3] It was intended that the homebound convoy, QP 9, should leave simultaneously, but that convoy, also of nineteen merchantmen, was delayed by twenty-four hours and departed on 21 March. The cruiser HMS *Kenya* was assigned a similar close escort role for this convoy, but it was unable to find the convoy and proceeded on alone, its captain no doubt preoccupied by the ten tons of Soviet gold he was carrying to the US as payment for the materiel delivered to the Soviets.[4] In support of the convoy escort, and guarding against another sortie by the German battleship *Tirpitz,* was a heavy covering force, comprising the battleships *Duke of York* (Vice Admiral Curteis commanding), *King George V,* the battlecruiser *Renown,* the aircraft carrier HMS *Victorious,* two cruisers, *Kent* and *Edinburgh,* and sixteen destroyers.

The imminent sailing of the convoys was known to the German commanders in *Gruppe Nord* and to Admiral Northern Waters via SIGINT reported from the *B-Dienst.*[5] Since the operation against PQ 12, Admiral Northern Waters had continued his debate with *Gruppe Nord* over command arrangements, and a divided command arrangement remained in place. Admiral Schmundt would have command of all U-boats east of the North Cape (26 degrees east) and would take over command of all boats in contact with the convoys wherever they were found. *Gruppe Nord* would retain control of U-boats west of the North

Cape. The shortcomings of the plan are immediately obvious, not least because the two commands operated on different radio frequencies and the U-boats would have to switch in mid-operation.[6] The submarine force was also divided. Schmundt sent his four available boats to the Murmansk coast (within his area of operations), while *Gruppe Nord* deployed four newly arrived U-boats south-west of Bear Island. The movement of U-boats to the Murmansk coast was identified at Bletchley Park from Enigma messages available on 20 March, and this was passed on by the Admiralty.[7] This led to the twenty-four-hour delay in the sailing of QP 9 from Murmansk. When the convoy did sail, it was protected by fog, snow squalls and high winds, and the U-boats were unable to make any impression; rather the opposite, as the minesweeper HMS *Sharpshooter* chanced upon *U-655* on the surface and was able to ram and sink it before it could submerge. The remainder of the voyage of QP 9 passed undisturbed by German activity.[8]

The surface units available to the Germans had also been increased during this period. The heavy cruiser *Admiral Hipper* left Brunsbüttel in Germany on 19 March and sailed for Norway, arriving on 21 March in Trondheim, where it anchored in a small fjord near to the *Tirpitz*. A series of Enigma messages concerning its passage were read successfully at Bletchley Park, including several transmitted on the evening of 19 March, and these were made available to the Admiralty only five hours later in the early hours of 20 March.[9] Unfortunately, neither British reconnaissance aircraft nor a torpedo striking force of Coastal Command Beauforts managed to find it.[10] Interestingly, the *B-Dienst* were able to pick up on the British air activity almost immediately. *Gruppe Nord* signalled *Hipper* on the afternoon of 20 March: 'B Service report lively recco activity on the part of 18 Group, chiefly from Wick and Leuchars', although Bletchley Park would not break this message for another three days.[11] Despite this additional strength, no plans were made for a sortie by large surface units. *Hipper*'s crew was insufficiently trained, and a number of working up exercises would be required before it was battle ready. The ongoing lack of fuel oil was also a factor. Instead, a plan was drawn up to relocate some of the German destroyers which would normally provide escorts for the larger ships and to allow them to operate against the convoys independently.

PQ 13 ATTACKED

Having left Reykjavik on 20 March, convoy PQ 13 was undisturbed for the first two days' sailing. On 23 March a course alteration was received from the Admiralty, turning the convoy due east in order to avoid a concentration of U-boats.[12] It is likely that this was a response to several Enigma messages decrypted on the morning of 23 March but originating from 20 March between *Gruppe Nord* and the four boats it had operating towards Jan Mayen island.[13] That evening, however, a fierce gale and Arctic storm blew up, which continued until the morning of 27 March, by which time the convoy had been hopelessly dispersed, with no merchant vessels in contact with any of the escorts. The same storm had also hit the heavy covering force, and with damage to his carrier HMS *Victorious*, as well as the destroyer *Tartar*, Admiral Curteis had turned back to Scapa Flow at midnight on 26/27 March. He had no hope of catching up with the convoy or influencing its defence.[14]

On the morning of 27 March, Captain Saunders, in HMS *Trinidad*, and the other escort commanders began an effort to round up their charges. Overnight on 26/27 March the disposition of the German forces became clearer at the Admiralty. Traffic on the German naval Enigma key pair for noon 25 March to noon 27 March started to become available in the evening of 26 March. This included the location of the patrol line of the *Gruppe Nord*-commanded U-boats off Bear Island, codenamed *ZIETHEN* by the Germans, as well as the patrol areas of the boats under Admiral Northern Waters' command off Murmansk.[15] This information was passed on by the Admiralty at around midnight on 26/27 March.[16] Movements northwards by the German 8th Destroyer Flotilla were also picked up, leading to a warning being issued at the same time to the convoy to expect surface attack.[17]

A further round of information became available on the afternoon of 27 March. A message to the *ZIETHEN* group sent repeatedly around midnight on 25/26 March was forwarded to the Admiralty at 3.25 p.m. on 27 March. This referred to both air and surface attacks supporting the U-boats. Further messages provided instructions to the German destroyer flotilla, en route to Kirkenes, to be ready to attack the convoys. A German air force message also reported a sighting of merchant ships on the morning of 26 March.[18] Warnings containing details of the air, surface and U-boat attacks were sent out in a series of Admiralty messages in the late afternoon and evening of 27 March.[19] Unfortunately, this was the last Enigma material available in time to influence the outcome of the action which followed on the journey of PQ 13. Once the German naval Enigma key for noon 27 March to noon 29 March came into operation, Bletchley Park, and hence the Admiralty, would be blocked out of naval traffic until the keys were broken in the late morning of 29 March, by which time the major battles were over.

The situation of the convoy on the morning of 28 March was as follows: the furthest east was the merchantman *Empire Ranger*, which was due north of the North Cape. Roughly 40 miles astern of it to the west was a group of six ships and two smaller escorts, and 35 miles west of that were the destroyer *Fury* and one merchant vessel. A further group of six ships with the remainder of the close escort were 65 miles to the west of *Fury*. Four other merchant ships were straggling and proceeding alone.[20] Captain Saunders in HMS *Trinidad* set about rounding up his charges. He steamed east until he picked up the *Empire Ranger*, then reversed course to the west to try to find the remainder of the convoy. Next, he encountered the destroyer HMS *Fury*, with the merchant ship *Harpalion*, before turning around again and resuming his journey eastwards. The improving weather, however, had brought out the German air force to attack the various scattered parts of PQ 13 which were now strung out within 150 miles of the north Norwegian coast and the airfields of Banak and Bardufoss. Air attacks were made on various parts of the convoy, including an attack on *Trinidad* itself. The *Luftwaffe* achieved two successes: the most easterly ship, *Empire Ranger*, was sunk at around 7.30 that evening, along with one of the most westerly, the straggler *Raceland*.

What the British did not know was that, at 1.30 p.m. on 28 March, the *8. Zerstörer-Flottille*, consisting of the Narvik-class destroyers *Z24*, *Z25* and *Z26*, had sailed from Kirkenes on a northerly course, intending to strike the predicted route of the convoy and track westwards along it until contact was made with the merchant ships. The German destroyer commander *Kapitän* Pönitz was guided by a series of reports of shipping provided by the German air force. These messages, as well as other instructions to the destroyer force, were intercepted in the UK during 28 March, but decrypts of this traffic would not be available until lunchtime on 29 March.[21] Also included in messages around this time was the instruction for the *ZIETHEN* group of U-boats to switch to the control of Admiral Northern Waters now that the fight was passing east of the North Cape.[22] Late in the evening of 28 March the German destroyers started to encounter evidence of their target. At 10.45 p.m. they came across the survivors of the sunken *Empire Ranger* in lifeboats and picked them up, before at 12.30 a.m. meeting the merchantman *Bateau*, which they duly sank, after the crew had been taken prisoner. The Germans then doubled back south-east for several hours before returning north onto the predicted convoy route.[23]

The three German destroyers then altered course west, which put them on a direct course towards the *Trinidad* and the *Fury*, who, having located most of their merchant charges on 28 March and left them in the hands of the destroyer HMS *Eclipse* and the smaller escort vessels, were once again on an easterly course. Contact was inevitable. It was made by *Trinidad*'s radar at 8.45 on the morning of 29 March, and visual sightings followed at 8.49. Saunders opened fire on the leading enemy ship at 8.51 a.m. The fight was by no means uneven; *Trinidad* fired a broadside of twelve 6-inch guns, along with secondary armament of eight 4-inch guns, while *Fury* provided another four 4-inch guns. The three German destroyers, meanwhile, mounted a total of twelve 5.9-inch (150mm) guns. Both sides scored early hits, and a running battle followed as the German ships attempted to dodge out of sight of the British cruiser in the morning mist, while working to the north and west in order to get closer to the likely location of the convoy.

Nonetheless *Trinidad* was able to close down *Z26* to within 1½ miles, taking advantage of the German vessel's disabled rear turret, which prevented it from returning fire in a stern-chase. The demise of the German destroyer seemed inevitable, and *Trinidad* drew abeam to fire torpedoes to finish it off. However, of the three tubes available, only one fired, as the other torpedoes had frozen in their tubes. Even more unluckily for the British, the only torpedo that launched malfunctioned, and instead of running straight towards the German ship, it somehow reappeared, heading directly for *Trinidad*. Despite Captain

Saunders' evasive manoeuvres, the torpedo impacted the cruiser below the bridge, causing significant damage and flooding. In particular, fuel-oil tanks were ruptured and many of the crew of the gunnery computer and transmitting station deep in the ship were drowned in fuel oil.[24]

The German *Z26* took the opportunity to disappear into the mist, hotly pursued by HMS *Fury*. Their course took them towards the portion of the convoy (eight merchant ships) protected by the destroyers HMS *Eclipse* and HMS *Oribi* as well as two Russian destroyers. With the sudden appearance of both *Z26* and *Fury*, a confused melee broke out, which included some friendly fire, before *Fury* broke off to return to *Trinidad* and *Z26* made off once again into the mist, pursued this time by HMS *Eclipse*. The British destroyer continued to bombard its German counterpart until *Z26* was left stopped, awash at the stern and listing. *Eclipse* was about to administer the coup de grace by torpedo when the other two German destroyers appeared on the scene, and the British ship withdrew in the face of superior numbers.[25]

At 10.50 a.m., *Z26* capsized and sank, and after picking up survivors, *Z24* and *Z25* abandoned the fight and set course for Kirkenes, arriving late that evening. *Trinidad*, despite its damage, managed to get underway and limped on to Kola escorted by *Fury* and *Oribi*. Although the risk of surface attack was over, the convoy had yet to pass through the patrol area of the eastern U-boats off Kola, and a further two merchant ships, the *Induna* and the *Effingham*, were lost to submarines. This raised the total loss of merchant vessels in PQ 13 to five ships out of nineteen, or just over 25 per cent. The whaler *Sulla* was also lost from the escort. Significant damage was suffered by *Trinidad* and *Eclipse*, the latter having been struck a number of times in the fight with *Z26*. Among the merchant losses, two had been sunk by aircraft, two by submarines and only one by surface attack. The German losses, meanwhile, amounted to one destroyer and the U-boat rammed by HMS *Sharpshooter* near QP 9.

REACTIONS TO PQ 13

The German commanders considered the operation against the two convoys to have been a 'notable success', but there were differing views on the tactics used and losses incurred. *OKM* stressed that the loss of *Z26* was reason to be even more cautious with surface assets. *Gruppe Nord*, meanwhile, argued that it was evidence that such attacks needed to be supported by heavy surface units to tackle the British cruisers.[26] The U-boats had clearly not lived up to their full potential, and Admiral Northern Waters once again criticised the divided command and the lateness of *Gruppe Nord* in handing over control of their boats to him. However, the deployment of his force to the east of the North Cape was also criticised, as it had not left enough time for the U-boats to fully develop their attack on the convoy before it reached Murmansk.[27]

New arrangements would be in place for the next pair of convoys. Not only was Schmundt placed in more or less complete command of the available U-boats, but there would also no longer be a geographic divide of command at the North Cape, and the whole effort against the convoys would be moved west to the areas east of Jan Mayen Island. Three patrol groups were formed: *NASEWEISS* (two boats), 50 miles east of Jan Mayen; *BUMS* (four boats), 150 miles east of Jan Mayen; and *ROBBENSCHLAG* (eight boats), just to the west of the Bear Island–North Cape passage.[28] GC&CS was able to identify the first two groups in Enigma traffic from the beginning of April, and this was available for the Admiralty to pass on to the fleet on 5 April.[29] The third group, however, escaped notice until a message of 8 April was deciphered on 10 April, by which time convoys had sailed and the *ROBBENSCHLAG* group had been re-tasked east to attack QP 10.[30]

On the Allied side, Admiral Pound, the First Sea Lord, was increasingly concerned at the losses sustained in the Arctic, and in this he was supported by Admiral Tovey as C-in-C Home Fleet. However, the political imperative to continue the runs was overwhelming and was endorsed at the highest level by both Roosevelt and Churchill. Thus, rather than diminishing in size as the weather grew more favourable for the Germans, the convoys actually increased. However, more protective resources were placed at Tovey's disposal. A number of destroyers and corvettes were removed from Atlantic duty with Western Approaches Command and allocated to the Home Fleet, allowing for up to ten of these larger escorts to accompany each convoy.[31] The Americans also balanced their demands for continuing convoys with a substantial naval contribution in the form of the battleship USS *Washington*, light aircraft carrier *Wasp*, the heavy cruisers *Wichita* and *Tuscaloosa* and six destroyers. These forces under US Admiral Giffen were placed under the command of the Home Fleet to augment the covering forces, although they did not begin operations immediately.[32] Representations were also made to the Russian government to provide additional assistance by both air and sea, but beyond the limited destroyer cover provided on the eastern part of the route, little extra help was forthcoming. Historian Richard Woodman summed this up when he commented: 'Though displaying both élan and gallantry, neither the Soviet navy nor its air force ever relieved the British Home Fleet of any appreciable share of the responsibility for the defence of an Arctic convoy.'[33]

PQ 14 AND QP 10

The outbound PQ 14 and returning QP 10 sailed on 8 and 10 April respectively. PQ 14 ran into thick ice after only a couple of days, and the bulk of the convoy was forced to turn back, only eight out of twenty-eight ships pushing on towards Russia. The remainder were joined by an escort of five destroyers and four corvettes, along with the cruiser HMS *Edinburgh*, flying the flag of Rear Admiral Stuart Bonham Carter, commander of 18th Cruiser Squadron (and a talented cricketer). The usual distant covering force of *King George V*, *Duke of York*, *Victorious* and a number of cruisers and destroyers was also at sea, although there were no indications from Allied SIGINT that any move by major German surface units was planned.[34]

QP 10 ran into trouble almost at once. The sixteen merchantmen in the convoy were sighted by the German air force when they were only just over 100 miles out from Kola Inlet, and air and submarine attacks began immediately. The most easterly of the U-boat groups, *ROBBENSCHLAG*, was redirected east of Bear Island to attack QP 10, as German SIGINT was able to confirm that PQ 14 was still some distance to the west and could be engaged later. This information gave Admiral Northern Waters a window of several days in which to attack the westbound ships, before returning to those eastbound.[35] In three days of subsequent fighting, four merchant ships were lost: *Empire*

Cowper sunk by air attack on 11 April, *Kiev* and *El Occidente* sunk by *U-435* on 12 April and *Harpalion* damaged by air strikes and later deliberately sunk by its escort on 13 April.[36]

Things might have been even worse for QP 10, as, on 11 April, the three serviceable destroyers of *8. Zerstörer-Flottille* – *Hermann Schoemann*, *Z24* and *Z25* – sailed from Kirkenes in pursuit of the convoy. Unfortunately for the Germans, terrible weather and visibility meant that the destroyers struggled to find the convoy; meanwhile, the U-boats in the area had to be cautioned against attacks on surface warships for fear of hitting their own destroyers.[37] As a result, the destroyers aborted and returned to Kirkenes. Admiral Schmundt was clearly dissatisfied with this effort, as a message was sent from Admiral Northern Waters to the destroyer group on 12 April: 'Report how weather has interfered with operation. Air recco is intended, so await the results of this. Only put in before this if operation cannot be carried out.'[38]

Chastised, the German destroyers headed out to the north again on 13 April, but they never made contact with the convoy. Nervousness also remained about enemy surface forces; several messages to and from U-boats asked for a tally of the escorting British destroyers, lest their own forces should be forced into a battle on unfavourable terms.[39] In the event, no further attacks were made on QP 10 after 13 April, and the remainder of the convoy, along with returnees from PQ 14, reached Reykjavik on 21 April.

Attention now turned to PQ 14. The convoy was located by the German air force on 15 April south-west of Bear Island, and Admiral Northern Waters concentrated a new U-boat group *BLUTRAUSCH* (which literally translates as 'Bloodlust') to attack it.[40] Submarine and air attacks continued on 15, 16 and 17 April, although these were not marked by any great success, with only one ship, the *Empire Howard*, lost – it exploded on 16 April after being hit by two torpedoes from *U-403*. Once again, deteriorating weather worked in the Allies' favour, as both the U-boats and the German air force struggled to keep track of the merchant ships. A new plan was developed to pick them up as they approached Kola Inlet, and in addition to U-boats and aircraft, the German destroyers once again put to sea,[41] but after a brief sighting of the cruiser HMS *Edinburgh* they too broke off, and the convoy reached Kola on 19 April without further loss.

PQ 15 AND QP 11

By the time the next pair of convoys sailed at the end of April, both sides had made further changes to their offensive or defensive arrangements. The British naval commanders remained sceptical of the whole enterprise. Stuart Bonham Carter wrote in his report on PQ 14 that it was principally luck and the weather that had saved them from greater loss:

> Under present conditions with no hours of darkness, continually under air observation for the last four days, submarines concentrating in the bottlenecks, torpedo attacks to be expected, our destroyers unable to carry out a proper hunt or search owing to the oil situation, serious losses must be expected in every convoy.
>
> The remains of PQ 14 were extremely lucky in the weather in that when the first heavy air attack developed on Friday 17th April, fog suddenly came down [. . .] on the following day [. . .] when a combined surface, submarine and air attack was expected, the weather again was on our side, fog and snow showers persisting all day, and on the final run in to Kola Inlet a strong gale from the north-west sprang up.[42]

Such good fortune could not be relied upon in the future, especially as the seasons advanced. Nonetheless, the prevailing political imperatives gave the Royal Navy no choice but to press on with operations.

New defensive measures were provided for the convoys. For the first time, PQ 15 would be accompanied by a merchant anti-aircraft ship, HMS *Ulster Queen*, a former cross-Channel ferry now equipped with six 4-inch anti-aircraft guns in three turrets, as well as smaller armaments, its boxy civilian lines and straight bows hidden under splinter camouflage paint. A CAM ship, the *Empire Morn*, was also added, with its catapult-mounted Hurricane fighter. In addition, the distant covering force was almost doubled in size, as the US Navy group at Scapa was deployed for the first time, adding a further battleship, two heavy cruisers and a destroyer group to the force. Unfortunately, however, due to the increased daylight, the Allied submarine screen off Norway had to be pulled back 150 miles from the coast to avoid sighting by German air searches. Up to five submarines were still present, but they were no longer able to observe Trondheim directly. The burden of identifying a sortie by German heavy units thus fell even more heavily on SIGINT and on the analysts of GC&CS.

On the German side, Admiral Schmundt concluded that none of the available forces operating alone was very effective, but that success lay in combined submarine, surface and, particularly, air attack. To that end, he attempted to secure even better coordination with the *Luftwaffe*.[43] His air assets were also enhanced at the end of April by the arrival in Norway of modified Heinkel 111 bombers of *KG26*, equipped to carry torpedoes. These aircraft were initially based at Stavanger, but several sub-units were moved to Bardufoss in order to be close to the convoy routes. These moves were detected by the British via *Luftwaffe* traffic and were reported to the Home Fleet in Admiralty messages between 26 and 28 April, at the time that PQ 15 was leaving Reykjavik.[44]

At the same time, however, Admiral Dönitz, as head of the U-boat forces, was pressing for a reduction in submarine numbers in the Arctic, as he felt they were more useful in the North Atlantic. Twenty boats were deployed against the Arctic routes versus eighty-five in the Atlantic, but the longer transit times to the Atlantic area of operations meant that a similar number of boats (sixteen to twenty) was in operation against convoys in each theatre at any one time. Against this baseline, Dönitz calculated that in March those boats in the Atlantic had sunk 96,000 tons of shipping, whereas those in the Arctic only 14,000 tons (14 per cent of the Atlantic figure). Again, for April he compared 120,000 tons in the Atlantic with only 26,000 tons in the Arctic (21 per cent). Thus, U-boats in the Atlantic were arguably five times more effective. He also argued that the long daylight hours, bad weather, strong escort forces and lack of repair facilities in the north made submarine operations there less effective.

His mathematics was flawed, in that it took eighty-five boats, not twenty, to achieve the losses measured in the Atlantic, and on that basis the numbers were pretty equal. In any case Dönitz's argument was in vain, as Admiral Raeder at *OKM* responded by upping Schmundt's force to twenty-six U-boats, arguing that their influence on the critical land battles on the eastern front justified their deployment. Schmundt also reorganised his submarine forces, moving his own headquarters to Narvik and shifting his submarine bases to Narvik, Tromsø and Hammerfest, all to the west of the North Cape, instead of Kirkenes. This placed them further from the Russian air threat to the east and closer to his main focus of operations between Bear Island and Jan Mayen.[45]

The third element of Schmundt's mix was surface units, but here he was less successful. The original intent of *Tirpitz*'s foray against PQ 12 was for a force of multiple units to operate together, but this had been foiled by the torpedoing of *Prinz Eugen*. *Admiral Scheer* was available, but it did not have sufficient speed to accompany *Tirpitz* on operations. *Admiral Hipper* had arrived in Norway in March but such was the poor state of its crew training that much working up would be required before it was any use operationally. The situation would not be resolved until late May, when *Lützow* arrived in Norway, allowing two pairs to be formed, consisting of *Tirpitz* and *Hipper* in Trondheim with two destroyers, and *Scheer* and *Lützow* in Narvik with six destroyers, the latter forming *Kampfgruppe Kummetz* under the vice admiral of that name aboard *Lützow*.[46] We will hear more of *Kampfgruppe Kummetz* in later chapters, but for now all of the German heavy units were effectively stranded by lack of fuel oil. Only the destroyers would continue to be available for operations.

Convoys PQ 15 and QP 11 sailed, as was routine, more or less simultaneously, the eastbound ships leaving Reykjavik on 26 April and those westbound two days later on 28 April. The newly expanded distant covering force sailed from Scapa on 27 April. As had been the pattern with PQ 14 and QP 10, the eastbound outward convoy had several days' sailing ahead of it before it reached the Germans' chosen battle area, while the returning QP 11 was available for attack almost immediately after leaving Kola Inlet. Both convoys had been sighted by the German air force by 29 April, and this allowed Schmundt to direct the seven U-boats still based out of Kirkenes to form group *STRAUCHRITTER* ('highwayman') to attack QP 11. Shortly after, in the early hours of 30 April, *U-88* made contact with the convoy and began sending homing signals to his colleagues.[47]

QP 11 had the usual escort of six destroyers and four corvettes. Initial support was also provided by Russian destroyers, although these did not stay with the convoy for very long. Also, to protect from the threat of German destroyers, the convoy was escorted by the cruiser HMS *Edinburgh*, returning from Murmansk after its escort of PQ 14. It was also, incidentally, carrying another five tons of Russian gold bullion, intended as payment to the US government for supplies delivered by the Allies.[48] Given the likely direction of approach of any German surface attack, Bonham Carter took *Edinburgh* about 15 miles ahead of the convoy to the west, in order to intercept an approach. Unfortunately, the smallness of the anti-submarine escort for the convoy meant that no ships could be spared to accompany *Edinburgh*, and it was forced to rely on its own anti-submarine defences, and a sharply zig-zagging course, for protection. Admiral Tovey, C-in-C Home Fleet, later acknowledged that this risk was taken on his orders:

the *Edinburgh* was to protect Convoy QP 11 against surface attack by enemy destroyers [. . .] the provision of this protection necessitated the *Edinburgh* being within close supporting distance of the convoy, and therefore exposed her to considerable risk of attack by U-boats operating against the convoy. The smallness of the A/S [anti-submarine] escort available for QP 11 did not enable me to provide *Edinburgh* herself with any A/S screen.[49]

Both Bonham Carter and Tovey would come to rue this strategy. At 10.17 a.m. on 30 April, *Kapitänleutnant* Max-Martin Teichert in *U-456* reported that he had sighted a 'Belfast-class' cruiser.[50] He was joined by *Kapitänleutnant* Günther Seibicke in *U-436*, and at 3.38 p.m. Seibicke reported that he had attacked the cruiser with four torpedoes, but all had missed.[51] Teichert would have better luck, as at 4.15 p.m. *Edinburgh* was struck by two torpedoes. The force of the explosion took its stern clean off and damaged the steering gear, but it was able to get underway at slow speed. There was no choice but to limp back to Murmansk, and *Edinburgh* painfully reversed course, escorted by two destroyers – *Foresight* and *Forester*, detached from the convoy – and two Russian destroyers.

The elimination of the cruiser threat altered the dynamics of the battle. Admiral Schmundt, who had initially declined to risk his destroyers against the bigger ship, sent them to sea at midnight on 30 April to find and finish off *Edinburgh* and its escorts. The 'Destroyer Group Northern Waters', consisting of *Hermann Schoemann*, *Z24* and *Z25*, put to sea at 1 a.m. on 1 May, but Schmundt seems almost immediately to have had another change of heart. He signalled the destroyers at 1.15 a.m. – 'operation against cruiser cancelled' – and re-tasked them to attack the now more vulnerable convoy.[52] A lack of firm purpose is detectable in these changes of policy, and this appears to have infected the commander of the destroyer force, *Kapitän zur See* Alfred Schulze-Hinrichs. Guided by shadowing U-boats, he was able to contact the convoy by early afternoon on 1 May. His three ships were detected on radar by the escorting destroyer HMS *Beverley* at 1.15 p.m. The four escorting destroyers immediately formed line ahead between the Germans and the convoy, and a gun and torpedo battle began between the two forces. Four times, the German ships approached the convoy over the next five hours, but each time they broke off the attack after a few minutes, despite the fact that their three destroyers vastly outgunned their four British opponents. The only loss was one Russian merchant ship, probably hit by a torpedo fired by the German destroyers.[53]

Schulze-Hinrichs sent several messages in the course of the afternoon to Admiral Northern Waters, but none recorded a decisive success, only that he was fighting a force of four enemy destroyers and was running low on ammunition and torpedoes, but that 'hits had been observed'.[54] Schmundt's reaction was to call him off the convoy and redirect his attentions back towards HMS *Edinburgh*, signalling: 'If still impossible to attack by 2000, discontinue task and operate against cruiser.'[55] This would be the third re-tasking of the German destroyer force since sailing only sixteen hours before. As a consequence, QP 11 was left to continue its journey unmolested and without further loss, arriving in Reykjavik at 7 a.m. on 7 May. Prior to the arrival of the German destroyers, the convoy had been attacked on the morning of 1 May by the German air force. This attack is principally significant as it was the first mission flown by the torpedo bombers of *KG26*, but all aircraft missed their targets and no damage was suffered.[56]

HMS *Edinburgh*, meanwhile, had been inching its way towards Murmansk, at times under tow, and at times under its own power but unable to steer effectively, making holding a course very difficult. The Russian destroyers were forced to withdraw due to lack of fuel, and so *Forester* and *Foresight* spent the night of 30 April–1 May keeping at bay the shadowing U-boats. Late on 1 May they were joined by a force from Murmansk consisting of the Russian warship *Rubin* and four British minesweepers, along with a tug. Hopes rose that the battered cruiser might be saved, but these were shattered when the German destroyers arrived on the scene at around 6 the next morning. Bonham Carter had ordered that, in this eventuality, the escorts were to fight their own battle without worrying about *Edinburgh*, but this order had not reached the minesweepers, who remained as close consorts to the cruiser throughout the following action, holding off U-boats and firing their diminutive salvoes at any German destroyer within range. *Edinburgh*, meanwhile, went to maximum speed (about 8 knots) but, without steering, sailed in erratic circles, engaging the enemy ships whenever its guns would bear.

The British drew first blood, *Edinburgh* hitting the *Hermann Schoemann* with its second salvo, destroying the German vessel's engines and bringing it to a stop. Unfortunately, at the same time *Z24* scored a series of hits on *Foresight*, also stopping its engines, and killing the commanding officer. The ensuing melee was fought with both sides making smoke, and highly variable visibility due to the changing weather. By the end of the engagement, at about 8.20 a.m., the Germans had managed to get *Z24* alongside the *Hermann Schoemann* and take off most of the crew before scuttling it; meanwhile, the two British destroyers were heavily damaged. *Edinburgh* had been hit by two further torpedoes and had to be abandoned, before *Foresight* sank it with its own last torpedo. The crew were mostly taken off by the attendant minesweepers, but just over fifty of its complement had perished in the action.[57]

Having recovered their shipmates, the two remaining German destroyers made off rapidly to the north-west and disappeared. This was despite the fact that their three principal British adversaries were stopped and heavily damaged, and could have been sunk by the Germans at their leisure. Nor did they attempt to re-engage with the convoy. This could be interpreted as a significant lack of offensive spirit on their part, but it must be remembered that, as they drew off, *Edinburgh* was still afloat and firing, and in the poor visibility it was difficult to determine how many British ships were present, as the minesweepers were also firing on the Germans and may have been mistaken for larger vessels. It would appear that Admiral Northern Waters was not aware of the fate of *Edinburgh* for some time, as U-boats were tasked with looking for it as late as the morning of 3 May.[58] Clearly, significant 'fog of war', both literal and metaphorical, hung over the Germans' understanding of the real situation.

Attention now turned to the outbound PQ 15. At 11.50 a.m. on 2 May, after hearing that his destroyers had broken off the fight, Admiral Northern Waters redirected the *STRAUCHRITTER* U-boat group (less the boats still hunting *Edinburgh*) to move west and engage the eastbound convoy.[59] The location of the Allied ships had been established by a Condor patrol on 30 April and their progress had been followed since then. An air attack by bombers on 1 May scored no hits, but a raid on 3 May was more successful. Torpedo bombers of 1 Coastal Group of *KG26* attacked at low level during the darkest part of the day and were not seen or detected by radar until very late. Three were shot down, but they managed to deliver torpedoes into three merchant ships, the *Botavon*, the *Cape Corso* and the *Jutland*, all of which were sunk.[60] After that, however, despite further air attack and the best efforts of the depleted *STRAUCHRITTER* U-boats, PQ 15 arrived in Murmansk on 5 May without further loss.

Four merchantmen sunk out of a total of thirty-eight sailing in the two convoys was not a disastrous loss. The cost for the Royal Navy, however, had been high. *Edinburgh* was sunk and two destroyers were heavily damaged. In addition, an accident in the covering force during fog led to HMS *King George V* ramming the destroyer *Punjabi* and cutting it in two, while damaging itself in the process. The escort of PQ 15 also forced a submarine to the surface, only to find it was a Polish boat, which subsequently had to be scuttled. In exchange for this, the Germans had lost a destroyer, with two more damaged, and several aircraft, but no U-boats.

For the Germans, the sinking of an enemy cruiser counted as a significant success. It was, however, a distraction from their main purpose, which was to interrupt the flow of supplies to Russia by sinking merchant ships. In the latter regard, the U-boats had been especially ineffective, achieving no hits on any merchant vessels of either convoy; of the four ships lost, three were sunk by aircraft and one by the destroyers. This can largely be blamed on Admiral Northern Waters and his decision to split and divert his submarine forces, firstly between the two convoys and later against the tempting target of the damaged *Edinburgh*. Penny-packets of one or two U-boats would always struggle against the convoy escorts, but a concerted attack by half a dozen or more stood much more chance of overwhelming the defences and scoring hits on the merchantmen. This was, after all, the rationale behind the *rudeltaktik* ('wolfpack') doctrine. Despite the revised command arrangements, *Gruppe Nord* also continued to interfere in operations, diverting two U-boats to chase *Edinburgh*, when they might have been better disposed against PQ 15.[61] In its post-war analysis of these operations, GC&CS offered the following summary:

> The operations against PQ 15 and QP 11, while constituting a tactical failure, had served to provide Admiral Northern Waters with some valuable object lessons. In the first place, it had been abundantly clear that the use of destroyers against a convoy with a cruiser escort was impracticable, no matter what apparently easy path to success was opened. In addition, the decision to split forces between three targets was shown to militate strongly against obtaining good results from any one of the attacks so delivered. Strongest of all the tactical implications in the action was the pressing need to incorporate in future operations the greatest possible strength of aircraft and heavy units.[62]

The emphasis here on air power is significant. The increasing influence of the *Luftwaffe* on the battle was partly due to detailed organisation and streamlining of its operations. A coordinated structure for convoy attacks had been developed. In this, responsibility for the various phases of a convoy sailing were distributed to different units. The British Home Fleet at Scapa was monitored by the aircraft of *Fliegerführer Nord-West* from Stavanger. Meanwhile, other units of his force based in Trondheim conducted routine patrols over the convoy routes. If a convoy was sighted, the Trondheim squadrons switched to covering Home Fleet and any shadowing force of heavy units that might be at sea, while following and attacking the convoy itself became the responsibility of *Fliegerführer Lofotens,* and in turn *Fliegerführer Nordost* as it passed eastwards. Attacks on the returning QP convoys were not a particular priority for *Fliegerführer Nordost,* but regular reconnaissance of Kola Inlet showed when QP convoys sailed, which was a clue to when a PQ convoy would also sail. This clear division of responsibility, unlike that of the navy, allowed for coordinated and effective operations.[63] Just how effective this could be would be revealed on the next three convoy sailings (dealt with in the next chapter).

A post-script to the story of the spring convoys, and a foretaste of the power of the *Luftwaffe,* was the fate of HMS *Trinidad.* Having been patched up in Murmansk into a seaworthy condition, the cruiser departed Russia on the evening of 13 May. It was accompanied by the destroyers *Somali, Matchless* and the rather battered *Foresight* and *Forester,* with Admiral Bonham Carter on board, fresh from his abandonment of *Edinburgh* less than a fortnight before. A cruiser squadron under Admiral Burrough was placed west of Bear Island to meet the returning group, and the Home Fleet covering force was also put to sea further to the south-west. In the event, however, this protection was of no avail. The *Trinidad* group was spotted by the German air force on the following morning, 14 May, and it was shadowed continuously by multiple aircraft thereafter. Dive-bombing of the group began at 10 p.m., followed by torpedo-bomber attack half an hour later. *Trinidad* was struck by one bomb forward of the bridge, starting a fire which soon became uncontrollable. At midnight the decision was taken to abandon it, and after crew and passengers had been transferred to the destroyers, it was finally sunk by a torpedo from *Matchless* at 1.20 a.m. on 15 May. Bombing of the surviving destroyers continued on 15 May, but no further hits were scored.[64] Bonham Carter gave his own opinion of his experience of having two cruisers sunk beneath him: 'I am still convinced that until the aerodromes in North Norway are neutralised and there are some hours of darkness that the continuation of these convoys should be stopped. If they must continue for political reasons, very serious and heavy losses must be expected. The force of the German attacks will increase, not diminish.'[65]

Sadly, those 'political reasons' continued to apply, and Bonham Carter's predicted losses would indeed be suffered by the remaining convoys of the 1942 Arctic summer.

THE INFLUENCE OF SIGINT ON THE SPRING CONVOYS

The quantity of SIGINT ultimately accumulated by Naval Section at GC&CS allows a detailed picture of German operations against these convoys to be reconstructed. Almost all the significant moves by German surface ships and submarines are recorded in messages contained in the surviving decrypts. However, due to the delays in the breaking of the various German cipher keys in use during each operation, the fact that any one message was read eventually is not proof that it was read in a timely enough way to be immediately operationally useful. Only by reconstructing in detail the timeline of each convoy and analysing not only the times when messages were sent by the German forces but also the times at which those messages were read at the Admiralty can the tactical value of that intelligence be assessed. Before examining the detail of this, however, it should be pointed out that late decryption was not useless decryption. All of this traffic contained longer-term information about enemy doctrine, strength, equipment and procedures which added to the detailed understanding both GC&CS and the Admiralty were able to build up of German forces in the Arctic. In fact, much of the value of Naval Section's work lay in this longer-term analysis. For the present, however, the discussion will be confined to short-term tactical information. The picture naturally breaks down into three parts: knowledge of the intentions of the German large surface units, knowledge of the activities of the smaller surface ships, in particular the destroyer flotillas, and, finally, understanding of U-boat operations.

The movements of German capital ships were mostly quite well understood on the Allied side. For example, when *Hipper* sailed for Norway between 19 and 21 March, this information was available from Enigma messages transmitted on 18 and 19 March and deciphered on 20 March, in time for an air attack on the enemy ship – albeit an abortive one – to be mounted. Similarly, once convoys PQ 13 and QP 9 were at sea, messages were intercepted concerning local exercises by *Hipper* around Trondheim, and at midnight on 26 March the Admiralty was able to signal the Home Fleet, fairly confident that the moves of German destroyers northwards were 'not connected with larger units'.[66] A follow-up message on the evening of 27 March confirmed that *Hipper* continued exercising near Trondheim.[67]

Very little traffic concerning large surface units was intercepted during the passage of PQ 14 and QP 10. For the analysts of Bletchley Park, this provided fairly strong negative evidence of any move by those ships, as no traffic associated with operations was detected. The Admiralty was thus able to report on 13 April (when the two convoys had completed about one-third of their journey) that no major enemy units were at sea.[68] This information was repeated at midnight on 14/15 April.[69] When PQ 15 and QP 11 put to sea at the end of April, there was more activity detected around *Tirpitz* and the other large German ships. The German fleet had been brought to high readiness on 21 April due to fears of an imminent attack on Norway but was stood down after the attack failed to materialise. The Admiralty reported this with the wry comment 'nothing is known of any [Allied] forces off the Lofoten Islands, the weather at the time was hazy'.[70] A similar scare occurred on 29 April, when *Gruppe Nord* warned the Admiral Commanding Battleships to 'expect a raid', but this fear was dispelled when it was realised that the raiding force was actually the distant covering force for PQ 15.[71] These messages were read at the Admiralty on 1 May, but as they did not reflect any aggressive move by the German ships, the information was not passed on to the fleet. It seems that, as often as not, no news was good news when it came to the large German ships. A lack of signal traffic could be interpreted as a lack of activity, and the Admiralty could be confident of their non-interference in events, at least in the short term.

The activities of the German destroyer flotillas were also followed via intercepts, but the usefulness of this information was heavily dependent on the length of time taken by the decryption process, and, while some messages were broken in time to be passed on, others were not, producing a mixed picture. During the passage of PQ 13, the moves of German destroyers first to Narvik and then to Kirkenes on 25 and 26 March were followed and passed on by the Admiralty to the fleet in the early hours of 27 March.[72] Later that same day, further intercepts showed that the destroyers had arrived in Kirkenes and were preparing to attack the convoys.[73] All of this information was available prior to HMS *Trinidad*'s encounter with the German ships on 29 March. Unfortunately, however, several decrypts describing the German force's movements once at sea, intercepted on 28 March, were not available until the afternoon of 29 March, by which time the surface-ship battle was already over.[74]

Similarly, when the German destroyers sailed again to attack QP 10 at lunchtime on 11 April, the relevant intercepts were not available to the Admiralty until late in the evening of 12 April, by which time they had already aborted their mission.[75] Again, when the Germans renewed their destroyer attack on the morning of 13 April, the messages were not broken until lunchtime the following day.[76] In the event, these delays were not significant, as the German ships did not press home their attack, but in other circumstances the wait for information might have been fatal. It is also notable that it was on 14 April that the Admiralty signalled that no threat was expected from major surface units, which, while true, had the potential to decrease readiness among the escorts for surface attack, at the very time when the German destroyers were at sea. The risk of inappropriate wider inferences being drawn from specific messages was ever-present.

In the case of HMS *Edinburgh* and QP 11, the decision by Admiral Northern Waters to commit his destroyers against the damaged cruiser happened to be signalled at 11.20 p.m. on 30 April, thirty-six hours into the 29 April–1 May key cycle.[77] Bletchley Park broke the keys for that period the following morning (1 May), allowing the Admiralty to send warning to Admiral Bonham Carter at lunchtime that day. This gave him time to brief his forces in preparation for an attack.[78] It is perhaps fortunate that the subsequent message from Schmundt to his destroyers only two hours later in the early morning of 1 May calling off their attack on the cruiser was not read at Bletchley Park until 3 May, nor indeed were those reinstating the attack later that day. Too close a following of the indecisive command on the German side that day would only have served to confuse the picture equally on the Allied side.

SIGINT was perhaps least tactically useful to the Admiralty in tracking the movements of enemy submarines. By far the largest portion of intercepted traffic was that sent to and from U-boats, so it may seem odd that this was not of greater value; however, a number of factors mitigated against its immediate relevance to the battles. The first of these was that German intelligence was good enough to predict when convoys were likely to depart, and Admiral Northern Waters, or *Gruppe Nord*, were usually able to pre-position their boats across the likely convoy routes in advance of the arrival of the convoys. This meant that orders to the already formed U-boat groups were usually executed with very little delay. Any re-positioning of boats could usually be completed within twelve hours, as the battle area (unlike in the Atlantic) was relatively small. This meant that a delay of twelve to twenty-four hours in decryption of a message, which was not unusual, often rendered it out of date. This was not so with surface ships, whose operations began further away in Norwegian ports and thus took longer to execute.

Linked to this was the fact that the sea space available to the convoys was very restricted, particularly in the key battle area between Bear Island and the North Cape. Thus, the scope for re-routing of convoys to avoid U-boat patrol lines was very limited. There was also relatively little that convoy escorts could do, even if they were forewarned of submarine attack, that they were not already doing. When the movements of large enemy surface units or the destroyer groups were detected in advance, the potential existed for the covering forces of Allied warships to manoeuvre and act independently against them. Against submarines, this was not an option. As the fate of the *Edinburgh* proved, to hunt U-boats with larger vessels was to invite disaster, and there were simply not enough dedicated anti-submarine vessels available to form hunter groups independent of the immediate screens around the convoys. This left the convoys with little choice but to await submarine attack passively and to rely on the expertise of their local escorts to chase off the attacking U-boats. Nonetheless, the poor record of the U-boats against these convoys suggests that the lack of relevant SIGINT did not put these escorts at much of a disadvantage.

One threat that decrypts did reveal in advance was that of the new German torpedo bombers deployed north in April 1942. Their first sortie against QP 11 was unsuccessful, but they were subsequently able to score hits on PQ 15. This was combined with the efforts of the existing bomber forces, who were successful in finishing off HMS *Trinidad*. The power of the air threat against the convoys was set to increase, and ever more complex air defence measures were required. How this was countered, both by SIGINT and other means, is a story for the next chapter.

CHAPTER SIX

'CONVOY IS TO SCATTER'

CONVOYS PQ 16 AND PQ 17, MAY–JULY 1942

SHIP-BOARD 'COMPUTORS'

In June 1940 Jack Purvis joined the RAF Volunteer Reserve. He was thirty-three years old at the time and since leaving school at fourteen had spent much of his life in the textile industry in Glasgow. His age made him ineligible to be called up, but he was determined to serve and so volunteered for the RAF. In his time working at J & P Coats, a thread manufacturer in Glasgow, Jack had, despite his lack of formal education, become fluent in both French and German, dealing with the textile markets in those countries, and in his spare time doing work as an interpreter for Rangers football club.

His linguistic skills were immediately recognised, and after only a fortnight of military training he found himself at Bletchley Park, working in Air Section as a 'computor' responsible for breaking low-level ciphers used by the German air force and analysing both German Morse and voice (R/T) traffic. Jack considered Bletchley Park to be 'a queer place in many respects', but nonetheless his talents led to his promotion to corporal and then sergeant. He was later posted to Cheadle, which was at the heart of the SIGINT operation against the German air force. It was during his time at Cheadle that Purvis was selected for a commission, and despite his own scepticism as to whether he was really officer material, he found himself in late 1941 an acting pilot officer.

After the mauling received by the Royal Navy at the hands of the *Luftwaffe* in April and May 1942, described in the previous chapter, it was decided that for the next convoy, PQ 16, at-sea interception of German air force wireless traffic, both W/T and R/T, would be helpful in giving early warning of enemy air attack. The Royal Navy had in fact been developing a ship-borne SIGINT capability since the spring of 1941, but suitably qualified linguists had proved hard to find and the relevant teams were slow to be rolled out. The Home Fleet did not receive its first Royal Navy intercept operators until 1943.[1] Instead, in the summer of 1942 the navy turned to the RAF for the relevant expertise.

As a consequence, Jack Purvis was summoned from Cheadle to Bletchley, and without even the chance to recover his belongings from Cheadle he was whisked first to the Admiralty, and then to Thurso to rendezvous with the destroyer HMS *Ashanti*. On board ship, he was 'to participate in Convoy PQ16 to Murmansk, in command of a mixed RAF and Naval unit, for the purpose of keeping the Commodore informed of enemy movements as learned from the interception and decoding of messages transmitted by the Luftwaffe'.[2]

To cover this new-found responsibility, he was promoted to flight lieutenant. On board *Ashanti*, the captain, Richard Onslow, who would be the escort commander for the convoy, made light of Purvis' secret role when introducing him to the other members of the wardroom:

> [Onslow] took me down to the wardroom to meet the naval offi-
> cers. He said that no doubt they were wondering why an RAF
> officer should be joining them, but explained that, whenever enemy
> aircraft was sighted, Flt Lt Purvis would open the box he had
> brought with him, take out his collapsible Spitfire and proceed to
> engage the enemy! This of course produced roars of laughter, and
> they understood then that the purpose of my presence was not to be
> questioned. However, from then onwards, I was always addressed as
> 'Spitfire'.

Jack Purvis served on *Ashanti* throughout PQ 16 and was later trans-ferred to the cruiser HMS *London* in order to perform the same role for PQ 17. Little did he know that he was about to experience some of the fiercest air attacks on any convoys ever conducted in the Arctic. After PQ 17, Purvis returned to Bletchley and went on to be an instructor, passing on his experiences at sea. For his service, he was mentioned in dispatches in January 1945.

PQ 16 AND QP 12

The concerns expressed by Admiral Bonham Carter on his return to the UK after the loss of *Trinidad* were widely shared at the Admiralty. As the Arctic entered the summer period of near-perpetual daylight and the weather improved, it became an ever more dangerous environment for convoys. Air attack was becoming a particular concern. Admiral Tovey requested that long-range fighters, or at least reconnaissance aircraft, might be stationed in Russia to provide cover for the convoys beyond the reach of UK aircraft, but Coastal Command did not have aircraft to spare.[3] Equally, Russian promises of additional air support proved to be mostly empty words. It was therefore with a considerable sense of foreboding that in late May the Home Fleet prepared to escort the largest Russian convoy so far, consisting of thirty-five merchant ships.

In addition to Flt Lt Purvis' on-board SIGINT team, a number of other protective measures against air attack were taken. The auxiliary anti-aircraft ship *Ulster Queen* was already in Murmansk and would be returning with QP 12, in its stead the outgoing convoy PQ 16 was accompanied by its sister ship *Alynbank*, which, critically, was equipped with radar in addition to anti-aircraft guns of various calibres. This was vital, as none of the other Royal Navy vessels in the close escort were radar-equipped, the only other set being carried by the CAM ship *Empire Lawrence* (which would be sunk before reaching Russia). In addition, every merchant ship was equipped with a barrage balloon which could be raised in the event of attack to interfere with overflight of the ships by enemy aircraft.[4]

PQ 16 departed Reykjavik on 21 May 1942. In addition to its escort of minesweepers and trawlers, it was joined in the following days by a force of five destroyers under Commander Onslow on the *Ashanti* and by Admiral Burroughs' 10th Cruiser Squadron, formed of HMS

Norfolk, Kent, Liverpool and *Nigeria*. The usual covering force of battle-ships and a carrier from the Home Fleet also took station to the north-east of Iceland to defend against a sally by the larger German surface units. There was some confusion due to fog, but all of the various component forces had collected together by 25 May, with the four cruisers spaced between the lines of merchantmen, and the destroyers and smaller ships in an anti-submarine ring around the outside.

At 6.30 a.m. on 25 May the convoy was sighted by a German FW Condor aircraft, which continued to shadow the ships for the rest of the day. At around 9 p.m. the first air attacks by the *Luftwaffe* began. These were to continue at irregular intervals for the next five days, until 5 p.m. on 30 May. Initially, the convoy survived unscathed from the air, but on 26 May Burroughs' cruisers broke off in accordance with orders not to risk themselves too far east and sailed to link with the homeward-bound QP 12. The loss of the cruisers' anti-aircraft firepower was to be keenly felt when the German air force returned to the convoy on 27 May. In a day of severe attacks, no fewer than six merchant ships were lost to bomb and torpedo attack: the *Alamar, Mormacsul, Empire Lawrence, Empire Purcell, Lowther Castle* and the *City of Joliet*. A further three ships were heavily damaged but able to proceed, while, in two cases, fires continued to burn on board. The anti-aircraft ship *Alynbank* recorded 108 individual air attacks, a surprisingly accurate tally, as German records show 101 sorties by Ju 88 and 7 by He 111 aircraft. The cost to the Germans was three Ju 88 bombers lost, although the convoy defenders believed they had brought down more.[5] Air attacks continued for three more days but without further loss to the convoy. The strain on the crews was enormous, as virtually everyone remained at permanent action stations for the best part of a week, sleeping at their posts in the brief intervals between combat. Physical as well as human resources ran low, and Commander Onslow became concerned for his dwindling ammunition stocks, at one point ordering only one gun-mount on HMS *Ashanti* to be fired at each wave of German aircraft. Despite their increasing defencelessness, the merchant captains sailed doggedly on. Onslow paid tribute to this in his report: 'We were all inspired by the parade-ground rigidity of the convoy's station-keeping, including the *Ocean Voice* and the *Stari Bolshevik*, who were both billowing smoke from their foreholds.'[6] PQ 16 reached Murmansk on 30 May, with six ships continuing to Archangel, now ice-free, where they arrived on 1 June.

The performance of the *U-bootwaffe* against these two convoys was rather less impressive. A six-boat wolfpack *GREIF* ('bird of prey') was formed on 14 May and initially took up a patrol line to the south-east of Jan Mayen Island.[7] This information had been discovered by GC&CS by 19 May and was passed on the same day by the Admiralty to C-in-C Home Fleet and 10th Cruiser Squadron (two days before PQ 16 sailed).[8] The wolfpack adjusted its position on 22 May, and again this was revealed in traffic intercepted during 22 May and broken twenty-four hours later on 23 May, towards the end of the 21–23 May key period. This information was passed on by the OIC to the fleet at 11.30 a.m. on 23 May.[9] This was followed by a German air force sighting of ships 'assumed to be PQ.16' late on 23 May. This too was passed on to the fleet, at around midnight on 24 May.[10] The subsequent sighting on 25 May and the air attacks that followed have already been described.

The first U-boat contact with PQ 16 was in the early hours of 25 May, and repeated attacks were made during the next forty-eight hours. A running battle was fought as escort vessels first detected and then drove off U-boats with gunfire and depth charges, while the submarines struggled into firing positions and launched multiple torpedoes. The battles can be followed in the frequent wireless reports intercepted from U-boats during the fight, but none of these were deciphered until late in the 25–27 May key period, by which time most of them were of only historical interest. Despite all this effort, only one merchantman was hit – the American *Syros*, torpedoed by *U-703* at 3 a.m. on 26 May. No U-boats were sunk, but several suffered depth-charge damage, and two had to break off the fight and return to port.

In contrast with the running air and submarine battle fought by PQ 16, the returning QP 12 had a passage from Murmansk described as 'singularly uneventful'.[11] The convoy was overflown by a group of German reconnaissance aircraft on 25 May, but these disappeared after the CAM ship *Empire Morn* launched its Hurricane, which claimed one Ju 88. Sadly, the Hurricane pilot was killed when his parachute failed to open on leaving the aircraft.[12] For the next four days the convoy was undisturbed, protected for much of the journey by fog, and it arrived in Iceland on 29 May.

RESPONSES AND PLANS: OPERATION *RÖSSELSPRUNG*

The Allied response to the loss of six ships out of thirty-five in PQ 16 was measured against prior predictions of heavy loss. Admiral Tovey described 'success beyond expectation'. Commander Onslow, who had been in the thick of the action, was pleased by his ships' performance but had a number of recommendations for improvement. These included better air defence in the form of more CAM ships, or ideally an escort carrier, as well as more radar. He also advocated for specially tasked rescue ships, as his escorts had become crowded with survivors from the sunken merchantmen.[13]

The Germans were less satisfied. Dönitz travelled to Trondheim on 30 May to meet with Admiral Schniewind and plan for the next round of operations. He wrote in the *BdU* war diary:

My opinion as to the small chances of success for U-boats against convoys during the northern summer [. . .] has been confirmed by experience with PQ 16. Owing to difficult conditions for attack (constant light, very variable weather and visibility, abnormally strong convoy escort, clever handling of the convoy, appearance of Russian aircraft forcing the U-boats to dive on sighting our own aircraft as well) the result, in spite of shadowing and a determined set-to by the boats, has been one steamer sunk and four probable hits. This must be accounted a failure when compared with the results of the anti-submarine activity for the boats operating [. . .] U436 [and] U703 have depth charge damage, unfit to dive to greater depths, three more boats have slight depth charge damage, the defects of which [. . .] will probably mean some considerable time in the dockyard.

He concluded: 'the German Air Force would seem to be a better means of attacking convoys in the north in the summer.'[14]

The picture was complicated by the fact that, while the operation against PQ 16 was in progress, Hitler had another of his periodic panics over the possible Allied invasion of Norway and ordered that all available U-boats should be sent north. Dönitz's view was the polar opposite. Not only had his U-boats been unable to prevent British landings in Norway in 1940, but since then they had been able to sink only eight ships from sixteen outbound convoys, and only one from the twelve return sailings, this at a cost of three U-boats lost and more damaged. The commander of the U-boat fleet believed that all his boats should be withdrawn from the Arctic and put to better use in the Atlantic. A middle course was steered by the commander of the navy, Admiral Raeder, who settled on a force of around twenty-four boats in the north, which would allow eight to be deployed against each convoy.[15]

Better still would be an operation which combined all of the resources at the Germans' disposal: air, surface and U-boats. It was obvious that a well-coordinated combined strike by all arms was required, and a plan was developed named Operation RÖSSELSPRUNG ('knight's move' in chess) to attack the next PQ convoy, probably in June. The weather would probably be good, but the ice would not have yet retreated completely to its summer minimum (reached in August), so the corridor available to convoys around the North Cape would be only 240 miles wide. This would allow surface forces based in the extreme north of Norway to reach the convoy before Allied heavy forces could intervene. Stocks of oil had also finally been built up which would allow for operations by heavy surface units, as well as U-boats and aircraft. Hitler had placed a prohibition on the use of large surface ships unless interference from the British Home Fleet could be ruled out, so the surface action was intended to take place to the east of the North Cape and Bear Island, well away from any British carrier group.[16]

Two German surface groups were formed: *Tirpitz* and *Hipper* at Trondheim with four destroyers as escort, commanded by Schniewind himself, and *Lützow* and *Admiral Scheer* at Narvik with six destroyers as *Kampfgruppe Kummetz*, commanded by the vice admiral of that name. The aim was that the two groups would move to more northerly anchorages once a convoy was expected, and then at the right moment they would pounce, the *Tirpitz* group attacking the shadowing cruiser force while the two pocket battleships went for the convoy itself, all of which would take place in the east out of reach of the heavy forces of the Home Fleet. Speed was essential, as well as seamless cooperation with aircraft and submarines, which would both track the convoy for the surface fleet and mount attacks in their own right.[17]

Admiral Schniewind issued formal orders for this operation on 14 June. Fortunately for the Allies, the Swedes were reading German communications to and from Norway, and by 18 June the full details of the plan were provided to British naval intelligence via their attaché in Stockholm, Captain Henry Denham. Ongoing Enigma intercepts had also allowed Naval Section at Bletchley Park to build up a complete picture of current German ship and U-boat dispositions and air strengths in Norway, so the Allies had a pretty good idea both of German intentions and of the forces available to carry them out.[18] At the same time, German SIGINT was providing the *Kriegsmarine* with confident predictions of when the next convoys, PQ 17 and the returning QP 13 (which they were able to identify specifically by their PQ numbers) were likely to sail, what route they would take and how they would be protected. Little was hidden from either side.

For the Germans, the challenge was, firstly, actually to find the convoy when it was at sea (not always straightforward) and, secondly, to find the Home Fleet shadowing force to ensure it could not interfere with their surface ships. For the Allies, the challenge was to monitor whether the German surface fleet would be tempted out of its anchorages in the fjords, and, if it were, what to do about it. Hints of the debacle which would follow were revealed in a telephone briefing between Sir Dudley Pound, First Sea Lord, and Admiral Tovey, C-in-C Home Fleet, who was still at anchor in Scapa Flow. Pound advised Tovey that in the event of a German surface attack, he (Pound) might be obliged to order the convoy to scatter. Knowing how vulnerable merchant ships sailing alone would be to aircraft and U-boats, Tovey described this idea as 'Sheer bloody murder', but he could not influence Pound to adopt any other policy.[19]

PQ 17 AND QP 13

Both PQ 17 and QP 13 sailed on 27 June 1942. PQ 17 consisted of thirty-four merchant ships bound for Murmansk (eight ships) and

Archangel (twenty-two ships), along with three rescue ships and an RFA oiler for the escort. The convoy was closely escorted by six destroyers, four corvettes, three minesweepers, two merchant anti-aircraft ships, four anti-submarine trawlers and two submarines. This force, First Escort Group (EG1), was commanded by Escort Leader Commander John Broome in the Destroyer HMS *Keppel*. Shadowing the convoy was 1st Cruiser Squadron (CS1), commanded by Rear Admiral Louis Hamilton aboard HMS *London*. His force included four cruisers – two British (HMS *London* and HMS *Norfolk*) and two US (USS *Wichita* and USS *Tuscaloosa*) – along with three British and American destroyers. Further afield, Admiral Tovey put to sea with a distant covering force of two battleships, his flagship HMS *Duke of York* and the American USS *Washington*, along with the aircraft carrier HMS *Victorious*, two cruisers and a large force of twelve destroyers.[20]

Knowing that an attack by German surface ships was likely, a screen of fifteen Allied submarines (eight British, six Russian and one French) was placed around the coast of northern Norway to report, and possibly interrupt, any German sailings. Air patrols over the Arctic Ocean and the ports of Norway were also stepped up. It was recognised by the Admiralty that if larger German warships were at sea, the cruiser force (CS1) would be no match for them, so it was arranged that the cruisers would go no further east than Bear Island unless it was confirmed that there was no surface threat.[21] This may have been a wise move to protect the Royal Navy's diminishing supply of cruisers, but it did not answer how the convoy itself would be defended in this eventuality.

In anticipation of PQ 17, a 'wolfpack' of ten U-boats was assembled on 21 June codenamed *EISTEUFEL* ('ice-devil') and spread in a patrol line across the expected path of the convoy. This fact was known to the Admiralty and passed to the fleet on the afternoon of 22 June, five days before the convoy sailed.[22] Increased Allied air reconnaissance flights at the end of the month over the Norwegian ports hinted to the Germans that a convoy might be imminent. This was followed by sightings on 28 and 29 June of a battleship and destroyers at sea north-east of Iceland and by a sighting of the forty ships of QP 13 off the North Cape. The sighting of QP 13 was circulated in a wireless message by Admiral Northern Waters during the evening of 30 June and was intercepted by

Bletchley Park and forwarded to the Admiralty at lunchtime on 1 July.[23] However, the German Enigma key change at 12 p.m. on 1 July meant that no further messages would be available to Allied commanders until the early hours of 3 July. This gap in information was a major consideration in Admiralty planning, and Admiral Tovey at sea with the Home Fleet specifically asked on 28 June to be kept informed of when current 'special intelligence' would be available and when not.[24]

German command decided that QP 13 was a secondary target only to be attacked from the air. PQ 17 was sighted by a U-boat (*U-456*) in the vicinity of Jan Mayen Island on the afternoon of 1 July.[25] Meanwhile, German air reconnaissance also sighted a separate large force including an aircraft carrier in the area of the Denmark Strait (the sea between Iceland and Greenland). This was Tovey's distant covering force and, as both sides knew, knowledge of its location was key to German planning.[26] It must have been disappointing for Admiral Northern Waters to report that aircraft reconnaissance had lost these ships again by the evening of 1 July.[27]

The eastbound and westbound convoys were due to pass each other near Jan Mayen Island on 2 July. An air attack on PQ 17 was planned for that evening, to be carried out by seven He 115 torpedo bombers of *Luftwaffe Küstenfliegergruppe 406*. Aircraft from this unit had already been shadowing the convoy. However, this attack was driven off with the loss of one aircraft without damaging the convoy. Messages referring to this attack had been transmitted as early as 9.30 that morning, but due to the delay in breaking the day's German naval key, these were not read at Bletchley Park until the following morning.[28] However, versions of this message were also intercepted which had been sent using the much more easily broken *Luftwaffe* daily key, and these were broken within a few hours. The Admiralty was thus able to send a warning to the cruisers of CS1 which were accompanying the convoy, at 11.13 a.m.[29] Unfortunately, the attack was later brought forward to 6 p.m., information which the Admiralty did not obtain in time to send a revised warning.[30]

Meanwhile, preparations were taking place for the planned attack by the German surface fleet. The *Tirpitz* and *Hipper* group was put on three hours' notice to leave Trondheim at noon on 2 July and sailed at

8 p.m., arriving at Westfjord (Narvik) at 2 p.m. the following day (3 July). At the same time, the *Lützow* and *Scheer* group left Narvik just after midnight, heading for Altenfjord. *Lützow* ran aground after a couple of hours and was sufficiently damaged to have to return to Narvik, out of action for the remainder of the battle. *Scheer* and its escorts arrived at Altenfjord at 5.45 p.m. on 3 July. These moves were identified by Bletchley Park overnight on 2/3 July as from midnight onwards a number of messages were intercepted which were unreadable because they were doubly encrypted in an *Offizier* cipher, but these, crucially, listed the Admiral commanding cruisers and C-in-C Fleet among their addressees. Admiral Schniewind, C-in-C Fleet, was aboard *Tirpitz*, which when in harbour was connected to landline communications. The fact that he was being contacted by wireless was a clear sign that *Tirpitz* was at sea. This information was passed to Tovey and to Admiral Hamilton with CS1 by Admiralty ULTRA message on the morning of 3 July.[31]

At this point, not only was the Admiralty concerned with the whereabouts of the German heavy forces, but the *Kriegsmarine* had the same problem, as contact with Tovey's Home Fleet force had been lost. On this basis, it was too risky for *Tirpitz* and its consorts to attack, and Hitler himself countermanded the orders. Instead, *Tirpitz* and *Hipper* would rendezvous with *Scheer* in Altenfjord, and the now three-ship force (lacking *Lützow*) would await events.[32] *Tirpitz* sailed from Narvik during the afternoon of 3 July and arrived at Altenfjord at 10 a.m. the following morning, but not without further depleting the available surface forces, as three of its escorting destroyers struck rocks and had to be left behind.[33] Clearly, German inshore navigation left something to be desired. Indirect hints of these moves were detected at Bletchley Park. A message from *Luftwaffe* command apologising that air cover for a naval operation 'CONCERT' would not be available due to weather was intercepted at 1.52 a.m. on 3 July.[34] This was deciphered by lunchtime and was passed to Allied commanders at sea, along with other information about the German surface ships, at 3.55 p.m.[35] Later on 3 July, Hamilton's escorting cruisers of CS1 were spotted by German aircraft, but this only confused the picture further for German commanders, as the report initially described three cruisers and a battleship, as opposed to the four cruisers actually present, and the message also hinted at the presence of an aircraft carrier in the vicinity.[36] The decision was taken to keep the German surface fleet in port until this force separated from the convoy.

Meanwhile, PQ 17 sailed on eastwards relatively unmolested. A number of U-boats from group *EISTEUFEL*, as well as reconnaissance aircraft, were shadowing the convoy. However, the weather was described as 'smooth as glass',[37] which combined with the prolonged daylight to make it very difficult for the U-boats to attack. As a result, only air attacks were made on the convoy, using homing signals from the shadowing U-boats to guide them to their target. Two air attacks were launched, one unsuccessfully on the evening of 3 July, and a second early on 4 July which scored one torpedo hit on a merchant ship, the American *Christopher Newport*, but failed to sink it.[38] It would later be abandoned, still afloat after attempts by the escorts to sink it had failed, and finally sunk by *U-457*, who came across it, attracted by the underwater noise of the Allied efforts.[39]

THE 'SCATTER' ORDER

The following day, 4 July, would be the decisive day for PQ 17. It was clear to Allied commanders that aircraft and U-boat reports were giving the Germans a good idea of the location of the convoy. The question was whether they would continue with air and submarine attacks or launch Operation *RÖSSELSPRUNG* fully and attack with their surface ships. The movement of these ships towards Altenfjord was not fully understood by Allied intelligence, but something was definitely afoot. However, the German Enigma key change at noon on 3 July had shut Bletchley Park and the OIC out of German communications for at least twenty-four hours, as the first new decryptions were not expected before the early evening of 4 July. Also, frustratingly, the weather over Norway prevented any direct air reconnaissance of the fjords to see where the German ships actually were.

At the same time, a crucial deadline for the Allied fleet was approaching. It had previously been decided that it was too dangerous for Hamilton's cruiser force to accompany the convoy further east than the longitude of the North Cape (25 degrees east), as it risked being trapped in the Barents Sea by the larger German surface fleet and would also be vulnerable to air and U-boat attack (two cruisers had already been lost on previous convoys, as has been described). Therefore, a decision about the cruisers needed to be taken. Also, if the German ships were at sea, then the opportunity for moving Tovey's Home Fleet group to intercept them, at least with aircraft from HMS *Victorious*, presented itself. At noon on 4 July, Tovey gave Hamilton permission to continue eastwards, but specified that 'Once convoy is 25 deg East or earlier you are to leave Barents Sea unless assured by the Admiralty that *Tirpitz* cannot be met.'[40]

As time passed on 4 July, tension rose in the Admiralty; news of the German fleet was awaited from the codebreakers at Bletchley, and this was expected early in the evening. In the meantime, both Naval Section at Bletchley Park and Commander Denning, who was responsible for following the German surface fleet at the OIC, were reasonably confident that no move had been made by *Tirpitz* and its consorts. They had several reasons for this:

- *Luftwaffe* intercepts, which did not suffer from the same delays as naval intercepts, showed that the German air force was still unable to find the Home Fleet. Schniewind was unlikely to put to sea unless this force had been firmly located.
- The Allied submarines at North Cape had seen nothing. If the German fleet had put to sea, it would have had to pass through their patrol line. (Indeed, when *Tirpitz* did sail on 5 July, it was spotted twice by Allied submarines.)
- No wireless traffic from *Gruppe Nord* to ships at sea had been identified, which would be expected if the fleet was out of harbour. (This pattern of traffic had been observed during *Tirpitz*'s previous sortie against PQ 12.)[41]

What happened next has been the subject of some controversy. The First Sea Lord Sir Dudley Pound was in the OIC when the first decrypted signals started to arrive from Bletchley Park. He was almost certainly there specifically to get as close to the unfolding battle as possible; however, as he died in 1943, he left no account of his thinking. An account of events, and his dealings with Pound, was, however, written by Commander Denning and deposited after his death in the archives of Churchill College, Cambridge.[42]

The first of the newly broken intercepts arrived in the OIC at 6.37 p.m. and 6.39 p.m. on 4 July. These were an exchange of signals between *Gruppe Nord* and C-in-C Fleet, but frustratingly they were in *Offizier* cipher and were unreadable.[43] These were followed by several U-boat messages locating the convoy, and a message from the *Luftwaffe* suggesting that their air reconnaissance continued to mis-identify one of Hamilton's cruisers as a battleship.[44] Also, and most significantly, a message was forwarded at 6.59 p.m., sent at 6.12 that morning, from the German C-in-C Fleet to Admiral Commanding Cruisers, stating that *Tirpitz* was arriving at Altenfjord at 9 a.m. and that its destroyer escorts were to be refuelled 'at once'.[45] This information was forwarded to the Allied commanders at sea in an ULTRA message at 7.18 p.m.[46] Denning wanted to add to this message the comment that *Tirpitz* was unlikely to have sailed, but he was overruled. Out at sea, Hamilton's cruiser force CS1 continued to shadow the convoy, but their deadline for turning back to the west was fast approaching. Hamilton had previously signalled that he would continue eastwards until 8 p.m. unless he received more information. At 7.30 p.m. he was signalled by the Admiralty 'further information may be available shortly [i.e. Enigma decrypts]. Remain with convoy pending further instructions.'[47]

According to Denning's account, as the intelligence started to arrive he was asked by Pound whether he could be sure that *Tirpitz* had not sailed. Denning explained that he could not offer definitive proof that it was still in Altenfjord, but the available negative evidence (as outlined above) was that this was the case. He also pointed to the recent evidence that the Germans had possibly confused Hamilton's CS1 cruisers with the Home Fleet battleships, and that this would be a further deterrent to their sailing. Pound remained unconvinced and convened a staff meeting beginning at 8.30 p.m. to discuss the situation. Denning did not go to the meeting, but his boss, the Deputy Director Intelligence Centre (DDIC) Admiral Jock Clayton, did attend. Before Clayton departed for the meeting, Denning was able to share with him the text of a message received by the OIC at 8.31 p.m., originating at 10.20 that morning, where the German Admiral Northern Waters had advised the *EISTEUFEL* U-boat group that there were 'No own naval forces in the operational area' and that 'Position of heavy enemy group [i.e. Tovey's Home Fleet force] not known at present, but is the major target for U-boats when encountered'.[48] This was further good (if negative) evidence that the *Tirpitz* group was not at sea, because the German command would be unlikely to give U-boats free rein to attack large surface ships if their own vessels were about to arrive in the battle area.

Other traffic received in the OIC between 8 p.m. and 9 p.m. revealed that, in the course of the afternoon of 4 July, the German naval command remained confused about whether CS1 contained a battleship. Despite a *Luftwaffe* signal sent at 2.10 p.m. correctly identifying four cruisers,[49] instructions to *U-457*, which was shadowing Hamilton's force, still referred to it as a 'battleship formation'.[50] This information was passed to commanders at sea in an ULTRA message at 9.10 p.m.[51] Incidentally, another message, sent at 4.45 p.m. and delivered to the OIC at 8.18 p.m., gave warning of an air attack on the convoy by twenty-three He 111 torpedo bombers.[52] However, by the time this message could be read, the attack was already underway, and a fierce air battle was being fought by the convoy and its escorts. Two merchant ships were sunk and the Russian tanker *Azerbaidjan* damaged.[53]

As this weight of inference but lack of concrete evidence about *Tirpitz* accumulated, Pound continued his meeting. His second-in-command, Vice Chief of the Naval Staff Sir Henry Moore, later recalled the experience: 'We talked for over an hour. Most of the time Admiral Pound sat with his eyes closed, saying nothing. He always did that. He looked asleep, but he always had an absolute track on what was going on. All the discussion was on the basis that *Tirpitz* was at sea. I was completely convinced of it.'[54]

In Pound's mind, it was possible, indeed likely, that the German surface group had sailed, perhaps as early as noon on 4 July. If so, they would be closing rapidly on the convoy and would reach it by around 2 a.m. on 5 July. Against such a force, Hamilton's cruisers would be no defence but would simply add to the potential destruction. The only option in the face of surface attack was to withdraw CS1 and 'scatter' the convoy to make it harder for the German ships to destroy the merchantmen. As a result, Pound drafted a series of signals giving orders to the ships at sea. At 9.11 p.m. he signalled Hamilton: 'Most Immediate. Cruiser force withdraw to westward at high speed.'[55] At 9.23 p.m. his second message read: 'Owing to threat from surface ships convoy is to disperse and proceed to Russian ports.'[56] After advice from his staff about the inexactitude of the term 'disperse', Pound sent a third, more explicit signal at 9.36 p.m.: 'Most Immediate. My 2123/4 Convoy is to scatter.'[57]

At sea, the response to these messages was a mix of fear and incredulity. When Commander Broome, commanding the close escort, raised the appropriate flag signal, he had to steam within hailing range of the convoy commodore Dowding and use a loudhailer to assure him that this was the correct instruction. As we heard in Chapter 1, he is reported to have added, 'Sorry to leave you like this. Goodbye and good luck. It looks like a bloody business.'[58] The convoy ships then adopted diverging courses as laid out in pre-arranged orders to spread themselves apart across the sea. Hamilton's cruisers were obliged to turn across the bows of the convoy and down its starboard side as they reversed course to the west. To many aboard the merchant ships, it appeared as if they were simply running away. Broome ordered all of his smaller escorts to continue east with the merchantmen to offer whatever protection to individual ships they could. He meanwhile took his six destroyers off to the west to join Hamilton's cruisers in what he assumed would be an imminent and unequal fight against the German surface squadron. If necessary, their outgunned ships would sacrifice themselves to give the convoy time to make its escape, but even if the German surface fleet was held up by this temporarily, the merchantmen sailing alone stood little chance against the inevitable air and submarine attack.

As the night wore on and no German ships were encountered, it started to appear that a significant blunder had been made. In the absence of a surface attack the convoy would have been much safer together under the care of its escort. In the early hours of 5 July, it was acknowledged that if the German ships had sailed as early as predicted, they would have made their presence felt by now. At 2.38 a.m. an

ULTRA message was sent from DDIC stating that 'It is not, repeat, not known if German heavy forces have sailed from Altenfjord, but they are unlikely to have done so before 1200B 4th.' The message added that the Germans were still possibly confused as to whether CS1 included a battleship, and that they had not located the Home Fleet covering force.[59] Both these two latter points can only be interpreted as arguments that *Tirpitz* was still in Altenfjord – an interpretation of the situation that had also prevailed six hours earlier, but which had not been signalled to the fleet.

By midnight 4/5 July, the Germans has a reasonably clear picture of what was going on. Both U-boats and aircraft reported the separation of the cruiser force from the convoy, and the subsequent scattering of the merchant ships.[60] However, the Home Fleet remained unaccounted for. This situation changed at 7 a.m. on 5 July when the *Luftwaffe* was able to finally identify Tovey's force 500 miles to the west of the convoy, at around 5 degrees east (halfway between Jan Mayen and Bear Islands).[61] Schniewind was quick to react, and the *Tirpitz* group was underway to sea between 11 and 11.30 a.m. *Tirpitz* reported its intended position at the exit to Altenfjord at 11.45 a.m. German time, just fifteen minutes before the Enigma key change would once again have blacked out Bletchley Park for another twelve or more hours, and this message was forwarded to the OIC at 2.20 p.m.[62] This information was forwarded to Tovey in an ULTRA message at 3.17 p.m.[63] Further confirmation of *Tirpitz*'s movements was given when it was spotted and unsuccessfully attacked by a Russian submarine at 5 p.m., spotted again by a reconnaissance aircraft at 6.16 p.m. and then finally reported by HM submarine *Unshaken* at 8.29 p.m., sailing eastwards past the North Cape.[64] In the event, however, it was clear to German command that with the convoy scattered there was no clear target for the surface group, and the individual merchant ships were being effectively dealt with by U-boats and aircraft. *Tirpitz* and its consorts were recalled, frustrated but unscathed, at 10.19 p.m. on 5 July.[65]

The German air force and U-boats had the scattered convoy at their mercy. With feeble resistance only from the few small escort craft continuing eastwards, the merchant ships of PQ 17 were picked off one by one. Twenty-four ships were lost (out of the original thirty-eight) to

U-boat and air attack, in some cases being bombed to a standstill and then finished off by U-boat torpedoes. Thousands of tons of vital military cargo were lost and over one hundred merchant seamen lost their lives.

Pound's order to scatter the convoy has become notorious in naval history. Patrick Beesly, who worked in the OIC, wrote that the order was 'totally and fatally mistaken' and that 'His rejection of OIC's views led to disaster.'[66] This view is repeated in any number of other popular accounts, and Pound's death soon after gave him no right of reply. The basic facts show that Pound's conclusion that *Tirpitz* was at sea when it wasn't was wrong, and his failure to take advice from his intelligence experts makes him personally culpable for that decision. However, the intelligence picture was complex, and relied more on inference than on hard facts.

A second argument in Pound's defence is that he only delayed the inevitable. Operation *RÖSSELSPRUNG* was a well-planned operation which actually presented the defenders of PQ 17 with an impossible choice: keep the convoy together and have it destroyed by the German surface group in the Barents Sea, or scatter it and have the ships sunk individually by aircraft and U-boat attack. Had Pound kept the convoy together, it would have provided it with perhaps thirty-six hours' respite, but the sailing of the *Tirpitz* group, unmolested, into the Barents Sea on 5 July would have sealed the fate of the convoy. Even had Hamilton's cruisers been risked further than 25 degrees east, it is unlikely they could have fought off Schniewind's fleet alone. Tovey's Home Fleet covering force had also effectively manoeuvred itself out of the battle by 5 July. On this basis, it can be argued that Pound was facing an impossible choice, and as Hinsley pointed out in his history of British intelligence, 'It does not justify the conclusion that the operational authorities in the Admiralty could have saved the convoy if they had accepted [Denning's] judgement.'[67] As soon as the *Luftwaffe* was able to confirm that the Home Fleet was out of the battle to the west and that CS1 contained only cruisers, the destruction of the convoy was inevitable. As the professional head of the Royal Navy, Pound is also to be commended for taking the fateful decision on his own shoulders, even drafting the signals himself. In a crisis such as this, the buck stopped with him.

Sadly, the fate of PQ 17 was not the only setback suffered in these operations. QP 13 sailed simultaneously on 27 June, as has been described, with a total of thirty-five merchant ships from both Archangel and Murmansk. They were escorted by five destroyers, eight smaller vessels and the anti-aircraft ship *Alynbank*. Despite very poor weather, the German air force was able to pick up the convoy on 30 June while still east of Bear Island, and again as it crossed with PQ 17 on 2 July. However, German attention was fixed on the outgoing convoy, and no attacks on the inbound ships occurred. The convoy divided north-east of Iceland on 4 July as the UK-bound ships headed for Loch Ewe and those returning across the Atlantic passed to the north of Iceland. Tragically, the northern element made a series of navigational errors which led the ships into a British minefield, rather than through the passage between the minefield and Iceland itself. The leading minesweeper HMS *Niger* was blown up on a mine and sank with heavy loss of life, and a further four merchantmen were sunk and two heavily damaged, one of which had to be beached subsequently.[68] These events tend to be overshadowed by the disaster unfolding further east, but the five merchant ships lost on QP 13 represent the highest loss on any returning convoy (five merchant ships, versus four on each of QP 10 and RA 53). They also demonstrate how hostile an environment the Arctic was, even without interference from the enemy.

PQ 17 AND SIGINT

From the outset of these operations, both the *Kriegsmarine* and the Royal Navy had a good understanding of the strategic picture and of the intentions of the enemy. The Germans knew the likely route and destination of the convoy, and their intelligence was detailed enough for them to refer to it by name as PQ 17. They also knew that it would be escorted by both close and distant covering forces, and that a battleship and aircraft-carrier group was likely to be at sea. The British, on the other hand, had a pretty complete understanding of the planned German operation from the Swedish intercepts shared in June and a thorough understanding of the German order of battle and the initial placement of their various assets.

Once the convoy sailed and the battle began, each side faced a range of intelligence problems. For the Germans, the main challenge was to find and follow the convoy. Although they knew roughly where it was, shadowing it directly with both aircraft and U-boats was problematic, with highly variable weather conditions and visibility. The shadowing U-boats were also frequently disrupted by attacks from the convoy's own close escort vessels. This battle to keep tabs on the convoy, and more importantly to position aircraft and submarines to attack it, was a continuing challenge for German commanders. Intercepts of U-boat traffic provide ample evidence of the struggles of the *EISTEUFEL* group to keep in touch with the Allied ships. It should also be remembered that a U-boat following a convoy in a shadowing position is in a very poor position to attack it. Attacks required the positioning of submarines across the path of the convoy, from where it could then manoeuvre around it or even submerge and attack from within the lines of ships. To do this required an ability not only to know where the convoy was but also to predict where it would be in the future. Significant use was also made of homing beacons operated by shadowing submarines to provide targeting for aircraft, and vice versa.

The secondary challenge for the German commanders was to locate the Home Fleet covering forces. While air and U-boat attacks could be continued without reference to these forces, the full surface operation envisaged in *RÖSSELSPRUNG* would not be possible, and indeed would not be sanctioned by the *Führer*, unless the location of Allied heavy units was known. There was a particular fear of carrier-borne air attacks, and so the location of HMS *Victorious* was key to German planning. Sightings of any Allied aircraft in the battle area drew close attention (attested in intercepted traffic) in case they might be signs of an aircraft carrier being within range. To achieve this, there seems to have been a reliance on air reconnaissance both by float-planes and by the longer-range FW 200 aircraft. There is little evidence in German signals traffic that SIGINT directed against Allied communications played a role; however, unless the key German units were at sea, this information could easily have been passed to decision-makers by land-line, and so would not show up in the Allied intercept record. It is notable that in the short period that *Tirpitz* was at sea it was sent at least one message passing on SIGINT. This was a message from *Fliegerführer Nord (West)* which reported the interception of a signal from an 'English Naval Unit', almost certainly the submarine HMS *Unshaken*, reporting the identification of two battleships and eight destroyers just west of the North Cape at 5 p.m. on 5 June.[69] It has been suggested that this indication that the British knew of *Tirpitz*'s departure was a factor in the decision to recall it only a few hours later at 2 a.m. on 6 July.[70]

For the British, the value of SIGINT can be considered in relation to the three types of threat faced by the convoy. Information about U-boats was of obvious operational relevance. It was helpful to know whether the convoy had been found or was currently being tracked, and if deliberate operations by a U-boat group were planned against it. In this, Bletchley Park was largely successful. As Hinsley described it: 'Enigma intelligence about the strengths and dispositions of the U-boats and the GAF's [German Air Force] forces was, as usual, excellent'.[71] However, given the limits imposed by the polar ice and the Norwegian land-mass, there was relatively little room for manoeuvre. Unlike in the Atlantic, where convoy routes could be varied quite widely to avoid U-boat patrol lines, the confined waters of the Barents Sea made this tactic less useful. Also, even if warning of an imminent submarine attack were intercepted in sufficient time for this to be communicated to the convoy escorts (which was unlikely due to decryption delays), there was little that the escorts could do that they were not already doing in terms of counter-measures, as they were already at maximum vigilance.

Similarly, planned *Luftwaffe* air attacks were rarely detected by SIGINT with enough warning to be useful to the convoy escorts. Several intercepts during the battle for PQ 17 reveal planned torpedo-bomber attacks. But these were typically read after the event or, at best, as the attack was in progress. Once again, this foreknowledge would have been of little help, since apart from the few minutes needed for the escorts to go to air action stations (manning their guns and re-positioning themselves closer in the convoy itself), there was no additional protection which could be provided. As has been mentioned above, the previous convoy, PQ 16, marked the first occasion when RAF W/T and R/T operators were deployed onto the cruiser covering force to try to intercept German air messages directly. Although these operators were able to detect German aircraft R/T chatter almost as soon as the aircraft took off from Norway, there was little extra the convoy could do to defend itself.[72] This situation would change with later convoys, where the escort force included aircraft carriers (converted from merchant ships). These allowed fighter air cover to be launched for the convoy if sufficient notice of an incoming attack was received. However, this was not the case with PQ 17. Convoy PQ 17 did include one CAM ship, the *Empire Tide*. It survived to reach Murmansk, but there is no record that it ever launched its aircraft.

As has been discussed, the most prominent role of SIGINT in the battle was to provide information about the whereabouts of the German major surface vessels, including *Tirpitz*. The problems encountered in both the acquisition and interpretation of this intelligence contribute significantly to the notoriety of the whole episode. In the exploitation of SIGINT, both Bletchley Park and their immediate customers, the OIC, faced a series of difficulties. The first of these was timeliness. As has been explained earlier, the forty-eight-hour key-change cycle adopted by the *Kriegsmarine* for its Enigma network meant that Naval Section at Bletchley Park went through alternate periods of famine and feast with regard to message decryptions. Traffic intercepted during the first two days of the battle, noon (10 a.m. GMT) 1 July to noon 3 July, did not start to be read until 5 a.m. on 3 July, and was lost again from noon on 3 July (10 a.m. GMT) until the evening of 4 July. This meant that much of the material on which the OIC had to base their assessments was as much as twenty-four hours old or more by the time they saw it.

The second issue faced by the Royal Navy's intelligence analysts was one of inference and interpretation. It was rare for messages to explicitly describe the activities of the German forces. More typically, the movements of major surface vessels had to be inferred from the activities of subsidiary units: arranging refuelling and docking facilities, providing air cover or de-mining access routes. There was also the problem of doubly-enciphered *Offizier* traffic. However, despite the fact that these messages were unreadable, their simple existence, and the identification of sender and recipient, could be very helpful. That the German C-in-C Fleet was required to receive any messages via W/T rather than landline was a good indication that he and his flagship were at sea rather than in dock. Both Naval Section and the OIC had become quite expert in interpreting these various indirect signs and could be reasonably confident in their conclusions. A key element of this process was the recognition of patterns of absence. Denning and his colleagues knew that particular types of naval activity generated a distinctive W/T 'signature', even if it only consisted of trivial traffic. In the absence of that distinctive traffic, it was a reasonable conclusion that those activities were not taking place, or to put it more specifically, that those ships were not at sea. In addition, intercepted messages were placed in an important wider context by knowledge of the German operational plans and strategic constraints. Knowing that German surface ships would not sail until the Home Fleet was located, the OIC could base a pretty good assessment of *Kriegsmarine* moves on negative reports from *Luftwaffe* reconnaissance aircraft.

Thirdly, however, the analysts of the OIC faced the perennial problem for intelligence officers: credibility. When faced with customers who did not understand the nuances of the SIGINT process, and who wanted definitive answers, it was hard for the intelligence staff to get their point across. Pound looked for this certainty, and positive evidence, but the OIC was not able to give it. An argument that the absence of proof that *Tirpitz was* at sea amounted to confidence that it *wasn't* was not enough for the First Sea Lord, who chose to act on the basis of the worst-case scenario. Denning explained that, while he could not predict when *Tirpitz* would sail, he would be able to detect this four–six hours after it had done so.[73] He was vindicated on 5 July when the German battleship finally left Altenfjord; this was revealed to the OIC by SIGINT within three hours and confirmed by submarine sightings within six hours, exactly as he had predicted. By then, however, it was too late for PQ 17.

1. Frank Birch was a naval codebreaker in the First World War. Birch spent the inter-war years as an academic and TV and radio personality before returning to the Government Code and Cypher School (GC&CS) to lead the German Naval Section. He rose to be head of the Naval Section and was instrumental in GC&CS' success against the *Kriegsmarine*.

2. F.E. 'Harry' Hinsley interrupted his studies at St John's College, Cambridge to join GC&CS at the age of twenty and rapidly made himself master of the communications systems of the German navy. He is seen here with Naval Section colleagues Elspeth Ogilvy-Wedderburn and Vera Bostock. This photo was taken in 1939 or 1940.

3. Admiral of the Fleet Sir John Tovey served as Commander-in-Chief of the Home Fleet from November 1940 until June 1943. He was responsible for the 'safe and timely arrival' of the convoys. He believed that Arctic convoys were unduly risky but had no choice but to support them as best he could with his limited resources.

4. Admiral of the Fleet Sir Bruce Fraser succeeded Tovey in command of the Home Fleet. He presided over the more successful portion of the Arctic campaign and was in command of the force that sank the German battlecruiser *Scharnhorst* in December 1943.

5. Admiral of the Fleet Sir Alfred Dudley Pound served as First Sea Lord (the professional head of the Royal Navy) until his death in October 1943. For much of 1941–43 he was unwell. His reputation is overshadowed by the fateful orders he gave to convoy PQ 17 in July 1942.

6. While not considered to be one of the Royal Navy's intellectuals, Admiral Sir Robert Lindsay Burnett commanded light cruiser groups at both the Battle of the Barents Sea and the Battle of the North Cape, proving himself an able and aggressive fighting admiral.

7. Aircraft carrier HMS *Victorious* lying at anchor in an Icelandic fjord. On her rear deck a Fairey Albacore torpedo bomber is visible with its wings folded. This aircraft is similar to those used in the unsuccessful March 1942 raid on the battleship *Tirpitz*.

8. Along with her sister ship HMS *King George V*, the battleship HMS *Duke of York* was a regular distant escort to the Arctic convoys. The battleship carried the flag of Admiral Fraser at the Battle of the North Cape in December 1943 when her 14-inch guns helped sink the battlecruiser *Scharnhorst*.

9. Anti-submarine trawler HMS *Northern Pride* was built in Germany before acquisition and conversion by the Royal Navy. She served as escort to a number of Arctic convoys and typifies the smaller vessels which braved the Arctic seas in this unglamorous role. The damage to her hull from the severe conditions is evident.

10. Light cruiser HMS *Belfast* seen here with a covering of Arctic ice and her turrets trained obliquely side-to-side to reduce the impact of waves breaking over the bows. *Belfast* was escort to many Arctic convoys and served as flagship to Admiral Burnett leading the cruiser force at the Battle of the North Cape.

11. *Großadmiral* Karl Donitz began the war as overall commander of German U-boats, and succeeded Admiral Erich Raeder as Commander-in-Chief of the *Kriegsmarine* in 1943. He disapproved of the use of U-boats in the Arctic, believing them to be more useful in the Atlantic, but orders from Hitler forced him to send his boats north.

12. *Generaladmiral* Otto Schniewind commanded the fleet, including the battleship *Tirpitz*, on which he sailed to intercept PQ 17 in July 1942. Later he became commander of *Gruppe Nord* directing German naval operations in Norway and the Arctic. In that role he oversaw the ill-fated sortie by the battlecruiser *Scharnhorst* in December 1943.

13. Admiral Oscar Kummetz commanded the cruiser and destroyer force *Kampfgruppe Kummetz* in both Operation *RÖSSELSPRUNG* against PQ 17, and later Operation *REGENBOGEN* against convoy JW 51B. On the latter occasion Kummetz had the convoy at his mercy, but his own cautiousness and contradictory orders from above denied him a victory.

14. *Konteradmiral* Erich Bey commanded destroyers in Norwegian waters until he was promoted and placed in command of a task force consisting of the battlecruiser *Scharnhorst* and a number of destroyers for Operation *OSTFRONT* against convoy JW 55B. He would be killed when *Scharnhorst* was sunk in the Battle of the North Cape.

15. German battleship *Tirpitz*, seen here at anchor in Altenfjord, was the largest ship in the German fleet and posed a massive threat to Arctic convoys. However, it never fired its guns in anger at an Allied warship and was sunk while at anchor by bombers from the RAF.

16. Along with *Tirpitz*, German battlecruiser *Scharnhorst* made up the backbone of the German surface fleet in the north in 1943. Fast and armed with nine 11-inch guns, *Scharnhorst* would be more than a match for any Allied forces other than the battleships of the Home Fleet.

17. Crew members of a German U-boat in the Arctic, May 1942. Despite their fearsome reputation German submarines struggled to make the impact their leaders hoped for in the Arctic. Their slow speed and the adverse weather conditions, combined with increasingly effective Allied anti-submarine tactics, meant the Germans paid a high price in U-boats sunk during the campaign.

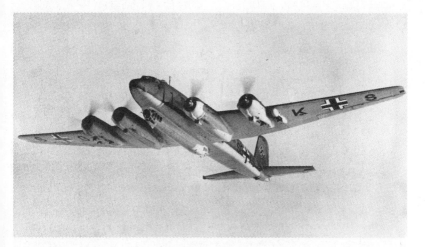

18. A Fokker-Wolff FW 200 Condor. Originally designed as a civil airliner, these aircraft provided the *Luftwaffe* with a crucial long-range maritime patrol capability. This long range allowed these aircraft to shadow convoys and to search the waters around Iceland to detect any sorties by the Royal Navy's Home Fleet.

19. Convoy PQ 17 forming up off Iceland. This photograph was taken by Ensign Howard Carraway, USNR, armed guard officer of the SS *Troubadour*. His ship was one of only eleven out of thirty-six merchant vessels to survive the journey to Russia with the convoy, while twenty-three were sunk by enemy air and submarine attack.

20. Merchant ship sunk during convoy PQ 17. This photograph is believed to have been taken from an attacking U-boat. The barrage balloon towed by the doomed ship to disrupt air attack can be seen floating just above the stern of the vessel.

21. Officers at work in the decoding room of HMS *Sheffield*; on the desk in front of the nearest officer can be seen a copy of the General Recyphering Table No. 2 for Naval Cypher No. 3. When this photograph was taken in 1941 this cipher was being broken regularly by the Germans.

22. Crew cleaning ice from the foredeck of the cruiser HMS *Scylla*. Accumulation of ice from frozen spray was a constant risk to all the ships involved in the Arctic campaign: if too much ice collected it could affect the balance of a ship and even capsize it.

23. Hut 4 at Bletchley Park in 1939. This hut was the home of GC&CS Naval Section from late 1939 until 1942. Members of the section can be seen relaxing in front of the hut after working on the construction of an air-raid shelter nearby.

24. Block A at Bletchley Park. Occupied in late 1942 this block became home to the much-expanded Naval Section for the remainder of the war. The exit door from the U-boat plotting room described by Caroline Rowett can be seen in the foreground.

CHAPTER SEVEN

'THE GOLDEN COMB'

CONVOY PQ 18, SEPTEMBER 1942

'BOB' BURNETT

Robert Lindsay Burnett declared his intention to join the navy aged seven. However, he had to wait as many years again before he got his wish, entering Britannia Naval College in January 1903 at the age of fifteen. He was a gifted sportsman, playing football, hockey and water polo. He would also go on to be the navy sabre-fencing champion. Some accounts suggest that the stocky and muscular young Scotsman used his athletic prowess as a cover for a certain lack of intellectual subtlety, but it did not stand in the way of a successful naval career. Burnett served as a junior officer around the world, on the China Station, in the Mediterranean and in the south Atlantic, before returning to the UK in 1911 to take advantage of his key talents and qualify as a Physical Training Instructor, or 'Leaper', as they were known in the navy.[1]

With the outbreak of the First World War, Burnett went back to sea, establishing the other strand of his career as a small-ships man, commanding the destroyers *Acheron* and *Nessus* in the Grand Fleet. When peace returned, he resumed his work in physical fitness, becoming Fleet Physical Training Officer for the Mediterranean, and later Assistant Director of Physical Training and Sports at the Admiralty. He also spent time in the 1930s as Captain (D) of the 8th Destroyer Flotilla on the China Station. Prior to that posting, he spent time as Executive Officer on board the battleship *Rodney*. He was there when it was taken over by Andrew Cunningham as captain (who would go on to become a celebrated Admiral of the Fleet). Cunningham observed that 'when the previous captain informed [Burnett] that he was coming as commander, he, Burnett had been told that that the ship had already as many brains as were needed and that was why he had been selected'. However, Cunningham clearly repeated this only in jest, commenting that Burnett was 'a man with a good hold and an excellent way with the men'.[2]

When war returned in 1939, Burnett spent a period as Naval ADC to the King, before becoming a shore-based commander of small ships, first as Rear Admiral (Minelayers) and later, in March 1942, as Rear Admiral (D) Commanding Home Fleet Destroyer Flotillas. In this role, Burnett based himself in Scapa Flow aboard the destroyer depot ship HMS *Tyne*. There he spent his time managing the destroyers of the Home Fleet in their various duties, both as escorts to the main units of the Home Fleet on their sorties as the covering force for the Russian convoys, as well as their work as escorts for the convoys themselves. Part of this role entailed the preparation of standing orders for how the ships were to react in various situations, as well as briefing and de-briefing the destroyer commanders between operations. In this, he was not universally popular. Roger Hill, captain of HMS *Ledbury*, recalled how, after the six fleet destroyers returned from PQ 17, five of the six captains (excluding Jack Broome) were summoned to a de-brief with Burnett:

we filed into his day cabin headed by Alistair Ewing of *Offa*.

He said 'Why did you leave the convoy?'

Ewing replied, flushing, 'Because we received an order.'

Burnett said, 'Well, I suppose it would be difficult for you to disobey an order.'

There was a pause. Ewing must have known of the explosion that was coming and said with quiet dignity, 'I think we should like to go.' And we all filed out of the cabin.[3]

Burnett also attempted to address the ship's companies of the destroyers concerned to 'explain' the Admiralty's decision-making over

PQ 17. This was not a success, and may have earned Burnett his subsequent nickname, 'Bullshit Bob'. However, this did not shake the confidence of Admiral Tovey as C-in-C Home Fleet in his commander of destroyers. As we shall see, Burnett was to go to sea with PQ 18 at the head of a force of eighteen fleet destroyers, into some of the fiercest combat of the Arctic war. He would subsequently go on to participate in all of the significant battles of the remainder of the campaign, as commander of cruiser force 'R' and subsequently as Rear Admiral/Vice Admiral Commanding 10th Cruiser Squadron on board HMS *Belfast*. As such, he will be a regular character in the ongoing story. Clearly, some liked him and some did not, but it was difficult to ignore the plain-speaking, red-bearded Admiral. Writing in 1957, Admiral Tovey gave his verdict on Bob Burnett: 'Admiral Burnett had more experience than any other officer in escorting Russian convoys and was in more actions in their support [. . .] I never knew Admiral Burnett to take anything but the right action, promptly and with the greatest Gallantry.'[4]

NEW SHIPS, NEW TACTICS

The political response to PQ 17 was to try and make up the lost ground. Churchill pushed for further operations, defended by ever bigger escorts. As he put it, 'I felt that this would be a very grave decision, and was inclined not to lower but on the contrary to raise the stakes on the principle of "in defeat defiance".'[5] The Admiralty, however, vetoed this, as the commitment of ships required and likely losses would almost certainly outweigh any benefit. Instead, convoys to Russia were paused for two months until September, when both the hours of darkness would be longer and the sea ice would have retreated to its northern limit, allowing the longer but safer passage north of Bear Island and skirting the southern tip of Spitzbergen. The ice-free months in the White Sea would also make it possible for the convoys to reach the more easterly but safer port of Archangel rather than Murmansk. A perhaps more pressing reason for delay was that the Royal Navy was preoccupied in August with its other convoy commitment, delivering supplies to Malta. Operation PEDESTAL in August involved over fifty warships escorting fourteen merchant ships to the island in the face of fierce Axis attack from both sea and air (only five merchantmen survived the trip). Home Fleet assets including the carrier HMS *Victorious* were sent south to join PEDESTAL, and it returned battered and in need of refit. At the same time, commitments in the Pacific forced the US Navy to withdraw its squadron from Scapa, removing a battleship and two cruisers, as well as a number of destroyers from Tovey's fleet.[6]

When Arctic convoys inevitably resumed in September, the C-in-C Home Fleet would be presented with the same three-pronged problem as had existed in the summer – German air, sea and sub-surface attack – but with fewer resources. The U-boat problem was the most manageable. Experience over the summer had shown that, while a convoy remained in being, it was very difficult for German submarines to inflict significant damage. No convoy could guarantee to survive unscathed, but losses from U-boats could be held within acceptable limits by a good close escort. The air question was more serious. The presence of large numbers of torpedo and dive bombers in northern Norway presented a threat which was best countered with equivalent air power. However, it was already an established principle that fleet aircraft carriers were much too scarce and vulnerable to be risked close to the North Cape, and, in any case, the Home Fleet's only carrier, HMS *Victorious*, was in refit. CAM ships were helpful, but they were an uneconomical 'single shot' solution.

The answer was provided in the form of escort aircraft carriers. These were merchant ship hulls converted in the US to become small aircraft carriers, with about half the flight-deck length and one-third of the displacement of fleet carriers. They were also slow, capable of only merchant-ship speeds rather than the 20 knots plus demanded of a warship. Their principal advantage, on the other hand, was their cheapness and, bluntly, disposability, although with a crew of over 550 men, the loss of one of these carriers would not be cheap in human terms. The first of these carriers to become available in the Arctic was HMS *Avenger*, based on a US-built passenger cargo ship the *Rio-Hudson*. It had been commissioned into the Royal Navy under lend-lease in March 1942 and in September 1942 had completed its working up with a squadron of twelve Sea Hurricanes and three Swordfish torpedo aircraft.

Avenger would lie at the heart of the air defence of PQ 18. An additional benefit of these carriers was that air patrols could also be mounted against U-boats, significantly extending the radius in which attacking submarines might be detected. The Swordfish aircraft could be equipped with depth charges, but just as importantly they could serve as 'eyes in the sky', vectoring surface escorts onto enemy vessels or, if nothing else, forcing the U-boats to dive at a distance from the convoy.

Other newly acquired anti-aircraft assets included the light cruiser HMS *Scylla*. Commissioned in June 1942, *Scylla* was equipped with high-angle 4.5-inch guns instead of the 5.25-inch guns of its sister ships. This led to it being mocked as the 'Toothless Terror' by rival ship's companies, but its performance as an anti-aircraft cruiser was to be proven in the Arctic. As on previous operations, the convoy was also provided with ship-borne wireless interception capability. The work of RAF Flying Officer Purvis and his team was described in the previous chapter. This was repeated for PQ 18 by a team of five RAF personnel and four naval ratings under the command of Flying Officer Gunn, placed aboard HMS *Scylla* to provide Admiral Burnett with real-time interception of enemy traffic. Gunn described his experience in a report for his superiors at Cheadle, in which he explained how he and his team brought additional receiving sets with them and were accommodated in the D/F Office, a small space aft of the ship's funnel, but with a direct telephone connection to the bridge.[7] Flying Officer Gunn also had a personal brief with Burnett aboard HMS *Tyne*, before both embarked on *Scylla*. More will be said about Gunn's work later.

The third problem was that of German surface ships, and in particular the heavy units including *Tirpitz*. As has been described in the case of the fleet carriers, it was considered far too risky to allow large surface units of the Home Fleet anywhere near the North Cape or into the Barents Sea unless it could be justified by a certain encounter with *Tirpitz* and its consorts. A force of four cruisers would be attached to PQ 18, but once again, in light of previous losses, these ships would turn back on reaching 25 degrees east – the longitude of the North Cape. How, then, to deal with a surface-ship attack east of Bear Island? That the Germans would attempt this was evident from the sortie of *Tirpitz* towards PQ 17. Tovey's solution was to provide a 'fighting destroyer escort' of a dozen or more destroyers, in addition to the close escort of the convoy. In the event of surface-ship attack, these ships could break away from the convoy and, while small, would by sheer numbers and their torpedo-firing capabilities present a formidable threat to the German fleet and, it was hoped, fend off the enemy at a distance. (We shall see in the next chapter the success of this tactic.) The difficulty with sending destroyers so far east was their lack of range, but this was overcome by the creation of a separate group of fleet oilers, which would lie up near the coast of Spitzbergen and provide a refuelling stop for the escorts. It was also recognised that if this escort was to pass significantly beyond Bear Island, then it was better to delay the returning QP convoy, so that the escort could transfer from one convoy to the other close the Russian ports, rather than meeting the QP ships mid-route.

A further defensive measure was the deployment of two squadrons of Hampden torpedo bombers, as well as Catalina and Spitfire reconnaissance aircraft, to bases in Russia. These aircraft would provide a direct threat to any German surface forces operating in the Barents Sea and potentially curtail the *Kriegsmarine*'s freedom of movement east of the North Cape. Equally importantly, the four photographic reconnaissance Spitfires forming part of the group would give the Admiralty more reliable cover of the fjords sheltering the German surface fleet, and advanced warning of its movements. Unfortunately, of the two squadrons of Hampdens which embarked on the 1,500-mile trip, only twenty-three of the original thirty-two aircraft reached their destination at Vaenga airfield: six crashed in Norway and Sweden, two made forced landings in Russia and one unfortunate was shot down by the Soviet air force. In the end, lack of Soviet cooperation meant that this deployment proved short-lived, and the aircraft were eventually donated to the Russians, while the crews returned home by sea.[8]

More importantly from a SIGINT perspective, the wreck of one of the crashed aircraft – Hampden G-George, which crashed near Vardo in Norway – provided the Germans with documents containing a complete set of wireless call-signs for the upcoming operation, as well as other information about the planning for PQ 18. This material was rapidly passed to the *B-Dienst*, who added it to their already thorough knowledge of Royal Navy wireless procedures. The damage was exacerbated by the fact that the details of the upcoming operation were shared with the Soviet air force, who in turn passed it by wireless to their various air commands, and this in turn was intercepted and read by German intelligence. The German authorities thus had a pretty full picture of what to expect: escort strengths, timings, routes and tactics.[9]

The final issue confronting Tovey, especially now that the escort arrangements were more complex, with numerous 'moving parts', was command and control. To this end, he remained in Scapa Flow, sending the heavy covering force of the battleships *Anson* and *Duke of York* to sea under his second-in-command, Vice Admiral Sir Bruce Fraser. This allowed him not only to stay in close contact with the Admiralty, but also to send instructions to his own ships without compromising the location of the covering force.[10] Unfortunately, the very complexity of the operation meant that use of wireless communications while at sea was almost impossible to avoid, as messages were required to coordinate oiling of ships, U-boat hunts, rescue of survivors and myriad other matters. Admiral Burnett would later record that some 1,840 messages were transmitted during the operation, many of which would have been audible to the Germans.[11]

From a German perspective, the destruction of PQ 17, while a marked success, was still not a flawless operation. Admiral Northern Waters had been able to collaborate with his colleagues in the *Luftwaffe* to sink a number of ships, but these losses were almost exclusively inflicted after the convoy was scattered. The *EISTEUFEL* wolfpack had no success at all against the formed convoy and was only able to pick off two stragglers already damaged by air attack. Only after the merchantmen were proceeding individually unescorted were the U-boats able to score any successes. Similarly, most of those ships sunk from the air were hit only after they had been denuded of their escorts and their anti-aircraft defences.

The surface fleet operation had been even more of a damp squib, and here the heavy hand of *Gruppe Nord*, Naval High Command and even the *Führer* himself restrained the fleet from meaningful operations. Admiral Schniewind, C-in-C Fleet, reopened the argument with his superiors that had previously been fought by Schmundt as Admiral

Northern Waters. Faced with the dilemma of how to use the surface ships without undue risk, the latter suggested that instead of sailing into the contested waters west of Bear Island to attack the eastbound convoys, risking a clash with the Home Fleet, the surface units should focus on the returning westbound convoys in safer waters east of the North Cape. The northerly summer convoy route would also leave convoys exposed in these waters for longer as they worked north towards Spitzbergen. Ironically, this was exactly the tactic for which the commander of the Home Fleet was struggling to find a solution. Bases for the German ships in Trondheim and Narvik were clearly unsuitable if those ships were to operate to the east of the North Cape, and so, with the agreement of Naval High Command, measures were put in place to build a fleet operating base at Altenfjord.[12] Shortly after this, in September 1942, Hubert Schmundt stepped down as Admiral Northern Waters to take command in the Baltic. He was replaced by the former Chief-of-Staff at *Gruppe Nord*, *Konteradmiral* (Rear Admiral) Otto Klüber.[13]

Meanwhile, the next convoy, PQ 18, was expected by the German forces sometime in early August. Intense air reconnaissance was conducted at a cost of over 1 million litres of precious aviation fuel, burned in 1,603 flying hours before it was decided that the convoy had been delayed and reconnaissance operations were scaled back. Interestingly, the German air force concluded that the scattering of PQ 17 was the result of their earlier air attacks, and so it prepared with some anticipation for repeating the process on the next westbound convoy. In particular, the *Luftwaffe* developed a new tactic to maximise their effectiveness against convoys: the *Goldene Zange* ('golden comb'). By September 1942 the two *Luftwaffe Gruppen* in northern Norway, *III/KG26* and *III/KG30*, had ninety-two He 111 and Ju 88 torpedo bombers available, as well as medium and dive bombers. The plan was that an almost simultaneous attack should be made on the target convoy, beginning with high-level and dive-bombing attacks to distract the defenders' anti-aircraft fire, before a force of up to forty torpedo bombers approached the convoy from its bow quarter, at wave-top height and in single line abreast, as little as 30 metres apart. All of these aircraft would release their torpedoes simultaneously at a range of around 1,000 metres from the target, creating a dense 'golden comb' of eighty torpedoes across a frontage of around 1,000 metres. It was hoped that this would overwhelm the convoy's ability to manoeuvre to avoid the dense wall of torpedoes and destruction would reign. What was not calculated was what would happen next for the torpedo bombers over-flying the convoy's air defences, and as no fighter cover was available so far from the coast, any interference by enemy fighter aircraft could be catastrophic. Indeed, once intelligence became available that a carrier might form part of the convoy escort, its prior destruction was given maximum priority. Even Herman Goering, Head of the *Luftwaffe*, commented on the proposal that 'The attack against the aircraft carrier must be so violent that this threat is removed.'[14] How well this plan worked in practice will be seen below.

PQ 18

PQ 18 departed Loch Ewe on 2 September 1942 bound for Archangel. The convoy passed to the west of Iceland, where more merchant ships joined, bringing the total to thirty-nine. They were accompanied by the usual escort of destroyers, minesweepers and A/S trawlers. In addition, a fighting escort of sixteen destroyers was provided under the command of Rear Admiral Burnett, with his flag aboard the anti-aircraft cruiser HMS *Scylla*. As well as *Scylla* and *Avenger*, the anti-aircraft defence was augmented by the two familiar auxiliary anti-aircraft cruisers, *Ulster Queen* and *Alynbank*. A force of three cruisers also accompanied the convoy under Vice Admiral Bonham Carter in HMS *London*. In total, fifty-one naval vessels of various sizes were involved in the operation.

On 5 September as the convoy reorganised at Hvalfjord in Iceland, it was identified by enemy reconnaissance aircraft, and German forces were warned of its imminent departure. Further sightings were made on 8 and 9 September which allowed *Luftwaffe* commanders to identify all of the various components of the convoy and its protecting forces. Allied knowledge of this discovery was quickly gleaned by Naval Section from intercepts of both low-grade and high-grade traffic from *Fliegerführer Nordwest*.[15] U-boats were immediately despatched to a series of intercept positions, with three sent north-west of Jan Mayen

Island and a further four close to Spitzbergen, as well as others en route. Again, this deployment was identified via intercepts, and it was reported to the Home Fleet on the evening of 10 September.[16]

By the time that message arrived, however, the convoy was already under U-boat attack, with first contacts being made at noon on 10 September. A running battle began between the convoy escorts and a varying number of U-boats for next three days but with limited success for the attackers; on the evening of 13 September, *U-88* was sunk by depth charges from the destroyer HMS *Faulknor*.[17] Undeterred, Admiral Northern Waters ordered more U-boats into the battle, forming a new wolfpack christened *TRÄGERTOD*. The focus of attention of the submarines is clear from the name, which loosely translates as 'the death of carriers'. Clearly, if the German air force was to make successful attacks on the convoy, the rapid disposal of HMS *Avenger* was a key objective. The U-boats were unable to reach the carrier, stationed in one of the inner columns of the convoy, but two merchant ships, stationed in the outermost starboard column – the *Stalingrad* and *Oliver Elsworth* – were both sunk by *U-408* on the morning of 13 September.

The first air attack arrived that afternoon. It began as planned with high-level bombing, which was ineffective, but that was followed by the planned torpedo attack by over forty aircraft. They swept in on the starboard bow of the convoy at wave-top height and in close formation, releasing their torpedoes within 2,000 yards of the ships. The convoy commodore, retired Rear Admiral Boddam-Whetham, responded promptly by ordering a simultaneous turn 45 degrees to starboard to point the bows of the ships into the path of the torpedoes, a procedure known as 'combing the tracks', which substantially reduced the likelihood of a hit. Unfortunately, miscommunication with the two ship columns nearest the enemy aircraft led to them maintaining course, presenting their flanks to the torpedoes. Six of the seven ships in those outer columns, as well as two further inside the formation, were hit and sunk. Two further raids were carried out later in the afternoon without achieving any more hits, but the damage had been done; ten merchantmen had been lost in a single day, at a cost to the Germans of one U-boat and eight torpedo aircraft.[18]

Signals were intercepted throughout the afternoon of 13 September which gave advanced warning of these air attacks. Some originated from *Fliegerführer Lofoten* and others from Admiral Northern Waters, and it is not clear which were enciphered in *Luftwaffe* keys and which in the new Home Waters key introduced at noon (10 a.m. GMT) on 13 September. None, however, were passed on in time to influence the battle. The time stamps show they were teleprinted from Naval Section to the Admiralty between 11 p.m. and midnight, long after the bombers had returned to base.[19] The Admiralty also sent two signals on the afternoon of 13 September reporting on the re-positioning of U-boat patrol lines and noting that the convoy had been found and was being shadowed by enemy submarines. Again, the ongoing battle between the escorts and attacking U-boats made this information somewhat superfluous.[20] As ever, the lack of a concurrent grasp by the Admiralty of events at sea meant that their judgement of what information would be useful to the fleet was severely hampered. Rarely was intelligence less than twelve hours old passed on, and often it was even more out of date.

The following day offered no respite. At 3.30 a.m., *U-457* took advantage of the brief twilight overnight, torpedoing the oiler *Atheltemplar*. It did not immediately sink, and consideration was given to towing it to join the refuelling group off Spitzbergen, but no escort could be spared for the tow, so it was abandoned. It was finished off that evening by Captain Heinrich von Hymmen with gunfire from *U-408*, adding to his tally of two ships sunk on 13 September. Balancing this loss, Swordfish aircraft from HMS *Avenger* tracked down *U-589* in the course of the afternoon and depth-charged it, before it was finished off by the destroyer HMS *Onslow*.[21]

The air battle began again at 12.35 p.m. on 14 September with an attack by twenty torpedo bombers at low level. This time, instead of lining up to attack the convoy as a whole, they singled out the air defence units, focusing their attack on HMS *Avenger* and HMS *Scylla*. Further raids followed in the afternoon by both bombers and torpedo aircraft, and although neither the carrier nor the cruiser were hit, a torpedo struck the *Mary Luckenbach*. Carrying around 1,000 tons of explosives, the freighter disappeared instantly in a massive explosion. *Luftwaffe* success was limited partly by the fact that HMS *Avenger* had changed tactics from the previous day, keeping a constant relay of

Hurricanes in the air throughout the day, maximising its limited deck space and ensuring that the incoming enemy aircraft formations were broken up by fighters. The result was twenty enemy aircraft shot down. Unfortunately, anti-aircraft fire from the convoy also brought down three Hurricanes, but all three pilots were recovered safely.

Air attacks continued on 15 September, but by this point the convoy was reaching the northward limit of the endurance of the attacking aircraft and no further damage was done to the convoy, at a cost to the Germans of three further aircraft shot down.[22] Again, messages were intercepted in the early afternoon of 14 September, giving several hours' warning of the subsequent air attacks, but none of these were read in time to be useful, all being passed to the Admiralty on the following morning.[23] A detailed breakdown of all the reported German air attacks on 13 and 14 September was passed to the Home Fleet on 15 September, but this was presumably in order to keep the C-in-C updated on events at sea rather than to allow him to influence the battle directly. A similar message reporting German claims of the sinking of the *Atheltemplar* was also sent a few hours later, no doubt for the same reason.[24]

Interestingly, among the intercepted messages on 15 September was an indignant report from Captain Clausen of *U-403*, reporting that he had been 'Attacked twice by He111 [. . .] seven bombs close by [. . .] type and national markings unmistakeable.'[25] Clearly, 'blue-on-blue' incidents were a problem when mounting joint service operations. German intelligence had revealed that the convoy escort included submarines, and it would appear that no effort to deconflict U-boat and air attacks either was attempted or, more likely, was possible. Nor was this the only setback for the U-boat forces. They continued to try to penetrate the ring of escorts around the convoy (supplemented by Swordfish aircraft from *Avenger*) without success. In the early hours of 16 September, HMS *Impulsive* depth-charged and sank *U-457*, and later in the morning both *U-255* and *U-378* were depth-charged by escort ships, the latter sustaining significant damage.[26]

No further damage would be inflicted on PQ 18 by submarines, and on the following day four U-boats were diverted to seek out the returning QP 14.[27] The air attacks, however, were not quite over. On 18 September a series of smaller-scale torpedo attacks were made as the convoy passed the entrance to the White Sea, using variants of the 'comb' tactics. One further merchantman, the *Kentucky*, was lost, but four German aircraft were shot down, three by ships' guns and one by the Hurricane from the CAM ship *Empire Morn*, which in the absence of *Avenger* (which had transferred to the westbound convoy) provided the convoy's only air cover. The pilot was able to land his aircraft in Russia and avoided the usually inevitable soaking which followed a CAM launch. The convoy arrived at Archangel on 19 September without further loss.

QP 14

The returning convoy, QP 14, left Archangel on 13 September, consisting of fifteen merchantmen and two rescue ships, with the usual Russian-based close escort of minesweepers and trawlers, as well as two auxiliary A.A. ships, the *Palomares* and *Pozarica*. The convoy set a course almost due north out of the White Sea, before passing the outbound PQ 18 on 16 September and meeting up with the destroyer groups and *Scylla* and *Avenger*, before making a more westerly course towards Spitzbergen on 17 September. The convoy was first located by the German air force on 15 September, but poor weather made it difficult to maintain contact, and nor were any U-boats immediately available, as some had been forced to return to base to replenish stores and others were still hunting PQ 18. A new patrol line across the path of QP 14 was not established until the evening of 19 September, and this was placed to the west of the southern tip of Spitzbergen. At the same time, however, Admiral Burnett redirected the convoy up the western coast of Spitzbergen. This allowed him to collect the oilers which had been based there, but also meant that when he resumed a westerly course he was significantly further north than on his outward journey. This placed the convoy at the limit of range of the German air force, who in the event left the convoy unmolested.[28]

The U-boats, however, were about to be rewarded with greater success. The minesweeper HMS *Leda* was sunk by *U-435* on the morning of 20 September, and that afternoon the merchant ship *Silver Sword*, one of the few survivors of PQ 17, was hit by a torpedo from

U-255 and had to be sunk by gunfire from its escorts. Worse still, that evening the Tribal-class fleet destroyer HMS *Somali* was hit by a torpedo from *U-703*. It did not sink but lost all power and had to be taken under tow and provided with electrical power by its sister ship *Ashanti*. Sadly, an eighty-hour struggle to tow the crippled destroyer in increasingly bad weather ended when it broke in two and sank on 24 September.[29] At around the same time, Admiral Burnett decided that, as he was out of reach of the Norwegian-based German bombers, his cruiser and aircraft carrier presented more of a liability than an asset, so *Scylla* and *Avenger* were detached to return home independently. He himself transferred his flag to the destroyer *Milne*, making the rather hazardous journey from the cruiser to the destroyer via a mess chair attached to the ship's crane.

Unfortunately, the departure of *Somali*, with both *Ashanti* and a group of escorting destroyers, as well as the three destroyers sent to escort *Scylla* and *Avenger*, left the convoy escort significantly depleted. It was also deprived of the anti-submarine patrols of *Avenger*'s Swordfish aircraft. This allowed the U-boat *U-435* to penetrate the escort screen and sink two merchantmen, the *Bellingham* (another survivor of PQ 17) and *Ocean Voice*, as well as the oiler *Grey Ranger*, all within five minutes, before successfully making its escape.[30] This brought the losses from QP 14 to two naval vessels, three merchantmen and an oiler (as well as a Norwegian-crewed Catalina flying-boat shot down while attacking *U-606* on 21 September). The convoy reached Iceland on 23 September and Loch Ewe on 26 September. The Germans had suffered no losses while attacking QP 14.

As with PQ 18, the intercepted messages passed on by Naval Section provided a commentary on, rather than a contribution to, the defence of the convoy. A significant volume of traffic was read between the U-boats at sea and Admiral Northern Waters, as he tried to vector them onto new patrol lines which would place them across the path of the convoy, and as the boats themselves reported their positions and their interactions with escort ships and aircraft. It is notable that the Enigma key which began at noon on 19 September was being read by the early hours of 20 September, so a sequence of messages sent early on 20 September were passed on by Naval Section as little as five hours after interception. For example, a message from Admiral Northern Waters repeating the reported grid positions of ten U-boats was intercepted at 1.25 a.m. and was teleprinted at 8.10 the same morning,[31] and a similar message moving boats to a new patrol line for 6.00 a.m. was intercepted at 3.34 a.m. and passed on at 8.36 a.m.[32] Much of this information was passed on to Home Fleet in the course of the morning of 20 September.[33] However, while it may have allowed the C-in-C Admiral Tovey to update his situation maps, it would have meant little to Admiral Burnett, whose overstretched escort forces were scurrying after constant ASDIC contacts and Swordfish patrol sightings. They knew where the wolfpacks were because they were busy fighting them.

TRACKING THE GERMAN SURFACE FLEET

No mention has been made so far of the activities of German surface forces during these battles, as they did not engage with or influence the progress of convoys PQ 18 and QP 14. However, that does not mean that they were entirely passive during the month of September 1942, and it is in the monitoring and tracking of the behaviour of these units that ULTRA provided by Naval Section played perhaps its most significant role.

In the interval between convoys PQ 17 and PQ 18 various operations were carried out by *Kriegsmarine* surface forces. The cruiser *Lützow*, which had been damaged by its grounding during the operations against PQ 17, was sent to Germany for repairs (it would return to Norwegian waters in November). It was replaced in the meanwhile by the light cruiser *Köln*, the only survivor of a class of three ships built in the late 1920s, its two sisters having been sunk in the invasion of Norway in 1940. The passage of these two vessels to and from Trondheim was followed by both SIGINT and information from the Swedes, as well as coast watchers and air reconnaissance. Unfortunately, as had been the case with similar previous ship deployments to and from Germany, there was little the Admiralty could do to intervene, and these operations passed without Allied interference.[34]

A more successful operation was that against the minelayer *Ulm* at the end of August. This vessel had been despatched into the eastern

Barents Sea to lay mines along the anticipated summer convoy route north from the White Sea and along the ice edge towards Spitzbergen. Not only did Enigma intercepts reveal its precise course, but by co-incidence the US cruiser *Tuscaloosa* was in the Barents Sea delivering supplies and personnel to support the RAF deployments described earlier. The escorting destroyers HMS *Onslaught*, *Martin* and *Marne* were detached to sweep along a given track, and in due course they overtook and sank the *Ulm* on the night of 25 August. Not only was this success achieved directly on the basis of ULTRA information, but, more unusually, specific facts derived from SIGINT were shared with ships which would not normally be privy to such highly secret material. Of course, the destroyer captains who might have raised an eyebrow at such specific orders were otherwise unaware of the source of the infor-mation.[35] They were simply told to sweep along a certain path and, if nothing was found, to return to *Tuscaloosa*; however, the point was made that no Allied shipping was present in the area at the time (*Ulm* was in fact sailing under a false Panamanian flag). The Germans, mean-while, failed to see anything unusual in radio silence from the mine-layer, and it was not until 5 September that its lack of response to specific messages made its loss apparent, a process followed in turn by Naval Section.[36]

A more critical task for Naval Section was of course to monitor the movements of the major German surface units in relation to PQ 18. In line with the strategy outlined earlier, when PQ 18 was detected by the Germans between 6 and 8 September, arrangements began to carry out surface operations east of the North Cape. *Scheer*, *Hipper* and *Köln*, as well as a number of escorts, were moved from Narvik to Altenfjord, departing on 10 September. Allied submarines had been deployed in patrol areas around the north coast of Norway in light of *Tirpitz*'s previous moves against PQ 17, and these picked up the German fleet move but were unable to attack it. Nonetheless, the Admiralty was able to report the move in the early hours of 11 September.[37] This was followed by Enigma information that *Hipper* was due to arrive in Altenfjord at 3 a.m. that morning, information that was passed on by the Admiralty only a few hours later at 6.40 a.m.[38] The absence of *Tirpitz* from the German striking force was confirmed that afternoon due to a combination of air reconnaissance of Altenfjord and routine radio traffic from *Tirpitz*. The OIC also noted that the force was commanded by the Admiral Commanding Cruisers Oscar Kummetz, aboard *Hipper*, which would not have been the case had *Tirpitz* been present.[39] This is another example of the kinds of intelligence inferences that were possible when the OIC and Naval Section had a thorough grasp of the *Kriegsmarine*'s order of battle and command structure. Harry Hinsley, in his account of this traffic in his official history, appears rather critical of Naval Section's performance on this occasion, stating that 'the Enigma provided no news of the German move until the early hours of 11 September'.[40] However, this seems harsh given that the news of the *Hipper*'s arrival in Altenfjord was forwarded by the Admiralty only three hours after the event.

The threat of a German surface-ship sortie reappeared on 13 September when a message was intercepted from Admiral Northern Waters, bringing the *Hipper* group one hour's notice to move. This message was intercepted at 4.30 p.m. and teleprinted at 11.06 p.m.:[41] a fast turnaround given that the full German Enigma key change had taken place at noon that day. The information was relayed to the Home Fleet shortly after.[42] This latter signal also included information from a later Enigma message that the German force had subsequently been moved back to three hours' notice;[43] nonetheless, the threat remained of an imminent sailing by the *Hipper* group. Air reconnaissance of Altenfjord was maintained for the next three days, and this, combined with SIGINT, allowed the Admiralty to confirm that all the German surface ships remained in place in Altenfjord and Narvik as late as 15 September.[44] Further intelligence was received from Sweden on 16 September that the Germans planned to use the *Hipper* group against PQ 18 east of the North Cape, after the air operations were over, but that *Tirpitz* was experiencing mechanical trouble and would only venture out in an emergency.[45] What Naval Section did not know at the time was that, after a further intervention from Hitler about not risking the ships, Admiral Raeder at German Naval High Command had cancelled the operation.[46] Monitoring of the German ships continued, with the Admiralty reporting on 17 September that routine radio traffic from *Tirpitz* suggested it remained at Narvik,[47] and on 19 September that 'So far as is known there have been no instructions to surface forces.'[48] This latter point was derived from Swedish sources, and was borne out by the subsequent lack of any further movement by the German heavy units during the passage of the two convoys. It is difficult to argue on the basis of a hypothetical situation, but given the mix of SIGINT and air and submarine cover, it would seem fair to suggest that had the *Hipper* group made a move against the convoys, Allied intelligence would have been able to pick this up at a relatively early stage. Also, unlike in earlier convoys, a contingency was in place in the form of the fighting destroyer escort to counter such a move had it occurred. A disaster like PQ 17 was unlikely to be repeated; indeed, the outcome of just such a sortie by the German fleet is examined in the next chapter.

BOTH SIDES WEIGH THE RESULTS

Overall, the September outward and return convoys had lost sixteen merchant ships, ten to air attack and six to U-boats. In addition, two warships and an oiler had also been sunk by U-boats. In exchange, the Germans had lost three submarines, with several others damaged, and forty-one aircraft had been shot down. While for the Germans this was not as overwhelming a success as that against PQ 17, it represented a reasonable tally of ships sunk. The most significant losses, eight merchantmen in as many minutes, had been inflicted in the torpedo bomber attack on 13 September. However, this success was not repeated in subsequent air attacks. There are several reasons for this. One reason so many ships were hit on 13 September is possibly the miscommunication within the convoy which did not allow all the ships to turn into the approaching wall of torpedoes. No ships which achieved the turn were hit, although it must be noted that these were in the columns furthest from the attack. More significant was the presence of HMS *Avenger* and its fighters. When its captain, Commander Colthurst, revised his tactics to ignore shadowing German aircraft and maintain a constant Combat Air Patrol (CAP) over the convoy, his Hurricanes were able, while not necessarily shooting down many bombers, to upset their formations and disrupt their aim significantly.[49]

The significance of the carrier to German planning is evidenced by the name of the wolfpack involved: *TRÄGERTOD*. Unfortunately, the U-boats were not able to fulfil their part of the combined mission by eliminating the carrier and freeing the air for the bombers. The 'comb' tactics also relied heavily on surprise, and once the cat was out of the bag after the first use of the tactic, no subsequent applications of it were as effective. It was also costly in aircraft casualties. The convoy's air defence, from *Scylla*, the auxiliary anti-aircraft ships, and indeed every gun in the convoy forced the attacking aircraft to fly through a formidable wall of fire, which caused significant German (as well as friendly) losses. No further opportunities were provided to the *Luftwaffe* to continue its successes in the Arctic. All of the torpedo-carrying He 111 and Ju 88 aircraft were withdrawn to the Mediterranean in November 1942, leaving only reconnaissance aircraft, a small force of bombers and the torpedo-carrying but slow He 115 seaplanes. What impact the continued presence of the aircraft of *KG26* and *KG30* in the north after 1942 might have had on the campaign remains a matter for speculation.

The *U-bootwaffe* had once again been found wanting. Nine ships sunk in exchange for three U-boats was not a ratio to bring smiles to the faces of Naval High Command. A number of other boats had been damaged and would be out of action for some time. The difficulties facing U-boats attacking well-escorted convoys have already been outlined in the last chapter. To these difficulties was added the burden of anti-submarine air patrols. Although *Avenger* carried only three Swordfish, their constant presence around the convoy significantly disrupted the U-boat commanders' attempts to close with their targets, and although they were not credited with any sole U-boat 'kills', the aircraft were instrumental in vectoring surface escorts onto several U-boats which were subsequently sunk. The toll on the crews of those three antiquated aircraft was huge. For eighteen days the aircrew were under almost intolerable strain both in the air and afloat. This was described by Telegraphist-Air-Gunner Les Sayer:

PQ18 was one of the most horrific experiences of the war for me. [. . .] We were flying Swordfish on anti-sub patrols so you could be airborne when these attacks were on or you could be on the carrier which was under attack anyway. [. . .] We didn't go all the way to Murmansk [*sic*]. We turned around because the captain of the *Avenger* said the Swordfish crews were so fatigued that he wasn't going to guarantee their safety. You did three hours in the air, three hours on standby, and three hours off. You did that for about three days and fed on Benzedrine tablets to keep you going. You didn't notice the tiredness until the whole thing was over.[50]

Their impact on the battle, however, was significant.

Admiral Northern Waters was once again theoretically in charge of U-boat operations but was in fact being second-guessed by his superiors as usual. The cancellation of the surface-fleet sortie on 14 September is symbolic of this. His relationship with the *Luftwaffe* appears to have been good, but his submarines were unable to live up to their part in the plan, and they were also subject to friendly air attack, as has been described. On this occasion, *Gruppe Nord* was largely a spectator on the operations, having no direct command role. However, it is interesting that even when they were not directly issuing orders to the Arctic U-boats it seems that the commanders in Kiel could not resist providing a wireless commentary on events. On 9 September C-in-C North signalled all U-boats in Northern Waters: 'I attach importance to successes against PQ 18 in relation to the whole front. I therefore wish all forces operating success equal to that achieved against PQ 17. Heil Hitler.'[51]

It is a myth perpetuated by Hollywood that Enigma messages frequently ended with the exhortation 'Heil Hitler', or that this was of any use as a crib for codebreakers, but it is interesting to note that several of the *Gruppe Nord* messages sent during this period ended with exactly those words. The message of 9 September was followed by the rallying cry on 12 September 'PQ 18 is here. Now for it!'[52] However, as the battle dragged on without decisive results the tone changed. C-in-C North signalled again on 16 September: '12 German U-boats are operating against PQ 18. So far U-boats have sunk 4 steamships [actually it was only three]. That is not good enough. Further successes are required. Your targets are of paramount importance.'[53]

A more congratulatory (and very long) message was sent on 18 September stating that the still only '4, probably 5' sinkings so far were a 'specially high achievement [. . .] only made possible by your fighting spirit and resolute will'.[54] Regardless of the tone of these exhortations, one has to wonder what a harassed U-boat wireless operator would have made of having to take down and decipher these tactically irrelevant observations in the midst of the battle.

The Allied reaction to the September operations was one of modest satisfaction. Losses had been incurred, but these were within acceptable limits (certainly compared with PQ 17) and it was clear that the various German efforts had not made the operation unviable. Twenty-seven out of forty ships had reached their destination. Regarding the U-boats in particular, Admiral Tovey observed: 'The comparatively heavy losses inflicted towards the end of the period were disappointing; but the surprising feature was their failure to achieve more in the earlier stages.'[55] He also noted the diminishing returns gained by the successive German air attacks, ascribing this to the heavy casualties suffered in the raids and the loss of skilled aircrews.

Admiral Burnett was less satisfied by events. He was of the opinion that things could very easily have been very much worse, and that it was only by good fortune that much greater losses had not been incurred. He wrote: 'I do not know how far this operation may be considered to have been a success or a failure, but I am convinced that had any of six circumstances been otherwise it must have been a tragic failure.'[56]

He went on to list a series of factors which would have led in his mind to disaster. Four of these related to the oiling operations; bad weather, or the loss of either the oilers accompanying the convoy or those in Spitzbergen, would have been catastrophic for the short-ranged destroyer escorts. He also quoted the failure of the German surface fleet to interfere in the operation, and shortages of anti-aircraft ammunition. In spite of this, he had nothing but praise for his destroyers and their crews: 'For eighteen days there was no let-up. When there was no air attack in progress there were countless A/S hunts, counter attacks and investigations, continuous zig-zagging in formation, moving positions on a large screen to fill gaps of others away chasing contacts, and during lulls, topping up with oil or running alongside to take on or transfer survivors.'[57] At a cost of almost complete exhaustion, the fighting destroyer escort had demonstrated its value.

One specific area of the operation for which detailed after-action information is available is the SIGINT team aboard HMS *Scylla*. Flying Officer Gunn's report, alluded to earlier, described how his team were able to follow German attempts to find the convoy via the reconnaissance flights of the Condors of *1/KG40*, and latterly the shorter-ranged BV 138 aircraft, using W/T (Morse) traffic, as well as following developing attacks via R/T (voice) communications.[58] A subsequent report from Air Section at Bletchley Park provided more detail of these operations.[59] Interestingly, when the weather was clear the attacking German aircraft would maintain radio silence, so little warning was obtained from R/T chatter; however, if the weather was cloudy, the pilots would start to guide one another towards the target, referencing holes in the cloud cover and issuing other directions which could be heard by the team on the cruiser.

Another piece of poor German wireless security was also exploited. The interceptors became accustomed to the constant broadcast of homing signals from the shadowing aircraft around the convoy. However:

> The ground control takes little or no part in the traffic as long as the shadowers are simply keeping contact and relieving each-other. When an attack is impending, he appears to grow nervous. He cannot hear the homing signals himself and when the attackers have taken-off he regularly sends the signal 'send homing signals on 365kcs' – this in spite of the fact that the a/c are sending D/F signals on 365kcs all the time. Moreover, he sometimes informs the shadower several hours in advance of the proposed time of attack.[60]

In his anxiousness to make sure he played his part in operations, the German controller was unwittingly giving the game away to his enemies – further proof, if it were needed, that much of the best SIGINT is derived from opponents' human error. Overall, Gunn concluded: 'The results obtained by the "Y" party, appeared to be very greatly appreciated by R.A.D. [Burnett] who assured me that the information provided had on several occasions proved of great value.'[61]

It was noted, however, that on these early convoys the ship-borne interceptors had little prior knowledge of what traffic to expect and were very much making things up as they went along. It was stressed that, in future, thorough briefing of operators on German orders of battle and operating procedures, frequencies, call-signs, etc., would make life a great deal easier.

QP 15 – THE LAST OF THE PQ–QP CONVOYS

Outbound convoy operations were once again suspended after PQ 18. The Allied invasion of North Africa in Operation TORCH absorbed all the available naval resources. The Russians, however, continued to press for more supplies, particularly in their own vessels, which were otherwise stuck in Iceland. This led to a number of ships making the journey independently, taking advantage of the fact that the northern route via Spitzbergen remained open, but the hours of daylight were reduced to almost nothing. Two Russian ships made the journey successfully, which led to the frankly ill-conceived Operation FB. Over a period between 29 October and 2 November, a series of ships sailed alone and at intervals, protected only by a chain of A/S trawlers distributed along the route. Of thirteen outward sailings, three turned back, four were sunk and one wrecked, leaving only five to reach their destination. Eight ships attempted the return journey, of which seven made it to Iceland.[62] Clearly, this was no solution to the ongoing convoy question. There was a further issue, in that a significant number of ships were lying in Archangel, and unless they departed soon the re-freezing of the White Sea would imprison them there when their tonnage was urgently required elsewhere.

In light of this, it was decided to run a return QP convoy in mid-November. QP 15 sailed from Archangel on 17 November with twenty-eight merchant ships and the usual escort of Russian-based corvettes and trawlers, as well as two Russian destroyers. Two groups of Royal Navy destroyers were despatched to the Barents Sea to provide a relay of escorts for the convoy, and a pair of cruisers, as well as further destroyers, stood by west of Bear Island to pick up the escort from that point. Unfortunately, the extremely bad weather, combined with the almost perpetual darkness, meant that the convoy was rapidly broken into small groups, and neither the destroyer groups or cruisers successfully made contact with them.

The operation was inspired in part on the Allied side by the knowledge gained from SIGINT of the departure of the German torpedo-bomber force from Norway at the beginning of November.[63] At the same time, however, German intelligence divined the Allied convoy plan in time to despatch a wolfpack, *BOREAS*, on 19 November to take station between Spitzbergen and Bear Island across the path of the convoy.[64] In turn, the Admiralty was able to locate the U-boats and signalled the convoy commodore, Captain Meek, to change his route south of Bear Island – a rare occasion when an Arctic convoy altered course substantially on the basis of prior intelligence of a U-boat patrol line. Ironically, while many of the merchantmen failed to receive this course correction, the two ships subsequently lost to U-boats, the *Goolistan* and the *Kusnetz Lesov*, both sunk on 23 November, had altered course to the southern route.[65] The remainder were collected and escorted into Loch Ewe between 30 November and 3 December. Admiral Northern Waters, meanwhile, had prepared a sortie for *Hipper* and its destroyers to exploit the lack of available Home Fleet warships and attack the convoy. This information was conveyed to the German Admiral Commanding Cruisers at 7 p.m. on 19 November and in turn was intercepted and passed on to the British Home Fleet at around 2 p.m. the following day.[66] In light of the extreme weather, however, the operation was subsequently postponed. This information was also obtained by the Admiralty and passed on later, on 20 November.[67] On this occasion, ULTRA had been able to keep pretty good tabs on the German surface fleet.

Outbound convoys would resume in December 1942 under the new JW code series, as will be described in the following chapters. As such, it is appropriate to reflect on the experience of the eighteen outbound and fifteen return PQ-QP convoys. The statistics are striking. The first twelve convoy cycles (outward and return) were carried out with the loss of only two merchant ships. However, this was to change in March 1942, as the next six cycles, PQ 13 to PQ 18, cost the Allies sixty-five merchant ships (19 per cent of those that sailed). Of these, thirty-six, or just over half, were sunk by aircraft, and the remainder mostly by U-boats, with only three lost to surface attack. Given that eighty-seven merchant vessels were lost from convoys in the campaign as a whole, the summer of 1942 was an unusually costly period. The impact of the arrival of the *Luftwaffe* torpedo bombers in the spring, and their subsequent departure in November 1942, was extremely significant. Over 40 per cent of all the merchant ship losses in the campaign were inflicted from the air on just six convoys during that period. It is hard to argue other than that the real threat to the seaborne route to Russia was not from U-boats but from torpedo bombers. Had this fact been fully understood by the parties concerned at the time, events might have played out somewhat differently, but that is speculation. As we have seen, there was little that SIGINT from Bletchley Park could do to assist in air defence, other than to keep an up-to date catalogue of the air power available to the Germans in Norway. There is no doubt, however, that ship-borne wireless interception (combined with radar) gave the convoys vital early warning of air attacks.

The events of the summer of 1942 have, however, skewed popular understanding of the Arctic campaign as a whole. This was concisely expressed by U-boat historian Clay Blair:

> The loss in a period of about eighty days of forty-three valuable ships in convoys PQ 17 (twenty-four) and PQ 18/QP 14 (nineteen), came as physical and psychological shocks to the Allies, and deservedly so. The news and newsreel reports and Allied and Axis propaganda that summer and fall, and talk among Allied merchant mariners and, later, war feature films, led to the impression that the 'Murmansk Run' was the most dangerous convoy route of all. However as Dönitz repeatedly informed Berlin, the Arctic was the *least* remunerative hunting ground for U-boats. Only a very few sank any more ships in that area. After the summer of 1942, the Luftwaffe was also ineffective against Allied shipping in the Arctic.[68]

The summer of 1942 was undoubtedly the worst period for the Arctic convoys from an Allied point of view, but it would not be repeated. The years 1941–1942 can be characterised as a period of desperate defence by the Allies. Starting in the winter of 1942 and continuing for the remainder of the war, the convoy battles would be different. Assisted by greater resources and better technology, in 1943 the Royal Navy would be able to take the fight to the *Kriegsmarine*, and the U-boats in particular, in a way that had not been possible in previous years. A strategy of defence would become one of attack, and ultimately dominance, in the Arctic.

DEFENCE

PART III
ATTACK
The JW–RA Convoys, 1942–1945

CHAPTER EIGHT

RAEDER'S LAST GAMBLE

CONVOYS JW 51–JW 53,
DECEMBER 1942–MARCH 1943

NAVAL SECTION MOVES HOUSE

C aroline Rowett left Cambridge University in the summer of 1942 and was expecting to don uniform shortly after, as she had been immediately drafted into the ATS (Auxiliary Territorial Service). However, it is likely that her talents had already been spotted by one of Frank Birch's scouts at Cambridge, as before she could begin her military career Caroline was summoned to the Foreign Office for an interview with the Head of Naval Section at Bletchley Park. Within a week, she arrived at Bletchley Park and joined the team in Hut 4 as a Foreign Office civilian working on U-boat intelligence. Morale in Hut 4 in June 1942 was low. Not only had Bletchley Park been able to make no progress in breaking the SHARK Enigma traffic introduced that January in the Atlantic, but, more recently, events in the Arctic were also taking their toll:

> My arrival in Hut 4 coincided with the reports of the PQ 17 tragedy, when a convoy on the Murmansk run was decimated by attacks from U-boats and surface vessels [*sic*]. The convoy route was subject to constant attack from enemy naval units based on the occupied Norwegian ports. 27 out of 33 escorted vessels were lost. The gloom in Hut 4 was indescribable.[1]

Caroline's work was dominated by the plot:

> The most immediately striking feature of the analysts' room in Hut 4 where I was to work was the large cork wall-drawing which covered one end of it. This represented a chart of the Atlantic and the Northern areas. Across this wall there appeared to crawl coloured caterpillars, with labels attached. There was also a scattering of labelled pins of a variety of colours. I was soon to learn that the caterpillars represented convoys, and their positions, course and speeds were all plotted currently as information was received.[2]

In August 1942, things were about to change. Naval Section had begun its operations in 1939 in the library of the mansion. By the end of 1939, Denniston reported on the grossly overcrowded Naval Section,[3] and in early 1940 it moved into Hut 4, initially only occupying part of the hut but later taking over the whole building, and spilling later still into Huts 5 and 9 and back into Rooms 49a and 50 in the mansion. In April and May 1941 there had been a proposal that Naval Section should move into Hut 14 (German) and Hut 15 (Italian), but the situation required a more long-term solution. The original plan in mid-1941 was for permanent splinter-proof office blocks to be built: a single-storey Block A (for Naval Section) and a single-storey Block B (for Military Section). This was altered in July 1941 to incorporate an upper storey to Block A (for Air Section). Planning and construction of the block, however, dragged on, delayed by lack of building materials and by lack of builders, and it was not finally occupied until August 1942.[4]

Birch was vociferous throughout this period in his campaign for better accommodation for his section. In December 1941, Birch wrote: 'for over six months this section has overflowed into other buildings [. . .] working in shifts has been extended throughout the section to make more room – even at the expense of efficiency.'[5] He was also exacting in his requirements for his own accommodation and argued for his own ground-floor office to be made larger in order that he could hold meetings without having to rearrange the furniture. Unfortunately, this proposal was cut from subsequent plans for the building, and a memorandum survives from November 1941 where Birch argued forcefully for its reinstatement.[6] In the end, he would get his extension, which survives to this day as an awkward bulge on the side of Spur 1 of the existing building.

Naval Section had been initially divided along geographical lines, with sub-sections dealing with each of the Axis powers, as well as smaller country-based teams. However, in 1941 these divisions became increasingly unsuitable. In particular, the entry of Germany into the Mediterranean and North African theatres alongside the Italians made separation of the two forces difficult. Increasingly, also, the work was becoming subdivided functionally, with different teams working on different technical aspects – research on unbroken systems, processing of broken systems, traffic analysis, technical intelligence, etc. Henceforth, this functional division of the section would become the model for its structure. This began in June 1941 when all German, Italian and Spanish naval cryptanalysis was combined into one sub-section under Wilfred Bodsworth, a pre-war member of GC&CS who had previously been head of the German sub-section.[7] Within this sub-section, the proportion of staff working on German material was smaller, as of course all naval Enigma material was being handled by Hut 8, leaving only medium-grade German codes to be attacked. It is notable that this reorganisation also coincides with the point (mid-1941) at which both German naval Enigma and Italian naval Hagelin C38m enciphered traffic became regularly and currently readable by Naval Section and Hut 8.

Naval Section moved into Blocks A and B in August 1942, occupying all the space allocated to them, as well as that earmarked for their Military Section colleagues, and it would appear that some further functional reorganisation in the section also occurred at that time. Work on cryptanalysis of German naval non-machine codes was separated into its own sub-section. Around this time a numerical system for distinguishing sub-sections was also introduced, and this section was christened Naval Section I while translation, analysis and forwarding to the Admiralty of all European enemy and neutral traffic was combined in a new section, Naval Section II.[8] Further numerical designations were given to other functions within the section.

The move to new accommodation, in combination with the restructuring, turned Naval Section into a large and powerful intelligence machine. By the end of 1943 there would be over six hundred people working in Naval Section alone, plus another hundred or more in Hut 8. The numbers for Naval Section would rise to over nine hundred by the end of the war. More than a third of these personnel worked on Japanese traffic, but the German sections expanded and were rendered more organised and efficient. As Rowett recalled, there was a certain nostalgia for the old life of the huts:

> By late September Block B [*sic*, actually A], which was to receive the denizens of Hut 4, was ready. Guess what! – Mary Ormsby left to get married and so it fell to me to go over there even before the benches and the shelving were fitted and before the paint was dry in many places, to replicate but in an expanded version on a wall of our future office the cork-based chart with which I was already so familiar. My last effort at cartography had been a dire experience but was nothing to this. At last it was done and soon we were all moving in.
>
> It was a big change from the old days of Hut 4. Inside, the dear old shack had been quite bright when the shutters were not up. Block B was dim even when it was sunny outside. The U-boat room was lucky however in having a door (probably a fire escape) which gave directly onto a grassy patch beyond which was the lake. During the day in good weather this door mostly stood open. This facility was particularly welcome to begin with in view of the fact that there was an overpowering smell of new concrete. The old smell of damp wood was almost preferable.[9]

Nonetheless, the change was both necessary and transformative. Naval Section would fight the remainder of its war with more staff, better facilities and an altogether more professional and indeed industrial approach.

CONVOYS RESUME

With Allied troops landed successfully in French North Africa by mid-November 1942, the Home Fleet was able to recover the forces it had been obliged to divert to Operation TORCH, and thoughts could be turned to the resumption of convoys to Russia. A significant backlog of fully laden merchant vessels was also accumulating in Iceland. It had originally been intended to suspend convoys until at least January, but the drawdown of German air force strength in Norway (revealed by SIGINT, amongst other sources), as well as the darkness and bad weather, encouraged the Admiralty to re-start operations sooner. They were also keen to continue the large-scale operations undertaken previously, and a thirty-two ship convoy (re-designated JW 51) was proposed. Admiral Tovey, on the other hand, felt that, in the likely weather conditions, the chances of keeping such a large body of ships together was very low, and that once the convoy broke up it would be much more difficult to defend. He advocated small, ten-ship groups.

Perhaps surprisingly, it was not until late in 1942 that any properly scientific thought was given to the best size for a convoy. Prior to that date, the Admiralty maintained a view that smaller was better and that around forty merchant ships in any one convoy was an optimum number. This pattern of sailing thirty to forty ships in any one convoy had been followed in the Arctic as well as the North Atlantic. Larger convoys were frowned upon, and those above sixty ships outlawed altogether. However, this was based on folklore and instinct as much as it was on science. In November 1942 a new Anti-U-Boat Warfare Committee was formed in the Cabinet. One of its first acts was to commission Professor Patrick Blackett, a former Cambridge physicist and mathematician, now head of the Admiralty's nascent Operational Research Department, to investigate convoy size and the best ratio of escort vessels to merchantmen. Blackett's team returned in January 1943 with a determination that, in fact, larger was better, in that convoys of fifteen to twenty-four ships could expect losses of 2.3 per cent of ships sailed, while for those of forty-five ships or more, that figure dropped to 1.1 per cent. A consequence of this was that Atlantic convoys grew larger in 1943, and convoys of up to eighty ships became common.[10] These calculations, however, did not take into account the problems of keeping together such a large group in the perpetual darkness of the Arctic, and in the face of frequent extreme weather; thus, while the convoys grew bigger in the Atlantic, the reverse happened in the Arctic. As Tovey described: 'After further discussions including a visit to London by my Chief-of-Staff, I was directed to sail the convoy in two parts of sixteen ships each, escorted by seven destroyers and some smaller craft; and the Home Fleet was reinforced by two 6-inch cruisers to allow of cruiser cover in the Barents Sea.'[11]

The Arctic convoys were also already treated differently to those in the Atlantic with regard to the number of escorts. Admiralty practice stated that Atlantic convoys should be escorted by escorts equal to the 'Number of merchantmen/10 + 3'.[12] Arctic convoys were always much more heavily escorted as a response to the confined waters and higher threat level. On the basis of the Admiralty calculation, the thirty-five merchantmen in PQ 17 would have been escorted by only seven ships. In fact, over twenty ships were involved in its close protection, not counting the heavy ships of the cruiser covering force and the Home Fleet. Similarly massive escort forces were required for convoys in the Mediterranean, showing how different convoy operations were in these waters compared to the broad oceans of the Atlantic.

Initially, the Admiral was wary of the U-boat threat and argued that, as previously, the cruisers should not go further east than the North Cape, but again he was overruled; the cruisers would accompany the convoys (at a distance) all the way to their destination. In the event, Tovey admitted that this was the correct decision: 'The Admiralty, however, were insistent that the cruisers should cover the convoys right through to Kola; this insistence was fully justified in the event, for otherwise the cruiser force would probably not have been present at the action on New Year's Eve.'[13]

As a result, two convoys were scheduled, JW 51A, which departed on 15 December, and JW 51B, which would depart a week later on 22 December. As well as the usual close escort of smaller vessels, the convoys were protected by half a dozen destroyers, and by the two light cruisers, *Sheffield* and *Jamaica* (with their own pair of destroyer escorts). The cruisers had the difficult mission of remaining near enough to the convoys to provide protection, but ideally up to 50 miles away in order to avoid detection by U-boats. This was no easy task in the poor weather and limited visibility of the Arctic in winter and was not entirely successful, as we shall see. The Home Fleet also provided their usual cover: Tovey sailed himself to cover JW 51A in HMS *King George V*, with the cruiser *Berwick* and an escort of destroyers, while JW 51B was shadowed by the brand-new sister ship of *King George V*, HMS *Anson*, along with the cruiser *Cumberland*. No fleet carrier was included with these covering forces, and no escort carriers were embedded with the convoys, but given the near perpetual darkness and the poor weather, air operations were unlikely to be especially effective, and nor was the German air threat considered to be very significant.

On the German side, there had been something of a re-shuffle of their naval strength in Arctic waters. *Tirpitz* remained a brooding threat in Trondheim, but it had begun a refit in October which would not be complete until January. Similarly, out of the two heavy cruisers *Admiral Scheer* and *Admiral Hipper*, *Scheer* had likewise returned to Germany to refit. The light cruiser *Köln* remained and was supplemented at Narvik in December by the light cruiser *Nürnberg*. In addition, the heavy cruiser *Lützow* returned north, arriving in Narvik on 12 November. It had been repaired in Germany following its grounding during the summer, and with its 28cm (11-inch) guns represented a significant additional asset. The movements of all of these ships were tracked successfully at Bletchley Park via Enigma traffic, and an attempt had been made by the RAF to intercept *Nürnberg* on its passage to Trondheim from the Baltic, but the aircraft failed to find their target.[14]

Enigma had also revealed a steady build-up in the U-boat forces in Norway, reaching a total of twenty-five boats, although the same intercepts revealed that no more than two or three boats were at sea at any one time, and activity was generally very limited, considering the number of U-boats present.[15] Nonetheless, there was pressure on the *Kriegsmarine* to show results, given the large force at their disposal. U-boat patrols continued throughout October and November, supported by limited air reconnaissance, but no eastbound convoys were discovered. It was inevitable, however, that the Allies would resume supplies to Russia eventually, and plans were drawn up accordingly. The strong convoy escorts made life difficult for U-boats, especially in poor weather, and air assets were very limited, so the German plan, Operation *REGENBOGEN* ('rainbow') relied on a surface-ship attack on the next convoy to be identified.

Unfortunately, although large on paper, the German fleet was less potent in reality. *Tirpitz* was out of action undergoing a refit, *Köln* was considered too poor a sea-boat in bad weather to keep up with other ships and *Nürnberg* was in use as a training ship. That left only *Lützow* and *Hipper*, and a destroyer escort of around six ships, available for the operation.[16] Even so, if these forces could find a convoy with only destroyers as escort, it was thought the escort could be quickly overwhelmed. The challenge was to avoid any British cruisers that may be shadowing the convoy. The answer to this was to operate east of the North Cape, as experience had shown that the British cruisers rarely ventured too far into the Barents Sea. Indeed, if the convoy turned out to have one light cruiser carrying the flag of the destroyer force, this would still not be an insurmountable problem. Accordingly, on 17 December *Lützow* sailed north from Narvik and joined *Hipper* to lie in wait in Altenfjord. This move was picked up by Naval Section from Enigma intercepts as early as 17 December, in particular *Luftwaffe* traffic organising air cover for *RUDELSBERG*, a codename for *Lützow*, which was quickly seen through.[17] U-boat involvement in the operation was limited due to the risk of misidentification of friendly ships, but a screen of four boats was deployed with the goal of finding and shadowing the convoy to provide location information for the surface ships. This too was known to the Admiralty from Enigma traffic.

THE BATTLE OF THE BARENTS SEA

Despite their preparations, the Germans missed convoy JW 51A. It sailed on 15 December from Loch Ewe and without calling at Iceland made its journey unmolested, arriving in Murmansk on Christmas Day, with some ships proceeding further east to Molotovsk in the White Sea.[18] Its successor, JW 51B, sailed from Loch Ewe on 22 December, albeit with only fourteen merchantmen. The convoy was joined by the 17th Destroyer Flotilla, sailing from Iceland. This consisted of six destroyers, *Obedient*, *Orwell*, *Obdurate*, *Oribi* and *Achates*, led by Captain Sherbrooke as Captain (D) in *Onslow*, although *Oribi* was later detached due to technical problems. The early part of the journey was uneventful, until on 29 December a fierce storm blew up which caused station-keeping difficulties and led to several ships straggling from the convoy, as well as substantially slowing their rate of progress eastwards.

Meanwhile, the cruisers *Sheffield* and *Jamaica*, codenamed 'Force R' under Admiral Burnett, had sailed with the previous convoy and followed a course 60 miles south of JW 51A, between it and any likely foray from Norway by the German fleet, and had arrived in Kola on 24 December. They sailed again on 27 December, heading west with their two escorting destroyers (*Opportune* and *Matchless*), intending to pick up JW 51B to the south-west of Bear Island and shadow that convoy in turn back east again. The departure of Force R from Kola was known to the Germans and alerted them to the likelihood of another eastbound convoy approaching in the next few days. A message to that effect from Admiral Northern Waters was intercepted on 27 December, although it was not passed to the Admiralty until around noon on 29 December.[19] In turn, this information was relayed to the Home Fleet and to Admiral Burnett and his cruisers a short time later.[20] It is likely that the departure of the cruisers was picked up by the *B-Dienst* during monitoring of Royal Navy communications, evidence that the Germans were still having significant success in breaking Allied codes.[21] Interestingly, however, they do not appear to have picked up on the change of convoy codes, as they erroneously refer to JW 51B as 'PQ 20'. This, incidentally, suggests that they were also aware of JW 51A ('PQ 19'), although they were not able to do anything to interfere with it.[22]

A U-boat was able to confirm German suspicions of the whereabouts of JW 51B on the morning of 30 December. *U-354* under *Kapitänleutnant* Karl-Heinz Herbschleb picked up the convoy immediately to the south-west of Bear Island and was ordered to begin transmitting homing signals.[23] This was the perfect chance, as the convoy was about to pass east of the North Cape and into waters that the Germans hoped would not contain British heavy units (cruisers and above). Unfortunately, at this point Admiral Kummetz, on board *Hipper*, and his new superior Otto Klüber as Admiral Northern Waters had to wrestle with the labyrinthine command structure of the *Kriegsmarine*. As has been outlined earlier, so tight was Hitler's grip on his major surface units that no one dared commit the ships to battle without authority from the highest level. Admiral Northern Waters in turn informed *Gruppe Nord* in Kiel, who passed the news to Naval High Command (*SKL*) in Berlin, and they passed it on to the Permanent Representative of the Commander-in-Chief of the Navy, Admiral Theodor Kranke, who was present with the *Führer* in his bunker at Rastenburg in East Prussia. Kranke read a message to Hitler from Admiral Raeder to 'inform [the] Führer that C-in-C Navy approves in principle the operational use of *Hipper, Lützow* and destroyers. Execution is in accordance with the decision of Group North dependent on the fact that according to existing information the escort with the convoy is not in fact superior.'[24]

On this basis, the *Führer* approved Operation *REGENBOGEN*, and word was sent back down the chain to put the wheels in motion. In fact, both Klüber and Admiral Kummetz, who would take the fleet to sea as Admiral Commanding Cruisers, had already begun preparations immediately on receiving the signal from *U-354*. The former Admiral signalled the latter at 1.02 p.m. on 30 December, ordering him to prepare his ships for sea immediately, while their planning staffs calculated a route and timings which would allow the German force to intercept the convoy at a suitable time the following day to maximise the available daylight for an attack.[25] This would allow for more accurate gunnery but also reduce the risk of torpedo attack from the British destroyers.

Before the ships sailed at 5.45 p.m., Admiral Klüber went aboard *Hipper* to brief Kummetz in person. This is perhaps where the indecision in the German plan set in, which was to be crucial later. Klüber's orders were 'on meeting the enemy: avoid a superior force, otherwise destroy [the convoy] according to tactical situation' – not the most decisive of commands. The waters were further muddied by the decision of Naval High Command to extend *Lützow*'s operations. After the completion of *REGENBOGEN*, *Lützow* was to proceed into the North Atlantic on a longer convoy-raiding cruise, codenamed *AURORE*. However, which was the more important operation was not stated, and its captain, Stange, was put in the position of trying to judge how far to commit to *REGENBOGEN* without compromising *AURORE*. The outcome of the subsequent battle would hinge, in part, on this lack of clarity and indecision on the part of the *Kriegsmarine* staff.

Almost nothing of any of these plans was known at the Admiralty. The Enigma messages concerning the sailing of Force R were read on the key in use from 12 p.m. on 27 December to 12 p.m. on 29 December. However, the sighting of the convoy by *U-354* and all of the subsequent communications during the battle took place using the 29–31 December key, and none of these messages were available to the Admiralty before the early hours of 1 January, by which time the action was over. To make matters worse, the last communication to the Home Fleet and to Burnett in Force R was sent at around 8 p.m. on 30 December. It read: 'There are strong indications that up to 0045/30 Admiral Commanding Cruisers [i.e. *Hipper*] was still in Altenfjord.'[26] While technically correct, this message could easily have led to false inferences, as by 8.15 on that evening Kummetz and his ships had already been at sea for two-and-a-half hours.

Kummetz's attack plan has been criticised, as he divided his forces, but in principle it was quite sound. *Hipper* and *Lützow* would follow divergent courses which would place them about 75 miles apart by the time they reached the convoy route. Each was accompanied by three destroyers, which would be strung out in between to provide a search screen. The intention was to approach the convoy from behind, using the warships' superior speed, with *Hipper* to the north and *Lützow* to the south. Whichever first encountered the convoy would engage and draw off the destroyer escorts, allowing the other ship to approach the convoy itself from the other side and destroy it at leisure.[27] As we shall see, this very nearly worked. It also neatly but unknowingly exploited the defensive plan Captain Sherbrooke had drawn up for the 17th Destroyer Flotilla's defence of the convoy. Sherbrooke's strategy, explained to his captains before sailing, was that if enemy surface ships were sighted, his destroyers would concentrate between the convoy and the threatened flank and attack aggressively while the close escorts covered the convoy with smoke as it changed course away from the threat.[28] This is exactly how the British ships responded on 31 December, and it very nearly played directly into the hands of the Germans.

In the early hours of New Year's Eve 1942, convoy JW 51B was at a point approximately equidistant between Bear Island and the North

Cape (73 degrees north. 29 degrees east), on a course slightly south of due east. Three of the merchant ships scattered by the storm had been reunited with the main body, while two escorts had gone in search of the remaining two strays. The trawler *Vizalma* had successfully tracked down the *Chester Valley* and was sailing in company with it about 45 miles to the north, while the minesweeper *Bramble* continued to hunt for the *Jefferson Myers* about 15 miles away to the north-east. Admiral Burnett, meanwhile, had rightly assumed that any German attack would sweep up from behind the convoy, and so placed himself and his cruisers to be both to the north of and behind the convoy track. This would allow him to detect an approach from the rear and with luck would also silhouette any enemy ships to the south in the faint daylight while he remained in shadow. Unfortunately for Burnett, his appreciation of the situation was off by about 150 miles. He had received a signal from the C-in-C on 27 December giving the estimated timings of the convoy. This signal suggested it would pass the longitude of Bear Island at around 4 p.m. on 30 December. In fact, the delay caused by the storm on 29 December put the convoy 20 hours and about 150 miles behind schedule, and on a more southerly track than originally anticipated.[29] As a consequence, although he didn't know it, Burnett's Force R (now minus its two destroyers, which had departed to refuel) was actually due north of the convoy and only about 30 miles away.

First contact between the two opposing forces occurred at 7.45 a.m. on 31 December, as *Hipper* sighted the convoy in the first glimmers of dawn, but as it was still too dark to engage safely, Kummetz drew off to the north-west while the destroyer *Friedrich Eckoldt* maintained contact.[30] The German destroyers were first sighted by their opponents at about 8.20 a.m., but there was confusion as to whether they were Russian ships come to escort the convoy. Sherbrooke detached *Obdurate* to investigate, but it was not until the three German destroyers opened fire on it that the matter was settled. At this point, the German destroyers were to the west (rear) of the convoy, with *Hipper* as yet undetected to the north. Sherbrooke's plan was immediately put into operation, and the destroyers of 17th Flotilla started to congregate on the north-western side of the convoy while the close escort made smoke. The German destroyers drew off to the north towards *Hipper*, and at

9.30 a.m. the cruiser became visible to Sherbrooke aboard *Onslow*. Sighting the British destroyers, *Hipper* turned to port to open its arcs and opened fire on *Onslow* and *Orwell* at 9.41 a.m. at a range of about 11,000 yards.

For the next hour, *Hipper* taunted the British destroyers, tracking broadly eastwards but changing course to keep at long range and avoid the possibility of torpedo attack, all the time hoping to lure the British ships away from their charges in the convoy. Aware of the convoy, and having lost sight of the German destroyers, Sherbrooke sent two of his own force, *Obedient* and *Obdurate*, back to keep an eye on the convoy. The convoy commodore had meanwhile turned JW 51B south-east away from the enemy in accordance with Sherbrooke's plan. At about 10.20 a.m. the uneven fight turned against Sherbrooke when *Onslow* was hit by a salvo from *Hipper* which took out the destroyer's A and B turrets and radar and badly injured Sherbrooke himself. On fire, with many casualties and its communications disabled, *Onslow* broke off to starboard, and its captain continued to command the ship and manage damage control, until reluctantly he was coaxed below, as his left eye had been dislodged and his face was a mass of blood. He would later be awarded the Victoria Cross both for his conduct of the battle and his personal bravery.

No matter how much heroism was displayed, the outlook for Sherbrooke's destroyers was bleak. The fight with *Hipper* was only likely to go one way, especially once the German destroyers entered the battle. However, help was on its way. To the north, the two cruisers of Force R were heading east when at 8.58 a.m. a radar contact was established away to the north-east. As this was where the convoy was expected to be, Burnett ran down the bearing to investigate, only to find the lone straggler *Chester Valley* under escort from *Vizalma*. At the same time, gun flashes were observed over the horizon to the south, but as these were not in the area where he expected the convoy to be, Burnett temporarily ignored them. By 9.45 a.m., Burnett was persuaded that the *Vizalma* was not the convoy, and the flashes continued to the south; meanwhile, a wireless message was received from *Onslow* reporting enemy destroyers in contact. In response, Burnett put his helm over and set off at 31 knots southward 170 degrees and 'steamed towards the sight of the guns'.[31] At this stage, the Admiral was unaware of the presence of the two larger German ships, only being aware of their destroyer escorts. However, at 10.30 a.m. two radar contacts were established on large vessels, one due south (*Hipper*) and another (*Lützow*) further away to the south-east, escorted by smaller vessels. Both were apparently firing on targets unknown to Burnett.

At around the time of Burnett's first radar contact (10.30 a.m.), *Hipper* had disengaged from Sherbrooke's destroyers when a snowstorm shut down visibility temporarily and was sailing north-east where, by unlucky coincidence, it came upon the minesweeper *Bramble* making its way back to the convoy after its unsuccessful straggler-hunt. The German cruiser and its destroyers made short work of the minesweeper, sinking its with all hands, but not before it was able to get off a W/T message reporting the contact. Although no British ships witnessed its destruction, HMS *Bramble* and its crew of 121 were widely mourned in the navy and the merchant fleet, as it had become a regular feature of the Arctic run.[32] Starting with PQ 2 in October 1941, *Bramble* had escorted no fewer than thirteen outward or return convoys.

Hipper then turned south-west again towards the convoy, which by this time had continued its starboard turns and was heading due south. Unknown to all parties, in the confusion the convoy was in fact on a directly converging course with *Lützow*, which was heading north-east and must have passed close across the bows of the convoy. Fortunately for the merchantmen, the weather closed in at that moment and a snow squall probably prevented the German plan from coming to fruition with the destruction of the convoy. Instead, Captain Stange, who was almost certainly aware of the presence of the convoy, decided to take his time and stand off to the north-east until the weather cleared. Unfortunately for him, with the imminent arrival of the British cruisers, his only window of opportunity for success had just closed. *Lützow* was sighted by the corvette HMS *Rhododendron* of the close escort, who first spotted its smoke to the south-west but then saw the ship itself steering north-east, only 2 miles off the convoy's port bow. By this time Sherbrooke's destroyers had rejoined and were making their way down the port (eastern) side of the convoy. *Obedient* also spotted *Lützow* at around 11 a.m., by which time the German cruiser had turned south-east and was tracking parallel with the convoy. The destroyers hastened to place themselves between the two and make smoke.

While the attention of the British destroyers was focused towards *Lützow*, *Hipper* reappeared to the north-east and resumed the fight. It engaged the destroyer *Achates* and soon scored crippling hits on the smaller ship, killing its captain, Lt Commander Johns, and forty others. Although its speed was much reduced, *Achates* gamely continued to hold station between *Hipper* and the convoy and made smoke. Meanwhile, the other destroyers turned north to tackle *Hipper*. In response, at 11.25 a.m. the German ship turned north-west, possibly in an attempt to draw the British destroyers away from the convoy and force them to split their effort between the two German ships. In this it was unsuccessful, as after a short time the destroyers turned back south-east again to return to the convoy.

Kummetz, on board *Hipper*, was also about to receive a rude shock, as while he turned towards the north-west his ship was sighted by *Sheffield* and *Jamaica* roaring southward down their radar bearing towards the battle. At 11.30 a.m. Admiral Burnett turned *Sheffield* to starboard to open his arcs and commence firing at 13,000 yards, followed shortly after by *Jamaica*. Such was the surprise that several salvoes from the British cruisers had already splashed into the sea around *Hipper* before its captain realised what was happening. Alerted to the danger, he then turned the German cruiser to starboard, making a clockwise turn towards the British ships. Soon after, however, *Hipper* was struck three times by 6-inch shells from the British ships. This was exactly the scenario that Kummetz had been ordered to avoid – contact with an unknown number of large enemy warships, as well as the destroyers he was already fighting – and he took the only decision permitted to him by his superiors. At 11.37 a.m. the Admiral ordered all German ships to break off to the west and end the action. Keeping the helm over to starboard, *Hipper* sailed in an almost complete circle before heading westwards at top speed, a speed somewhat reduced by flooding in the no. 3 boiler room.

In an attempt to conform to the movements of the German ship, Force R had turned in a similar near-complete circle, and as they steered to resume the chase to the west, other ships appeared out of the gloom and snow close by. These were the two German destroyers accompanying *Hipper* – *Friedrich Eckoldt* and *Richard Beitzen* – returning from the final destruction of *Bramble* off to the east and trying to reunite with their parent ship. Possibly mistaking *Sheffield* for *Hipper*, the *Friedrich Eckoldt* passed within half a mile of *Sheffield*. The British cruiser made no such error, and with main guns at minimum elevation it pounded the enemy ship with all weapons that would bear, including its 4-inch secondary armament and even its 3lb and 2lb anti-aircraft mounts. Within ten minutes, the German destroyer was a flaming wreck, at which point Force R resumed their pursuit of *Hipper*.

Lützow, meanwhile, obeyed orders from Admiral Kummetz and reversed course back to the north-west, passing up the east side of the convoy. It was briefly able to fire on the merchant ships, causing some damage to the steamer *Calobre*, but its fire was soon masked by the smoke laid by the British destroyers, and it broke off the engagement and followed *Hipper* westwards. A few shots were also fired by its destroyer escorts but hit nothing, the only part those ships would play in the battle. The whole German force then fled to the west. Force R gave chase, and shots were exchanged at around 12.30 p.m., but by 2.00 p.m. Admiral Burnett lost radar contact and called off the hunt, concerned to return to the convoy which was his primary responsibility.

While Force R was away to the west, fires continued to burn on the British destroyer *Achates,* and it heeled over until the crew could actually walk down its hull plating. Many of its complement were taken off by the trawler *Northern Gem* which came alongside. The coxswain of *Northern Gem* was somewhat surprised by the reactions of some of the *Achates* crew to the loss of their ship: 'Then as the men in the water started swimming towards the Gem, we stood on our deck and listened in amazement as we heard their voices giving out with a rendering of "Roll out the barrel". Here they were in dire peril, not only from drowning, but freezing to death if we could not get them out of the water within a few minutes, singing at the tops of their voices.'[33]

Many men were pulled from the water by the crew of the *Gem*, some of whom climbed down their own scrambling nets to help frozen survivors out of the water. The destroyer finally sank at around 1.30 p.m. Unfortunately, this detonated the stock of depth charges on the sinking ship's afterdeck, and the concussion from this killed any remaining men still in the water. At that point, *Northern Gem* was forced to abandon the rescue and rejoin the convoy. Out of *Achates'* complement of 194 men, 80 survivors had been recovered.

Convoy JW 51B suffered no further disturbance from the Germans and arrived in Kola Inlet on 3 January 1943. Burnett sailed his force westwards to catch up with the returning convoy RA 51, which had left Murmansk on 30 December. In turn, he handed the convoy over to the cruisers *Kent* and *Berwick*, which had been sent out for the purpose, and *Sheffield* and *Jamaica* made for Iceland, arriving on 2 January. RA 51 also sailed on unmolested and arrived in Loch Ewe on 11 January.

BEST-LAID PLANS?

There is little doubt that Captain Sherbrooke, and his successor in command of 17th Flotilla, Commander Kinloch of *Obedient*, had won a stunning defensive victory against superior forces. This fact was quickly recognised by both sides. Admiral Tovey summed up the general degree of British satisfaction:

> The conduct of all officers and men of the escort and covering forces throughout this successful action against greatly superior forces was in accordance with the traditions of the service. That an enemy force of at least one pocket battleship, one heavy cruiser and six destroyers, with all the advantage of surprise and concentration, should be held off for four hours by five destroyers and driven from the area by two 6-inch cruisers, without any loss to the convoy, is most creditable and satisfactory.[34]

Both British commanders skilfully balanced extreme aggression against larger enemy ships with an awareness of other possible threats to the convoy, sallying out and then doubling back to their charges, constantly interposing themselves between the convoy and their adversaries and making smoke to protect the merchantmen. The intervention of Burnett's force at a crucial moment was also fundamental to Allied success, a fact which Tovey was modest enough to acknowledge was only possible due to his own cautious cruiser strategy being overruled by the Admiralty.

German performance was (and is) much more open to question. Operation *REGENBOGEN* worked almost perfectly up until the moment of actual contact. German intelligence, a mix of limited air reconnaissance and SIGINT from the *B-Dienst*, had provided Admiral Northern Waters with good information about when to expect a convoy and along what route. A U-boat had then picked up the precise location of the convoy and was able to shadow it and provide homing signals for the surface ships. Kummetz's plan to bring his two heavy units alongside the convoy on both sides was also successful, and *Hipper* did a good job of engaging and drawing off the destroyer escort. All that remained was for *Lützow* to deliver the coup de grace and destroy the convoy. But this did not happen. The only available explanation is that the German commanders were so intimidated by their orders to avoid risk, and to preserve their ships, that they were paralysed when faced with real combat. The captain of *Lützow* also had his decision-making clouded by his two-fold mission which combined *REGENBOGEN* with *AURORE*. The Official Historian, Stephen Roskill, expressed this view explicitly: 'Though the German Admiral has been criticised for dividing his forces, it is to be remarked that events worked out almost exactly as he planned; the *Lützow*'s force passed very close indeed to the south of the convoy while almost all its escorts were engaged with the *Hipper*'s force on the other flank. It seems that only the over-caution of the *Lützow*'s Captain then saved the convoy from utter destruction.'[35]

Even had Captain Stange not wanted to risk his major unit, the option remained for his destroyer escort to attack the convoy with torpedoes, a move which might have proved equally fatal to the merchantmen, and yet the smaller German ships continued to sail in close concert with their larger sister. Commander Kinloch expressed his bafflement at these tactics: 'The inactivity of the German destroyers is inexplicable. They made no attack on the convoy and in two engagements were following astern of their cruiser without taking any part.'[36]

Vice Admiral Kummetz later tried to explain this lack of activity by his escorts, blaming the weather and poor visibility leading to confusion and possible misidentification: 'To make a destroyer attack was out of the question, owing to possible confusion with the enemy. As our action developed I should no longer have been able to assemble our own destroyers round *Hipper* before darkness and would thus have left her without destroyer protection at a difficult period.'[37]

There is an element of truth in Kummetz's argument. After all, when his destroyers did detach themselves in pursuit of *Bramble* they struggled to find *Hipper*, and one made the fatal mistake of sailing towards *Sheffield* instead. However, a more decisive admiral would have considered this a gamble worth taking when the prize at stake, the destruction of a convoy, was there for the taking.

From an intelligence point of view, while the Germans were well-supplied with information but failed to exploit it, the British ships were in the opposite position. Although the Admiralty had been able to provide a good account of the general strategic situation and was able to warn Force R that their own movements, and those of the convoy, were probably known to the enemy, they failed to give any warning of the sailing of the German surface fleet, and indeed sent a message which was both out of date and potentially misleading, saying that they were still in Altenfjord. Nor was Admiral Burnett provided with good information about the position of his own forces. The convoy position update he was given was hopelessly wrong, and nearly led to serious consequences when he sailed after spurious radar contacts in the almost opposite direction. Only a message from Sherbrooke and the fact that he could see gun flashes on the horizon led him to the right course. In fact, at no point did Admiral Burnett ever see convoy JW 51B, and he fought the battle in ignorance of its real position. That the Royal Navy was able to win the battle in the face of this handicap is testament to the skills, bravery and above all initiative of those involved. Sadly for the Germans, initiative was no longer fashionable in the *Kriegsmarine*.

A final note on the battle for JW 51B concerns the German submarine force. Beyond providing a shadowing U-boat to follow the merchantmen, no submarine attack was organised against the convoy. Despite the large number of boats available in Norway, there was some debate over their usefulness at that time of year, and eleven boats had been made available to Admiral Dönitz for operations in the Atlantic.

In addition, as soon as the surface fleet was at sea it was necessary to de-conflict the two arms, and a message was sent on the evening of 30 December banning U-boats from attacking surface warships, and vice versa, for fear of attacks on friendly forces.[38] Thus, the U-boat arm was prevented from making any useful contribution. The lack of joint effort by the various surface, sub-surface and air assets available to the Germans during this period was summed up by the GC&CS historian: 'Nearly a year after the campaign had first been launched, U-boat participation in strength was subject to the will of the *B.d.U.*, and the employment of bomber aircraft was reduced to the minimum; only the discredited main units remained in their former strength, and they constituted a most dubious instrument of German offensive strategy in the Arctic.'[39]

FURY AT THE *WOLFSSCHANZE*

German disappointment in the outcome of operation *REGENBOGEN* was increased by the manner in which the results were reported. Kummetz and the surface ships, not unnaturally, maintained radio silence while they sailed back to Norway, for fear of being pursued by the British. However, Admiral Northern Waters was anxious for news of victory. One witness was available, *Kapitänleutnant* Herbschleb, aboard *U-354*. Perhaps caught up in the moment, Herbschleb had signalled at 10.56 a.m. on 31 December: 'Battle has reached its culminating point. I can see only red!'[40] Quite what he meant by this is not clear, although gun flashes would have been visible and *Onslow* was on fire at that time, but a degree of hyperbole is present, whatever may have been visible through his periscope. Patrick Beesly, who was serving in the OIC at the Admiralty at the time of the decryption of this message, observed that it 'caused some hilarity in the Submarine Tracking Room'.[41] Admiral Klüber, on the other hand, seized on this news and jubilantly and prematurely forwarded it to the *Führer*. He meanwhile messaged Kummetz for more news, to which the Admiral Commanding Cruisers wisely sent no response.[42] Frustrated, Klüber instructed Herbschleb to search the battle area, firstly for evidence of a destroyed convoy, and secondly for any survivors from the unfortunate

Friedrich Eckoldt.[43] Despite his efforts, Herbschleb reported 'searching the battlefield in vain', seeing two fires, and meanwhile being harassed with depth charges by British destroyers.[44] Undiscouraged by these reports, Klüber sent a jubilant message to Herbschleb:

> Well done as a finish to the year!
> Carry on into the New Year!
> A New Year toast to my Ice-wolves![45]

This may just have been by way of New Year greeting (the UK intercept time, 10.05 p.m., was just after midnight German time), but the tone is remarkable in the circumstances. As an interesting aside, U-boat command continued to send domestic news to its U-boats, and ten minutes earlier a message had been sent to *U-354* for *Leutnant* Rainer, an officer in its crew. It read: 'It's arrived, going on well, Dora, Best Wishes.'[46] It would seem *Leutnant* and Mrs Rainer had some good news to share for New Year 1943.

Hitler, meanwhile, awaited further news of his victory. The first he received was a report on the BBC giving the real course of events. He was furious and flew into one of his towering rages. The Chief of the Navy, Admiral Raeder, was summoned on New Year's Day to explain, or rather to receive the brunt of the *Führer's* wrath. Raeder pleaded sickness and waited five days for the storm to abate, but this was to no avail. When he at last arrived at the *Wolfsschanze* (the *Führer's* secret headquarters near Rastenburg, Poland), Hitler ranted that the surface navy was entirely useless, and that in light of its lack of success it should be scrapped en masse and the guns relocated as shore defence batteries. Raeder argued against this, and was supported by Klüber, who made the rather specious argument that although no damage had been done to the convoy, the battle would remind the British of the potential of the German surface ships and would continue to tie up the Home Fleet.[47] Hitler would not be swayed from his 'irrevocable resolve', and, faced with such humiliation, Admiral Raeder resigned.[48] Hitler was somewhat taken aback by this development and argued for Raeder to stay, but the *Generaladmiral* was adamant, and he stepped down, succeeded on his own recommendation by the erstwhile *Befehlshaber der U-Boote* Karl Dönitz.[49]

The *Führer* expected that, as a U-boat man, Dönitz would acquiesce to the scrapping of the surface fleet, and initially his new chief was in agreement with this radical plan; indeed, he began drawing up the orders for the disbandment of the force. A gradual drawdown would leave no major surface units in commission by the end of 1943. As he talked to his colleagues, however, Dönitz revised his opinion, and on 26 February he returned to Hitler with a new plan to save key units including *Tirpitz, Scharnhorst, Scheer, Lützow, Prinz Eugen* and *Nurnberg.* Once he had overcome his astonishment at this *volte-face*, the *Führer* grudgingly agreed, and it was decided that *Tirpitz* and *Scharnhorst*, with escorting destroyers, would form a northern group in Norway, while the rest of the fleet returned to the Baltic for training and to await events. Thus, the surface navy was reprieved, for the moment at least.[50]

Almost nothing of this dramatic debate was known to the Admiralty in London. In fact, the appointment of Dönitz led to a belief in London and Scapa in a more active German surface-ship policy than hitherto. Gradually, evidence was developed from various sources that all was not well in the surface fleet. An Enigma message in March revealed the medical inspection of ships' crews for potential transfer to the U-boat fleet, and this was confirmed by interrogation of U-boat prisoners of war. In January, however, Enigma traffic revealed the likely transfer of *Scharnhorst* from the Baltic to Norway, which confirmed that the threat from German heavy units in the Arctic was likely to continue for the foreseeable future.[51]

As part of his takeover of command, Dönitz released a bellicose message to the fleet. In it, he reminded his sailors that 'From every individual I expect unqualified obedience, extreme courage, and devotion to the last breath. It is in these things that we uphold our honour. Gathered about our *Führer*, we will not lay down our arms until victory and peace have been won. Hail our *Führer!*'[52]

It is somewhat ironic that, unbeknownst to him, Dönitz's message was of great assistance to Bletchley Park. It was repeated verbatim on numerous Enigma networks, as well as on less secure dockyard ciphers. As a result, it provided the perfect crib for breaking those keys.

1943 SAILINGS CONTINUE

The next eastbound convoy, JW 52, sailed within a week of the arrival of RA 51, leaving Loch Ewe on 17 January 1943. The convoy was provided with similar protection to its predecessor, with a force of seven destroyers accompanying it, and a shadowing cruiser force consisting of HMS *Kent*, *Glasgow* and *Bermuda* under Rear Admiral Hamilton. Despite being contacted by U-boats west of Bear Island and coming under air attack by four He 115 torpedo aircraft, the convoy reached Kola unscathed on 27 January. Much of this success was attributed to the effective use of ship-board direction finding (known as H/F-D/F or 'Huff-duff') by the escort, which not only allowed them to run down and drive off U-boat attacks, but also allowed the convoy's senior officer, Commander Selby, in *Onslaught*, to maintain a high speed and frequent changes of course to avoid known submarine locations. Unfortunately, these tactics made it extremely difficult for the cruiser force to keep station on the convoy at a distance safe from U-boats but close enough to be useful in the event of surface attack. The same problem had arisen with JW 51B, and disaster had only narrowly been avoided, so Admiral Hamilton was quick to raise it with the C-in-C Home Fleet on his return. The only solution Tovey could offer was to remind all concerned that it was the duty of the convoy escorts to signal their position as often as possible when this was assumed to be known to the enemy (i.e., when they were being shadowed or under attack), and that the cruisers should keep close tabs on these transmissions.[53]

Instead of sailing a return convoy simultaneously with the outgoing one, as had been usual practice, RA 52 was delayed until the arrival of JW 52. This was due to delays in unloading the ships in Murmansk, where they were under constant air attack by the *Luftwaffe*. The escort ships of the outgoing convoy had forty-eight hours' rest in Russia before sailing on 29 January with only eleven of the hoped-for twenty-four merchantmen so far unloaded. These eleven ships were escorted by no fewer than nine destroyers, as well as the usual close escort and distant covering forces. U-boat attacks began on 1 February, but with such a large escort only one successful attack was made, with *Kapitänleutnant* Reche in *U-255* sinking the American freighter *Greylock* on 3 February.[54]

Admiral Tovey attributed this loss to fatigue among the escort crews, who by this point had been at sea (and mostly at action stations) for nineteen days with little respite.

The last pair of convoys to sail in the winter of 1942–1943 were the outbound JW 53 and the returning RA 53. The former was larger than its predecessors, with a total of twenty-eight ships sailing on 15 February, although several were delayed and had to catch up with the main group. Not only was it a very large convoy, but the advancing year meant that there was a great deal more daylight than there had been in January. As a consequence, the Admiralty laid on a very large escort, reminiscent of that for PQ 18. No fewer than thirteen destroyers were sent as ocean escort, led by the cruiser *Scylla*. The usual close escort was also provided, along with an escort carrier, *Dasher*, and a cruiser covering force of *Belfast*, *Sheffield* and *Cumberland*. The principal threat to this operation was the weather. A severe storm blew up during the first four days out, and six merchantmen had to abandon and return to Scotland. More dramatically, the carrier *Dasher* developed cracks in its plating and had to return, and HMS *Sheffield* was severely damaged. The cruiser had its guns trained abeam to ease the impact of the breaking waves on the gun mounts, but a large wave ripped the armour plate entirely off one turret, forcing it to abort its mission. The ships of the convoy were widely scattered, but a combination of weather and aggressive defence prevented any meaningful attack by U-boats or aircraft. All twenty-two merchant ships reached Kola battered but intact by 28 February.

The return convoy of thirty ships, RA 53, left on 1 March accompanied by the same large escort which had protected the outgoing group. This time, the U-boats were more successful, sinking the *Executive* near Bear Island. Once again, the weather deteriorated, and when ships began to straggle, the U-boats took advantage, and a further two – the *Richard Bland* and the *Puerto Rican* – were sunk, while the *J.L.M. Curry* foundered and sank in the gale. Further convoys were planned, but the arrival of *Scharnhorst* with *Tirpitz* and *Lützow* in Altenfjord (discussed in the next chapter) and the lengthening daylight hours made these a risky undertaking. Furthermore, the convoy situation in the Atlantic was becoming critical and the resources of the Home Fleet were sorely stretched. As a result, JW and RA 54 were postponed indefinitely, and convoy operations to Russia ceased until the following winter.[55]

Compared with the brutal experience of earlier in 1942, the Allies had reason to be pleased with the winter convoys between November 1942 and March 1943. Of the seventy-three merchant ships which had sailed for Russia, none had been lost to enemy action, and this had been achieved at a cost of one destroyer (HMS *Achates*) and one minesweeper (HMS *Bramble*). Of the eighty-three ships making the return journey, the Germans had sunk only six, of which four had been stragglers outside the envelope of protection provided by the escorting warships.[56] Escort forces were stronger, more experienced and had better defensive technology than ever before, and U-boats were finding it harder and harder to penetrate their shield around the convoys. The power of the *Luftwaffe* in the north was also substantially diminished. Never again would massacres on the scale of PQ 17 and 18 occur in the Arctic. However, the two most powerful ships of the *Kriegsmarine*, *Tirpitz* and *Scharnhorst*, still lay in wait in the fjords. Not until these two threats had been successfully dealt with could anyone be confident of ongoing supplies to Russia.

CHAPTER NINE

'WE WILL FIGHT TO THE LAST SHELL'

CONVOYS JW 54–JW 55B,
SEPTEMBER 1943–JANUARY 1944

A WINDOW ON THE WAR

In the early hours of Christmas Eve 1943, Sheila Holding was on duty in Naval Section. As the fifth Christmas of the war approached with still only glimmers of final victory, and with D-Day still six months away, it must have been a bleak time for everyone, with little to celebrate. After growing up in Colchester, Sheila had joined the WAAF in 1942 at the age of twenty as a teleprinter operator. She had been posted at Bletchley Park since the summer of that year. Despite being in the WAAF, she was assigned to Naval Section, as all communications in and out of Bletchley Park were run by the air force. Her workplace was a small upstairs room on the northern corridor in Block A. The next-door room housed Naval Section II. This team was right at the heart of the section, as it was their job to translate successfully decrypted messages into English and then decide if, or to which customers, they should be sent on. The section was headed by Walter Ettinghausen, a Jewish émigré and fluent German speaker who would go on in 1948 to become the Director of the Foreign Ministry of the newly created state of Israel. The rest of the section consisted of three 'Watches' of half a dozen people, with a male civilian head, a couple of other civilians and two or three Wrens in each. Whichever watch was on duty around the twenty-four-hour cycle would process incoming decrypted messages and produce translations. In turn, these would be passed through a hatch in the wall to three teleprinter watches, each of four or five WAAFs, of whom Sheila was one. The operators would then transmit the messages, most often to ID8G at the Admiralty, within the OIC.

Unlike many of the staff at Bletchley Park, the significance of whose roles remained mysterious to them, and their connection with the war rather tenuous, Sheila and her colleagues had a ring-side seat for the war at sea. As she described:

> At Station X [codename for Bletchley Park] our teleprinters were all on direct lines to the Admiralty and what made it so interesting was the fact that the messages we were sending, having first been intercepted then decoded into plain German, were then translated into English for onward transmission in plain language whereas I learned later that others were sending just groups of figures; very boring.
>
> [. . .] All the messages I typed up always started 'To: ID 8 (G)', which was the Admiralty and then 'From: N S' (Naval Section Bletchley Park) which was our call sign. The text would be in plain language and thus we were always very well informed on Naval matters. The messages were typed directly onto the Teleprinter and I know it came out at the Admiralty instantaneously as I was typing it.[1]

Sheila recalled a number of her colleagues: the WAAFs on her side of the hatch, Maisie Stewart, Jill Rodgers and Diane Townsend, as well as the watch personnel next door, 'Walter Ettinghausen, his brother Ernest (who did much of the translating from German into English) and two WRNS Officers, Ann [Toulmin] and Thelma [Ziman]'.[2] A fascinating sidelight on the events unfolding in the Barents Sea that Christmas is provided by the fact that each teleprint sent from Naval Section to the Admiralty included the initials of the watch officer responsible for the translation and of the teleprinter operator who sent it. Sheila was on watch on Christmas Eve when the first breaks of the German Enigma key in use since 10 a.m. (noon German time) on 23 December started to come through. Three messages were forwarded between 3.12 and 3.14 a.m., originated by *Fliegerführer Nord (West)* early the previous afternoon. These described the German air force identification of convoy JW 55B south-east of Jan Mayen Island. These bear both Sheila's initials, 'SMH', and those of Ernest Ettinghausen, 'EE', who no doubt drafted the translations.[3] Surviving teleprints show that Sheila and Ernest were at their posts again in the early hours of Christmas morning, as the *Luftwaffe* continued to shadow the convoy,[4] and would continue to be there for the next few nights, as other messages testify. However, it would fall to others to read and despatch the most important news of the season. At 11.31 p.m. on 26 December a deciphered naval Enigma message was teleprinted bearing the initials of the Head of 'B Watch', Charles Leech, and WAAF Corporal (later Flight Sergeant) A. Marshall:[5]

```
TO I D G 8                          ZIP/ZTPG/195207
FROM N S
2170 KC/S         T O O 1945     TOI 1941/26/12/43

F.O. CRUISERS and C.O. OF `SCHARNHORST` REPORT
AT 1815
TO:  THE FUEHRER
     WE SHALL FIGHT TO THE LAST SHELL

2331/26/12/43+CEL/AM
```

Out in the Barents Sea, *Konteradmiral* Erich Bey and his captain, Fritz Hintze, aboard the German battlecruiser *Scharnhorst*, were surrounded, their burning ship shuddering to the repeated impacts of torpedoes from circling Allied destroyers. Their last wireless message was addressed to the supreme leader and purposely repeated the words of the last message sent by Admiral Lütjens aboard the sinking *Bismarck* two years earlier. The *Kriegsmarine* had fought its last sea battle with capital ships, and lost.

CHANGES AT THE TOP

In many respects, life in the Royal Navy continued in wartime as it had in peace, with the minimum changes made to accommodate the inconvenience of conflict. One of these habits was promotion and career

progression. In May 1943 Admiral Tovey reached the end of his scheduled two-and-a-half-year term as C-in-C Home Fleet. He was duly
reappointed to Commander-in-Chief, The Nore, responsible for the
east coast, and raised from Admiral to Admiral of the Fleet in October.
There he went on to be instrumental in the planning for the landings
in Sicily in 1943 and Normandy in 1944. His obvious successor at the
Home Fleet was his former deputy, Bruce Fraser, who hoisted his flag as
C-in-C Home Fleet aboard the battleship *Duke of York* on 8 May 1943.
Fraser already had experience of the Arctic, and, at fifty-five years old,
was in John Winton's words 'at the peak of his career'. The same historian went on to describe him as 'one of the most able and lovable
admirals the Royal Navy has ever produced'.[6] From early in his career
he had possessed the ability to spread happiness and affability wherever
he went, and he was widely admired by his subordinates. However, he
also possessed a quiet steel when required to exert his authority or issue
a reprimand. He was, in short, a great leader of men. He was also a
gunnery expert, having not only served as a gunnery officer on ships
and as fleet gunnery officer in the Mediterranean, but having also
actually sat on the committee which designed the 14-inch guns on his
flagship *Duke of York*. He would put this knowledge to good use in
December 1943.[7]

A further change in command followed. The First Sea Lord, Dudley
Pound, was in declining health. This came to a head when he suffered
a stroke while accompanying the Prime Minister to the Quebec confer-
ence in September 1943. He offered his resignation to Churchill on
20 September and died a month later, on Trafalgar Day 1943. His
obvious successor was 'ABC': Admiral Andrew Cunningham, then
C-in-C Mediterranean, whose legendary status within the navy was
already well established. The Prime Minister, however, was characteris-
tically wary of someone with such popularity and a reputation as a
strong personality. Nor did he know Cunningham well, and so he
offered the role to a man with whom he was better acquainted, and
perhaps of whom he had the better measure: Bruce Fraser. Fraser was
flattered to be asked but felt that he was not ready, and that he still had
unfinished business at sea. According to Churchill, Fraser responded: 'I
believe I have the confidence of my own fleet, but Cunningham has the

confidence of the whole Navy. I haven't even fought a battle yet. If one day I should sink the *Scharnhorst* I might feel differently.'[8]

The Prime Minister acquiesced, and ABC became First Sea Lord. Churchill was prone to embroider his recollections of these moments, so Fraser's remarks about sinking the German battleship may have been recalled with a good deal of hindsight, but the fact remains that Fraser would go on to achieve both, becoming First Sea Lord in 1948.

At his disposal, Fraser had a rather reduced force in the Home Fleet. The *Duke of York* was one of a class of five modern battleships, the others being *King George V*, *Howe* and *Anson* (*Prince of Wales* had been sunk off Malaya in 1942). In June 1943 both *King George V* and *Howe* were sent to the Mediterranean, leaving Fraser with his flagship and *Anson*, supplemented by the ageing First World War battleship *Malaya*, which was withdrawn from service before the end of the year. To supplement this, an American squadron of two battleships and destroyer escorts was attached to the Home Fleet, but this force spent much of its time at Hvalfjord in Iceland as security against a breakout into the Atlantic by the remaining German capital ships. The US navy also provided the aircraft carrier USS *Ranger*, which was particularly useful as Fraser was otherwise without a fleet carrier. In addition, there were the two cruiser squadrons: 1st, consisting of five 8-inch gun ships of the *Kent* and *London* classes, and Burnett's 10th, comprising five 6-inch gun ships. The real shortage, however, was of destroyers; of the four flotillas theoretically part of the Home Fleet, amounting to over thirty vessels, only about half were available for use in the Arctic, as others were detached to the Channel and Atlantic, or as far afield as the Mediterranean.[9]

As was alluded to in the previous chapter, there had also been a re-organisation of German forces in the Arctic as a result of Dönitz's assumption of supreme command of the *Kriegsmarine* and his arguments with Hitler about the large surface ships. The northern forces after the summer of 1943 would consist only of *Tirpitz* and *Scharnhorst* in Norway, with a suitable destroyer escort force, while the remainder of the large surface fleet ships were either decommissioned or retained in the Baltic. Bletchley Park was not able to provide any insight into the conversations between Dönitz and the *Führer*, but Naval Section was able to keep good tabs on the movements of the ships involved. Thus, when *Scharnhorst* departed for Norway for the first time on 11 January, both Allied submarines and RAF Coastal Command were ready and waiting. However, as soon as the Germans became aware that the ships had been sighted by the RAF the move was aborted and *Scharnhorst* returned to the Baltic. It tried again on 25 January, but once again Enigma decrypts had provided warning as early as 20 January, and as soon as the force was spotted by the RAF the operation was once again cancelled. In the end it was third time lucky for the *Kriegsmarine*. When *Scharnhorst* made another attempt in March, ambiguities in the available SIGINT, and simple bad weather, allowed it to reach Narvik on 11 March undisturbed.[10]

Almost immediately after the arrival of *Scharnhorst* in Narvik, a flurry of messages were intercepted on the German fleet Enigma key *NEPTUN* (known at Bletchley Park as BARRACUDA). This key was so little used that Naval Section had never broken it, but the passing of messages between *Lützow* and *Tirpitz* was highly suggestive. Were they headed south to the Baltic? Or would *Tirpitz* move from Trondheim to Narvik? The Germans' plans became apparent when on 22 March Enigma revealed that *Tirpitz*, *Scharnhorst* and *Lützow* had all moved to Altenfjord, and that reconnaissance flights were being flown in search of suspected Allied convoys. It was partly in light of this dangerous concentration of force that convoys to Russia were once again suspended at the end of March, as described in the previous chapter.[11]

It was not until September 1943 that the German surface fleet became active once again. A plan was developed in August to send *Lützow* into the Kara Sea with a force of U-boats, but in the end only the U-boats carried out the operation. A great deal of German air force reconnaissance activity took place in connection with the Kara Sea sortie (Operation *SIZILIEN*), and this was followed by Bletchley Park. Unfortunately, traffic relating to this operation was combined with similar preparations for a second mission, Operation *ZITRONELLA*, and disentangling the two and making sense of the decrypts became very difficult. It later transpired that *ZITRONELLA* comprised a sortie by *Tirpitz* and *Scharnhorst*, along with ten destroyers, to bombard the Allied garrison of Spitzbergen, land a raiding force of German troops and destroy the wireless and meteorological stations there. This was surely a sledgehammer to crack a nut, and of only propaganda significance. It was, however, the only time *Tirpitz* would fire its main armament in anger, albeit at a rather trivial target. What might have been of far more significance was if Enigma had given sufficient warning for the Home Fleet to intercept the German capital ships outside the shelter of the fjords. In the event, the first clear news of the sortie was only received when the station on Spitzbergen reported that it was under attack, and by the time the Home Fleet had sailed it was obvious that the German ships would be safely back in Altenfjord before they could be intercepted.[12]

From a SIGINT point of view, this incident reveals that plentiful intelligence did not always mean easy interpretation. Enigma was pretty good at forecasting when the German surface fleet might be about to do *something*, and a mix of SIGINT and air reconnaissance was pretty good at identifying when they had begun to do it. Often the *something* was fairly obvious, for example if a convoy was at sea to provide a target, but if the *Kriegsmarine* had in mind another operation altogether, figuring out what it might be could be very difficult. A similar problem was highlighted at the end of September. In accordance with Dönitz's plan, *Lützow* left its berth in Altenfjord on 23 September and made its way south down the Norwegian coast to undergo a long-overdue refit before taking up duties in the Baltic. Messages concerning the preparation of air cover for the journey were intercepted from 21 September onwards, supported by air reconnaissance sightings and coast-watcher reports of its departure. Discussions followed in the Admiralty about how to respond, and a sortie by the Home Fleet escorting the US carrier *Ranger* was proposed, as well as an air strike by 18 Group Coastal Command. In the end, a strike was flown by the now land-based 832 Squadron of the Fleet Air Arm from Sumburgh in the Shetlands (coincidentally, the same squadron which had unsuccessfully attacked *Tirpitz* in March 1942; see Chapter 4). They aimed to attack *Lützow* as it rounded the eastern-most point of the Norwegian coast at Stadlandet, but the difficulty of computing its exact course and position meant the aircraft never found it and it passed into the Baltic undisturbed.[13] The escape of *Lützow* can be counted an intelligence failure on the part of the Admiralty and RAF, a point expressed by the Official Historian, Stephen Roskill: 'None the less it may well puzzle posterity how it came to pass that, after almost exactly four years of war, a German pocket-battleship was still able to steam from Vestfjord to the Baltic in complete immunity.'[14] It is hard to dispute this judgement.

OPERATION *OSTFRONT*

In September 1943 the Admiralty started to consider the resumption of convoys to Russia. Various factors influenced this decision. First was a significantly improved situation in the Atlantic. After something of a crisis in the late spring, the final closure of the Atlantic air gap by long-range aircraft, and the scaling down of the German U-boat effort in that theatre, meant that resources were once again available to the Home Fleet in the Arctic. Secondly, the threat from the German surface fleet was much reduced. *Lützow* had departed in September, and that same month Operation SOURCE, an attack by midget submarines on *Tirpitz* while it lay berthed in Kaafjord, had put the German battleship out of action until the following spring. (This operation, and its SIGINT aspects, are investigated further in the next chapter). This left only *Scharnhorst* and a flotilla of five destroyers available for action against the convoys.[15] At the same time, diplomatic pressure was being applied by Russia for a resumption of supplies. Admiral Fraser attended a meeting at the Admiralty on 28 September, where it was suggested that, starting in November, a convoy of thirty-five to forty ships should be sent every month until February 1944 – a total of four convoys. Fraser, however, like Tovey before him, was opposed to large convoys, as station-keeping and manoeuvring of such a large body was impossible in the dark winter months, and so a fortnightly cycle of smaller convoys was proposed; each convoy, starting with JW 54, would be split into two parts, 'A' and 'B'.[16]

The first task was to recover the merchant ships which had spent the summer in the Russian ports, and so the first sailing was of homeward convoy RA 54A. A destroyer escort was sent to Kola on 23 October, and the convoy of thirteen ships began its return journey shrouded in fog on 1 November. It reached Loch Ewe unscathed on 14 November. The first two outward half-convoys, JW 54A and JW 54B, totalling thirty-two ships, followed a week apart on 15 and 22 November, and a return convoy, RA 54B, of eight ships arrived in Loch Ewe on 9 December. None of these convoys suffered any loss. The German U-boat force in the Arctic numbered only twelve boats at this period, and while a patrol line had been maintained all summer in the North Cape to Bear Island gap, this consisted of only four boats at any one time, and as the season drew on and air reconnaissance became increasingly difficult, it was hard for these boats to find the convoys or make much impression on them when they did.[17]

Nonetheless, both sides knew that this situation would not continue. Having earned his surface fleet a reprieve from Hitler, Dönitz was under pressure to show that these ships were still useful. The massive Soviet successes on land starting with the Battle of Kursk in the summer of 1943 meant that any blow that could be struck against Russian forces was vital, even if it only had propaganda value. Indeed, as early as March 1943 Dönitz set out his strategy in a memorandum to his commanders:

> The conditions required for successful operations by surface ships against traffic in the Arctic will occur very seldom [. . .] Whenever such an opportunity occurs it must be seized with determination, but with due observance to tactical principles.
>
> It may also sometimes be considered necessary to attack heavily escorted convoys with all available forces; orders to deliver such an attack will be given if the convoy in question is deemed to be of such value that its destruction is of primary importance to the situation as a whole.[18]

Unfortunately for the German Commander-in-Chief, in November 1943 Dönitz suffered a significant change in subordinates. Admiral Kummetz, who had commanded fleet operations in the north since June 1942, went on leave to Germany for medical treatment, and he was replaced by Rear Admiral Erich Bey. As the former type-commander for destroyers, Bey had spent almost no time on capital ships and little time in the north. Undaunted, Bey drew up a plan for a potential convoy attack, and on 2 December this was endorsed by the Naval Staff, who advised 'it might be expedient to employ *Scharnhorst*, in spite of the experiences of 31 December 1942' (i.e., the Battle of the Barents Sea).[19]

The next convoy to sail was JW 55A, which left Loch Ewe on 12 December. Admiral Fraser felt sure that by this point the Germans must be aware of the resumption of the convoys and that a significant attack was imminent. All the usual precautions were taken: the convoy was provided with a 'through escort' of eight Home Fleet destroyers, it was shadowed by Burnett's cruiser squadron consisting of *Belfast*, *Norfolk* and *Sheffield*, and the C-in-C himself followed at a distance with his covering force of the *Duke of York*, *Jamaica* and four destroyers. No escort carriers accompanied the convoy, as operating from them in darkness was almost impossible. Fearing (or perhaps hoping for) a sortie by *Scharnhorst*, Fraser followed the convoy all the way to Murmansk, where it arrived unmolested on 21 December. Having taken the opportunity to meet his Russian opposite number Admiral Golovko in Murmansk, Fraser returned with his force to Iceland.[20]

In Germany, meanwhile, Dönitz and his staff were aware that the Allied convoy cycle had resumed, and on 18 December the *Grossadmiral* was able to obtain the *Führer*'s permission to mount an all-out attack on the next convoy to be detected. Orders were duly prepared by him and Admiral Schniewind for Operation *OSTFRONT*, a codename which by contrast with the earlier *ZITRONELLA* and *SIZILIEN* probably gave a strong hint to Allied codebreakers of the purpose of the operation. The *Scharnhorst* and its escorts were brought to six hours' and then three hours' notice for sea, and increased air reconnaissance was organised by the *Luftwaffe* to find the next convoy and its shadowing forces. These preparations were quickly identified by Bletchley Park. Patrick Beesly described Ned Denning at the OIC being woken from his bed in the early hours of 20 December to see a series of intercepts of traffic from the afternoon of 18 December laying out these various German preparations.[21] This information was forwarded as ULTRA to

Admirals Fraser and Burnett at around 8 a.m. that morning, but by then it was accompanied by the caveat that on 19 December the *Luftwaffe* had postponed its air search of the convoy due to the terrible weather.[22]

JW 55B departed Loch Ewe on 20 December with nineteen merchant ships and an escort of eight destroyers. On Christmas Day its course would take it past the returning RA 55A (which left Russia on 22 December) at the usual convoy crossing-point near Bear Island. In anticipation of this sailing (possibly informed by the *B-Dienst*), the *Eisenbart* ('ironbeard') U-boat group, consisting of four boats, was directed to a north–south patrol line to the south-east of Bear Island. This move was identified at Bletchley Park in the early hours of 20 December and passed on to the fleet later that morning.[23] The weather continued to be terrible during 21 December, and German air reconnaissance remained impossible. Further messages were intercepted reflecting this, and during the afternoon, Bey's fleet was stood down to six hours' notice for sea. This fact was known at the Admiralty later that evening and immediately passed on to the fleet.[24]

The *Luftwaffe* was able to find convoy JW 55B eventually on the afternoon of 22 December as it was passing east of Iceland. Initial reports caused some consternation, as they described a force of '40 troop transports' as well as an aircraft carrier. Admiral Schniewind at *Gruppe Nord* interpreted this as Hitler's long-predicted Allied invasion of Norway, and he gave orders for the *Eisenbart* U-boat group to be recalled to the defence of the Norwegian coast.[25] These orders were, however, rescinded when the air force revised its report of troop transports to one of ordinary merchantmen, and the German navy returned to its original plan for intercepting the convoy, bringing the surface warships once again to three hours' notice.[26] Again, all of this information was passed on to Fraser and Burnett, both of whom had departed for sea on 23 December. Burnett in 'Force 1', consisting of his three cruisers, left Murmansk to provide cover for RA 55A, which had sailed on 22 December. He would shadow that convoy westwards until it passed the outgoing JW 55B, at which point he would switch his attentions to the latter's ships. Fraser, meanwhile, sailed with 'Force 2', made up of *Duke of York*, *Jamaica* and his destroyers, to take up a covering position to the west ready to pounce if *Scharnhorst* emerged from its lair in the fjords.

The German air force was able to maintain contact with JW 55B throughout 23 and 24 December, and the U-boat forces, now numbering seven boats, were directed to intercept. However, all of this activity had been followed via intercepts, and Admiral Fraser was kept thoroughly informed by the Admiralty. This was summed up in a post-war report by Geoffrey Colpoys (Deputy Director of the OIC):

At 0049/18 December four U-boats known as the 'Arctic Group', reinforced by three more from the Baltic, were ordered to take up positions along a line 135 miles east of Bear Island. On the 19th these seven boats were ordered to move further westward. Much signal traffic to and from these U-boats was read giving positions of attacking areas, warnings of intended reconnaissance flights, reports of hydrophone contacts, etc. This information was passed out by Ultra.[27]

Fully informed though Admiral Fraser was on 24 December, he was increasingly concerned that the critical moment for a Battle, if there was to be one, was fast approaching. The two convoys were nearing the danger area between Bear Island and the North Cape, while his two surface-covering forces were still a long way from both convoys. The Admiralty had advised him at 10.25 a.m. that as recently as 7 a.m. that morning the German surface group appeared not to have sailed, but if it were to do so it could cover the 400 miles from Altenfjord to the convoy in less than twenty-four hours.[28] In light of this, Fraser took the unusual decision to break radio silence just after noon on 24 December to signal his various forces. He ordered the as-yet-undetected RA 55A to adopt a more northerly course and, if possible, to detach four of its escorting destroyers to join the outbound convoy. He later ordered JW 55B to reverse course for three hours to delay its progress eastward, which would keep it away from any enemy forces for the few remaining hours of daylight on 24 December.[29] In the event, the convoy escort commander Captain McCoy in *Onslow* knew that to attempt this manoeuvre in the prevailing weather would be impossible, and so

219

he simply slowed his ships for a few hours, achieving roughly the same effect.

It was a bold decision by Fraser to break radio silence in this way. He knew he risked interception and D/F by the Germans; however, he was in an even more precarious position than it might first appear. His plan relied on exact knowledge of all the 'pieces' on the game-board that was the Barents Sea. The convoys and their two protecting forces were still far apart, in almost perpetual darkness. Also, his destroyers would soon be at the limit of their fuel, so he could not afford to lose any time in searching for either friends or enemies. He was right to be nervous. His signals were intercepted both at Kirkenes and at Cuxhaven on the German coast. This created a very poor angle for a German D/F fix, as both stations were on a very similar bearing from the position of Force 2, but this was nonetheless passed on to Admiral Schniewind at Kiel at 6.30 p.m. He described his own response: 'The British unit whose bearings have now been acquired at an extremely acute angle, appears to be approximately 180 nautical miles astern of the convoy. This may be an approaching covering force. We must take into account the presence of a second enemy force in the Barents Sea, unless it is thought the fix is so unreliable that it emanates from the convoy itself or from a straggler.'[30]

Curiously, despite the obvious inferences of this message, Schniewind seems to have been anxious to explain it away and continue with the proposed operation. He continued, 'There is nothing revelatory about this message,'[31] a remark which seems at odds with the extreme caution which was usually a characteristic of *Kriegsmarine* operations. This attitude would become more apparent in the next twenty-four hours. The *Luftwaffe*, however, seem to have taken the report seriously, as by midnight 24/25 December they were planning a sortie by radar-equipped aircraft to look for 'what is thought to be a battle group approaching from the southwest, which has been D/F'd'.[32]

The following morning was Christmas Day, and Captain McCoy, escorting the convoy, expected it to be quite busy. He signalled his merchant counterpart, convoy Commodore Boucher: 'Situation today. Enemy will probably attack us today with U-boat and possibly surface craft. Four more Home Fleet destroyers should join us PM today. *Duke of York* is about 100 miles astern and coming up at 19 knots or more. Three heavy cruisers somewhere ahead. Happy Christmas.'[33]

McCoy was a little premature in his prediction, but he would not have long to wait. Unknown to him, at 8.00 a.m. his convoy sailed over *U-601*, and its captain Otto Hansen was quick to report it and take up a shadowing position as other U-boats were vectored to his location.[34] Although the U-boats made no impression on the convoy in their subsequent attacks, this nonetheless seems to have been the decisive moment for the German commanders. While Admiral Bey (still aboard *Tirpitz* at this point) and Captain-of-U-boats Norway Peters, who was standing in as Admiral Northern Waters at Narvik, were both anxious about the weather and the possible British covering battlegroup, their superiors, Schniewind at *Gruppe Nord* and Dönitz in Berlin, knew that it was now or never. If the convoy were to be attacked, 25 or 26 December were the only suitable days, when a fast surprise attack could be carried out by *Scharnhorst* and its destroyers, with the chance that they might make it back to safety before the covering forces could intervene. The political imperatives pressing down on the *Kriegsmarine* were also intense. Accordingly, the surface ships were brought to one hour's notice for sea at 1 p.m. on Christmas Day, and at 3.27 p.m. local time Bey received the order from Peters: 'OSTFRONT 1700/25/12'.[35] The German battleship and its escorts departed Altenfjord at 7 that evening.

In addition to these messages, a flurry of other traffic was read by Naval Section on the night of 25 December as minesweepers and aircraft made arrangements for the passage of the German battlegroup. On this basis, at 2.17 a.m. on 26 December the Admiralty was able to signal fairly confidently to Fraser and Burnett: 'SCHARNHORST probably sailed 1800A/25th December.'[36] The decision was taken also to share the news with the units at sea which were not cleared for ULTRA, such as Captain McCoy, with the outbound convoy, and so the more blandly worded 'Admiralty appreciates Scharnhorst probably at sea' was sent to all warships in the Arctic at 3.19 a.m.[37] Royal Marine Lieutenant Bryce Ramsden was aboard the cruiser *Jamaica* when the news was piped to all hands. He recalled the significance of the moment: 'For a second my heart stopped beating, and I tried to digest it. [. . .] A sense of the inevitable came over me. I was embroiled in a great machine of movement and purpose. Something big was going to happen.'[38]

The die was indeed cast, and what made the result perhaps more inevitable was an exchange of messages after *Scharnhorst* was at sea, not read by Bletchley Park as they were sent in either *Offizier* cipher or the fleet key BARRACUDA. Both Admiral Bey and Admiral Northern Waters (Peters) were becoming increasingly concerned about the deteriorating weather. The German destroyers were poor sea-boats and would struggle to keep up with *Scharnhorst*, and might even be at risk of severe weather damage. At the same time, air reconnaissance would be impossible, so the likelihood of detecting any Allied covering forces would be very low. Meanwhile, Dönitz signalled Bey on the evening of 25 December:

> Important enemy convoy carrying food and war material to the Russians further imperils our heroic army on the Eastern Front. We must help.
>
> Attack convoy with *Scharnhorst* and destroyers.
>
> Exploit tactical situation with skill and daring. Do not end engagement with a partial success. Go all out and see the job right through. Best chance of success lies in superior firing power of *Scharnhorst*, therefore try to bring her into action. Deploy destroyers as appropriate.
>
> Break off according to your own judgement. Break off in any circumstances if faced by heavy units.
>
> Inform crews accordingly. I have every confidence in you.
>
> *Heil und Sieg*
> Dönitz Grossadmiral[39]

In subsequent exchanges, both sides expressed their views on the situation. Dönitz would later argue in his memoirs that he left Bey with absolute discretion as the commander on the spot, but it is hard to reconcile this view with phrases like 'Do not end the engagement with a partial success. Go all out'.[40] In the event, Bey did not survive to give his side of the story, but it seems he was given very little choice but to make an attack on JW 55B come what may, and take the consequences.

THE DEATH OF THE *SCHARNHORST*

In the early hours of 26 December the situation around the North Cape was as follows: homebound convoy RA 55A was more or less out of danger, 220 miles west of Bear Island and heading west. Convoy JW 55B was 50 miles south of Bear Island on a course of 70 degrees (slightly north of due east). Admiral Burnett and his cruisers were 150 miles east of the convoy and sailing on a south-westerly course towards it. Admiral Fraser was approaching from the south-west but still over 200 miles away. Meanwhile, *Scharnhorst* and its escort of destroyers from 4th Destroyer Flotilla under Captain Johannesson were heading due north from the North Cape, perhaps 100 miles from the merchantmen and their escorts.[41] At 4 a.m. Admiral Fraser once again broke radio silence, this time to alter the course of the convoy to 45 degrees (north-east), a course which should take it as far as possible from the German surface group. He also ordered Burnett to close with the convoy, while requesting positional information from all parties and signalling his own. Again, his signals were successfully D/F-ed by the Germans; however, this information does not seem to have filtered through to Admiral Bey. Once again, the German air force seems to have been more alive to the situation than the navy. An air reconnaissance flown by radar-equipped flying-boats successfully detected Force 2, and a report was forwarded at 10.12 a.m. of up to five enemy units, including 'one heavy unit'. Unfortunately for Bey, this report was not given much credence, as it was based on radar, not visual sighting, and it is possible that the five ships sighted were interpreted as the Germans' own destroyer squadron, separated from *Scharnhorst*. In any event, the information was not passed along the command chain until it was too late to make a difference.[42] Indeed, by the morning of 26 December, SIGINT by both sides had ceased to be relevant to the outcome of the battle. Patrick Beesly in the OIC summarised the situation: 'During the course of Boxing Day another dozen German signals were decrypted, but fascinating though some of them were, none was received in time to be of operational value. O.I.C. had already played its part. It was now up to those at sea.'[43]

The German battlegroup continued on a northerly course until 8 a.m. on 26 December, at which point Admiral Bey became concerned that he might have overshot the convoy and so nearly reversed his course onto a heading of 230 degrees (south-west). He spread his destroyers out into a wide search line perpendicular to their course and manoeuvred *Scharnhorst* to a position 10 miles behind his escorts. Ironically, this move nearly came off; his destroyers passed within 30 miles of the convoy's escort screen, but no sightings were made, and from that point on Captain Johannesson's destroyers sailed out of the battle and would play no further part in proceedings.[44]

A few minutes later, at 8.40 a.m., HMS *Belfast* in Force 1 picked up a radar contact on a bearing of 295 degrees, 18 miles away to the north-west, almost exactly in line with the likely position of convoy JW 55B some 30 miles beyond. This was the *Scharnhorst*, which by this time was on a northerly heading, possibly because Bey had made fleeting contact with the convoy on his own radar. Burnett's force ran down the bearing to close the range, until at 9.30 a.m. HMS *Norfolk* opened fire with its 8-inch guns, followed shortly after by the two 6-inch armed cruisers. By this time, *Scharnhorst* had reversed course again and was heading south, and as *Norfolk*'s shells fell around it and scored several hits, *Scharnhorst* bore around to the south-east and increased speed. Bey's plan was to break away from the cruisers and circle around them anti-clockwise towards the north in order to come back towards the convoy from the north-east. Burnett did not have the speed to pursue directly, so he took the bold decision to break contact and place himself between the convoy and the north-easterly direction from where he felt *Scharnhorst* might return.

Burnett had been in constant contact with Fraser during the brief action, and the C-in-C was rather perturbed to hear that his subordinate had voluntarily relinquished contact with the enemy. Some sharp signals were exchanged, and both men spent several hours worrying that the chance to catch the enemy battleship might have been lost. Meanwhile, Fraser redirected the convoy north and detached four of the escorting destroyers to reinforce Burnett's shadowing group. As the hours passed, Fraser became increasingly disheartened, and at noon he reversed the course of Force 2 to head for home. This would not last long, however, as, just as Force 2 was turning away, at 12.05 p.m. *Belfast*'s radar in Force 1 once again picked up the enemy ship approaching from the north-east, just as Burnett had predicted. Force 1 was steaming north-east almost directly towards *Scharnhorst* in line abreast, and so Burnett was able to alter course to starboard and create a firing line with all turrets on his cruisers able to bear on the target. *Scharnhorst* also turned towards the south-east, opening its own turret arcs, and a gun battle ensued for the next twenty minutes, with both sides scoring hits and both believing that they had got the better of the engagement. *Norfolk* was hit twice, knocking out 'X' turret and suffering engine-room damage, while at least one hit was sustained by *Scharnhorst*. Again, however, Admiral Bey chose not to press home his advantage and instead increased speed away to the south-east. After some confusion over communications, Burnett sent his destroyers in pursuit to attempt a torpedo attack, but they never reached a position to shoot, and instead took up the pursuit of the enemy ship as it sailed rapidly southwards.

Prior to this second encounter, the German commander had summoned his destroyers back towards the calculated position of the convoy, and for two hours they bore down on the merchant ships, but at 12.18 p.m. they were misled by an out-of-date U-boat message locating the convoy elsewhere, and they altered course to the west, missing their target by as little as 8 miles. Meanwhile, after his second encounter with the cruisers of Force 1, Admiral Bey gave up on his mission and set course south for Altenfjord. At 3 p.m. he sent a message to Johannesson and his destroyers to do the same. He was, however, still being shadowed by Burnett's destroyers, and later the cruisers were able to catch up to radar range, and *Belfast* took over shadowing duties. Burnett did not press his luck – had Bey reversed course to engage him it might have been a stiff fight between the battleship and the three cruisers, and so long as the German ship continued on a path which would bring him into contact with Fraser and Force 2, Burnett felt it best not to disturb him. Instead, he remained in radar contact, supplying Fraser with frequent positional updates.

One of the mysteries of these events is that there can be little doubt that the exchanges between Fraser and Burnett were heard by the German wireless intercept services. The Germans certainly knew that a second force was at sea, and that *Scharnhorst* was in significant peril, and yet Bey sailed on apparently oblivious. At 4.17 p.m. Fraser got his reward – *Scharnhorst* appeared on *Duke of York*'s radar on a bearing of 20 degrees (almost due north) and a range of 23 miles. The Admiral allowed the range to fall to 6 miles before ordering *Belfast* to light up the target with star-shell. The cruiser's shots fell short, so *Duke of York* illuminated the enemy with its own 5.25-inch secondary guns, before opening with her 14-inch main broadside at 4.51 p.m. Hits were observed almost immediately, showing as small green sparks along the enemy's dark silhouette. *Scharnhorst* reacted within five minutes, using its own secondary armament to illuminate the British ships before opening up with its 11-inch main battery, although its firepower was reduced as its forward 'Anton' turret was disabled by an early hit from *Duke of York*.

Bey once again tried to make a run for it. He turned north, and then east, increasing his speed and the distance between the two forces. Fraser had split his four destroyers into two pairs on either side of the enemy ship, but he initially forbade them from engaging, something he came to regret as the enemy ship drew away from him eastwards into the darkness. Each ship jinked periodically to bring its full broadside to bear before resuming the stern-chase, which the German ship was winning by several knots of speed. Once again, Fraser saw his prize slipping from his grasp. He signalled Burnett: 'I see little hope of catching *Scharnhorst*.' However, at around 6.20 p.m. a 14-inch shell from *Duke of York* penetrated *Scharnhorst*'s stern and entered its machinery spaces and boiler room. Despite the best efforts of the engineers and damage-control teams, its speed started to fall from 29 knots to 22, and the range showing on British radars started to fall once again. By 7 p.m., in addition to the bombardment by *Duke of York* and *Jamaica*, Fraser's destroyers had caught up with the battleship and scored three torpedo hits on it. This brought it almost to a halt and allowed Burnett's cruisers and destroyers to add to the carnage with both gunfire and torpedoes. The outcome was inevitable. By 7.48 p.m. *Scharnhorst* had sunk, but such was the confusion of ships, and the large pall of smoke over its position, that it was difficult to be sure. *Duke of York*'s radar operators were initially reprimanded for losing contact, before it was realised that there was no ship left to produce an echo. Only when *Belfast* had illuminated the scene with star-shell and revealed wreckage, oil and a few survivors in the water was Fraser content that the battle had been won.

With the German destroyers running for home, JW 55B was safer, but still at risk from U-boats. However, the *Eisenbart* group was called off the convoy later that evening and directed to look for survivors from *Scharnhorst*.[45] When this proved fruitless, the U-boats were re-tasked on a new patrol line, but by then it was too late, and JW 55B arrived in Kola without loss on 27 December. The returning RA 55B was also allowed to depart undisturbed on 31 December and arrived in Loch Ewe on 8 January 1944.

CONGRATULATIONS FROM THE ADMIRAL

At 8.35 p.m. on 26 December 1943, Admiral Fraser signalled to the Admiralty the terse message: 'Scharnhorst sunk'. He received an equally reserved reply: 'Your 26/2035. Grand. Well done.' While no doubt deeply relieved and satisfied, Fraser was anything but triumphant. He later wrote 'we had to sink her, unpleasant as it was.'[46] For anyone at the scene, there was a strong sense of camaraderie with the enemy, and a feeling of 'there, but for the grace of God'. The U-boat threat meant that the British warships could not linger at the scene, and a brief sweep by the destroyers *Scorpion* and *Matchless* recovered thirty-six men from the water. None were commissioned officers, and their average age was just twenty-two. Admiral Bey and Captain Hintze, along with 1,930 other members of the crew, were lost with *Scharnhorst*, by any standards an enormous loss of life, and one which exceeded the Royal Navy's total loss in the whole Arctic campaign.

Nonetheless, the intelligence teams at the Admiralty and at Bletchley Park had reason to be satisfied. Not only had the convoys got through undamaged, but SIGINT had been able to track the movements of the German surface forces in sufficient and timely enough detail to bring them to battle. Captain Colpoys at the OIC gave expression to this satisfaction:

> The steady flow of special Intelligence up to the time that our forces made contact with the enemy enabled the C. in C. to keep C. in C.

Home Fleet and C.S. 10 [Burnett] regularly informed of German surface, aircraft, and U-boat moves. The interval between the time of origin of a German message and that of the Ultra signal based thereon varied from five to twelve hours. The value of special Intelligence in this particular operation can be judged by the fact that it provided the only source of information on 'Scharnhorst's' departure from Altafjord. It also revealed the enemy's ignorance of the odds with which he was called upon to contend.[47]

At the same time, the success of the operation also owed a good deal to the bold tactical choices of Fraser and Burnett when presented with the available intelligence, and a healthy dose of good luck. Operations discussed in previous chapters have shown that, in the darkness of the Arctic winter, finding the enemy was still little more than a large game of blind man's buff, and even with the best intelligence, ships could pass close by without realising each other's presence. There were also significant near misses: the German destroyer force twice almost intercepted convoy JW 55B, and in the absence of the covering forces and with the detachment of a number of destroyers from the escort, this could have been disastrous. Five larger German Z-class destroyers let loose on a convoy protected only by older British destroyer types and smaller vessels would have rapidly caused havoc among the merchant ships.

The other key factor in the outcome of the Battle of the North Cape, as 26 December 1943 became known, was the attitude of the German commanders. As has already been described, Admiral Bey did not live to defend his choices, and he was quickly scapegoated by his superiors searching for someone to blame for the disaster, but it is still hard to justify some of his decisions. On first contact with Burnett's Force 1, *Scharnhorst* was actually between the cruisers and the convoy, and there are suggestions that he had made radar contact. An aggressive move north-westwards into the convoy would have allowed him to do significant damage to the merchantmen and still have a path of escape westwards. Later in the day he could at any time have taken the battle to the British cruisers with a reasonable chance of success. Nor did Bey bring his destroyers into the battle to any effect once he had voluntarily separated from them. Admiral Cunningham summed up his views seven years later in his autobiography:

> But as usual Hitler's Navy had showed little of the fighting spirit of the Imperial German Navy of 1914–18. It was rather like the *Admiral Graf Spee* over again. When the *Scharnhorst* made contact with our cruisers the second time she turned and fled for home. She was a ship of great tonnage and high speed, armed with 11-inch guns. Her three opponents were smaller, weaker and slower. In the weather and visibility then prevailing, by all the tenets of naval warfare, she should have been able to brush the *Belfast*, *Sheffield* and *Norfolk* aside, attack the convoy, and have broken away in safety after destroying it. But the will was not there. No wonder Hitler was displeased.[48]

Hitler was indeed upset, describing Bey's actions a 'criminal error'.[49] However, both the *Führer* and his subordinates Dönitz and Schniewind bear some responsibility. Their orders to Bey were on the one hand assertive that he should 'go all out', but on the other placed heavy responsibility on him not to risk his ships against any substantial enemy forces. This was a contradictory mandate which was ultimately impossible to fulfil, as events tragically showed. It would also appear that, once Schniewind had determined on the completion of the operation, he was prepared not only to ignore the reservations of his subordinates at sea concerning the conditions, but also to overlook evidence that the Home Fleet's heavy covering force was at sea and a threat to *Scharnhorst*. Charitably, it could be argued that the intelligence on this was unclear, but in previous operations that very lack of clarity had been good grounds for caution, or even abandonment of similar projects. Once again, it seems German Naval High Command knew what it wanted but was unwilling to take the risk, and possibly pay the price, to get it.

We heard at the opening of this chapter how a select few in Bletchley Park's Naval Section were privy to the relevant decrypts concerning the sinking of *Scharnhorst*. However, they were not the only ones to be given a privileged insight into the battle. Admiral Fraser travelled to Buckinghamshire a few weeks after the event to meet the codebreaking teams who had so assisted him at sea. Two civilian members of staff, both working in the Hollerith punch-card section of Block C, which was used to assist with naval Enigma decryption, recalled the event. Peggy Munn was informed of the sinking almost immediately:

On 26 December 1943, our boss came out and said, 'We have some good news, the British fleet have sunk Scharnhorst'. We had all heard the reports on the Pathé news at the cinema and everywhere that the Scharnhorst was Hitler's best and biggest battleship. To think that we, the British Navy, had sunk it was a cause for celebration, hugging each other and jumping up and down. I couldn't believe that we, doing this card system, could help a man at sea to sink a battleship. It was amazing and really helped us to link what we were doing with the outside world and the war effort.[50]

A few weeks later Peggy received even more personal thanks, from the Admiral himself:

Six weeks later the admiral came into Block C and stopped at the end, but I hadn't seen him as I was too busy with my three machines. [. . .] He then came over, put his arms around my shoulder and gave me a hug, and said 'We have come to thank all you girls and everyone at the park for helping us to sink the Scharnhorst. It was a wonderful thing for us and we couldn't have done it without you'. He then waved to all the girls, some of them looked up, waved back and thought 'Who's that?' He then gave me another big hug and asked me what I was doing; of course as I didn't know what I was doing it was a bit difficult! So I said, 'It's rather complicated and might take some time to explain'. He nodded wisely and said 'Yes, I understand'. He was a lovely man. It is my best memory of Bletchley Park, being cuddled by the Admiral of the Fleet that sunk the Scharnhorst![51]

Admiral Fraser gave a lecture in the mansion at Bletchley Park, but as not everyone could go; there was a ballot and, somewhat to Peggy's chagrin, she lost out. However, her colleague Joan Glover was able to attend:

Another episode was when we'd been working until late in the evening and suddenly news came through that, because of our efforts, the Scharnhorst had been located in the Norwegian fjord. We were thrilled to be part of that but thought no more about it. A week or so later [sic], Admiral Sir Bruce Fraser came to Bletchley Park and asked to see the people involved in deciphering the message. So over we went to the mansion, to hear the whole story, which of course was very moving as it was a hard fought battle. The next morning, I was in my billet and heard the news on the radio, about the capture [sic] and sinking of the Scharnhorst, with the loss of so few men, which of course was totally different to what Sir Bruce Fraser had told us. It was marvellous to know we were doing a useful job.[52]

It is hard, in some ways, to reconcile the happy recollections of these veterans to the grim realities of the battle in the Arctic, but there is little doubt that there was a strong thread linking the mysterious, possibly even meaningless, work that they and their colleagues did at Bletchley Park with the success of the Home Fleet out at sea. All but one of the *Kriegsmarine*'s northern-based capital ships were now gone. It would take another eleven months to finally finish the job.

CHAPTER TEN

KILLING THE 'BEAST'

CONVOYS JW 56–JW 67, JANUARY 1944–MAY 1945

THE CHESS-PLAYERS OF HUT 8

A s was described in Chapter 2, the actual breaking of naval
Enigma at Bletchley Park was the preserve of the 'German
Navy Enigma Processing and Decryption Section', housed in,
and universally known as, 'Hut 8'. The section was moved out of its hut
in 1943 and placed in larger quarters in Block D, to the north of its
customers in Naval Section in Block A, but the 'Hut 8' title stuck,
forcing the renaming of the original hut as 'Hut 18' to avoid confusion.
As the father of many of its processes, Alan Turing was Head of Hut 8
from 1940, but Turing was not a man for the day-to-day running of a
section. His mind was elsewhere, solving other cryptanalytical puzzles,
and so in 1942 he was replaced in charge of the hut by his deputy,
Hugh Alexander.

Conel Hugh O'Donel Alexander, to give him his full name, was an
Anglo-Irish mathematician, who at the time of his recruitment to
GC&CS had just turned thirty. In the early 1930s he had excelled at
mathematics at King's College, Cambridge, where he was a couple of
years ahead of Turing. He pursued post-graduate mathematics at
Cambridge for a year before leaving to become a mathematics teacher
at Winchester School. His real passion, however, was chess. Having
mastered the game as a child, he was British champion in 1938 and was
on the British team for international Chess Olympiads in 1933, 1935,

1937 and 1939. This brought him into contact with the somewhat eccentric John Spedan Lewis, founder of the department store, and in 1938 Alexander gave up teaching to become an employee of Lewis.[1] His exact role remains obscure, but his principal function appears to have been to be the resident chess professional in a public chess lounge that Lewis opened on the top floor of his London store. This rapidly became a mecca for top chess-players in London and was developed into the National Chess Centre by Alexander and Lewis in September 1939.[2]

Unfortunately, the National Chess Centre would be completely destroyed when the John Lewis store was bombed in September 1940, and much of the irreplaceable chess history preserved there, including the British Chess Foundation library, was destroyed with it. When war broke out, Alexander was in Buenos Aires, Argentina, representing Great Britain at the Olympiad. He and his team-mates were forced to abandon the competition and rapidly board a steamer home. These team-mates included Harry Golombek and Stuart Milner-Barry, both of whom would join Alexander at Bletchley Park. The recruitment of chess-players (as well as crossword-puzzle enthusiasts) has become part of the mythology of Bletchley Park. As is so often the case, the prosaic truth is that this was not a significant recruitment criterion; however, it happens that, in this case, all three men were chess masters. It should be noted, however, that both Alexander and Golombek were King's graduates, and Milner-Barry studied at Trinity, so it is equally likely that their path to Bletchley Park was via the King's/Trinity 'old boy' network which furnished GC&CS with a great many of its senior figures. Milner-Barry was recruited to Bletchley Park by Trinity alumnus and Head of Hut 6 Gordon Welchman, and Milner-Barry in turn recruited his friend Hugh Alexander.

All three men went to work in Hut 6 on army and air force Enigma, but in the spring of 1941 Alexander and Golombek moved to work with Turing in Hut 8. Alexander would spend the remainder of the European war in Hut 8, taking over from Turing as head in 1942. He seems to have run a 'happy ship', as well as a productive one. Hut veterans variously described him as 'tall and good looking, a little bit shy'[3] or 'a great chatterbox',[4] but most of all he was a good manager of people. Rolf Noskwith, another Trinity-ite, who worked for Alexander in Hut 8 described the atmosphere of the hut: 'I had a much easier relationship with Alexander, who was extrovert, and had lots of things to talk about [. . .] They [Alexander and Wylie] were very easy to relate to. One of the lucky circumstances of Hut 8 was that it was a very pleasant place to work, due, particularly, to Alexander.'[5]

Not content with his congenial managing of the breaking of naval Enigma, Hugh Alexander took a sideline interest in Japanese cipher systems. Such was his success with this that by early 1945 he was appointed Head of Naval Section II J, responsible for breaking Japanese naval codes. His responsibilities as Head of Hut 8 were passed on to Patrick (A.P.) Mahon, who took over in April 1945 and was responsible for writing the post-war history of the hut, and from whom we will hear more later in this chapter. After the war, Alexander returned briefly to John Lewis, but such was his taste for codebreaking that he returned to GC&CS (by then renamed GCHQ) and continued to work on codes and ciphers, becoming head of the cryptanalysis section at GCHQ in 1949. He resisted further promotion and carried on in that role until 1971, when he retired; he died only a few years later in 1974.

Sadly, it seems Hugh Alexander's success as a cryptanalyst was at the expense of his chess. After the war, he was again British champion in 1956 and was on the British team for the Olympiads in 1954 and 1958, but the nexus of the post-war chess world was in Eastern Europe and the Soviet Union. The secret work carried on by Alexander in GCHQ precluded him from travel behind the Iron Curtain, and so, although he would write a number of acclaimed books about the great chess clashes of the Cold War era, he was never able to try his own skills against the Grand Masters of the age. His life-long friend and collaborator in both chess and cryptanalysis, Stuart Milner-Barry, mourned him in *The Times* thus: 'One could have wished for nothing else but that vivid and vigorous presence, that quick, clear and energetic mind, the passion for intellectual argument, the practical kindness and spontaneous understanding with the young – all this will be sadly missed. To have been so close a friend for 50 years is indeed good fortune.'[6]

THE END OF *TIRPITZ*

The destruction of *Scharnhorst* in December 1943 left only one German capital ship as a threat to Allied operations outside the Baltic. However, this was not just any ship, it was the largest and most powerful ship in the western theatre of the war: *Tirpitz*. Until it was permanently disposed of, the German battleship remained a constant threat to any Allied activities in the Arctic and a preoccupation for the Home Fleet, the Admiralty and even the Prime Minister, who gave it the nickname of the 'Beast' in recognition of its brooding threat.[7] Nor was it simply a physical threat. *Tirpitz*'s propaganda value to both sides was enormous; it was the pride of the *Kriegsmarine* and represented their continued capacity to threaten the Royal Navy, while on the other side the inability to sink it irked the Admiralty, and the ship's destruction, when achieved, would be a moment of public triumph. This latter factor was possibly an influence on the final attacks against it, as will be described later. The great ship was also a preoccupation for naval intelligence and the subject of hours of analysis, both at the OIC and at Bletchley Park. Its life and movements were studied on the basis of not only Enigma intercepts but also information from SIS coast-watchers, air and submarine reconnaissance and information from Swedish interception of German land communications. Together, these sources combined to give a constant commentary on the ship and its state of readiness. As historian John Winton described it: 'She almost certainly took up more staff time and thought, more space in OIC Special Intelligence summaries, and more text in ULTRA signals, than any other single ship. In the end, ULTRA was to play a major part in her life and death.'[8]

A recent assessment suggests that the files of the NID at the Admiralty contained at least 145 SIS coast-watchers' reports on *Tirpitz* alone.[9] While the number of Enigma decrypts concerning it has not been calculated, it is likely that it also runs into the hundreds. However, to tell the story of *Tirpitz* it is necessary to back-track somewhat to the summer of 1942. *Tirpitz* would be subject to repeated attacks over the next two years. These can be divided into three main efforts: a clandestine sub-surface effort in 1942–1943, a carrier-borne air attack in the summer of 1944 and, finally, a heavy bomber attack in late 1944. SIGINT would play its part in each of these phases.

After its indirect but crucial role in operation *RÖSSELSPRUNG* and the destruction of PQ 17, *Tirpitz* retired to Bogenfjord, near Narvik. However, it had been at sea for over a year and was due for refit. As Hitler was reluctant to see it return all the way to Germany, arrangements were made for refit in Trondheim. In light of the ship's previous visits to Trondheimsfjord, SIS arranged in February 1942 for direct observation of those waters. Norwegian agent Bjørn Røholt travelled to Trondheim from the UK and was able to establish wireless reporting by his colleague Magne Hassel, who actually lived within the German naval-controlled zone overlooking the fjord. In due course, on 23 October 1942, *Tirpitz* anchored in Foettenfjord, an inner spur of Trondheimsfjord. This was the moment for which the Admiralty had been waiting, and Operation TITLE was immediately launched. This operation involved an attack on *Tirpitz* by a pair of Chariots – essentially, manned torpedoes – which would deliver mines to destroy the battleship. The Chariots were to be delivered by a Norwegian trawler, the *Arthur*, which would sail into the fjord and deliver the Chariots within striking distance of the target. The trawler would then be scuttled, and all involved would escape overland to Sweden. The SIS team in Trondheim secured information allowing false documents to be prepared for the *Arthur* to pass the various German checkpoints en route, and in this it was entirely successful. Unfortunately, choppy seas led to the towed Chariots breaking loose from *Arthur* and sinking, and the whole project had to be abandoned, all but one of the participants escaping successfully to Sweden.[10]

Undisturbed by this abortive effort, *Tirpitz* completed the refit and on 11 March 1943 departed Trondheim for Altenfjord in the north, where it joined *Scharnhorst* and *Lützow*. As described earlier, this concentration of force was a factor in the suspension of Allied convoys for the summer of 1943. Again, its departure was observed by coastwatchers, information which reached London only three hours after the sailing.[11] Its new home was also placed under observation by the Norwegians, in this case agent Torstein Raaby, who sent detailed plans of the anchorage in Kaafjord to London via Sweden.[12] A second method of underwater attack had meanwhile been developed. These were the 'X-craft', small, 50-foot midget submarines, with a crew of four and capable of carrying two detachable explosive charges, each consisting of 2 tons of explosive. The X-craft had entered service in early 1943, and *Tirpitz* and its companion warships were the obvious target. An attack on the German northern fleet was planned for September 1943, but it was not known exactly where the German ships might be stationed at that time, so an intense intelligence effort was launched. In August 1943 the OIC produced a special report assessing all information available from decrypts about the various possible anchorages in Norway,[13] and this was backed up by air reconnaissance and agent reports. Additional anxiety was created in the Admiralty when, having been inactive for several months, the German fleet sallied forth on 8 September for Operation *ZITRONELLA*, the bombardment of Spitzbergen, described earlier. This was troubling news, because the X-craft attack was scheduled for 20–25 September, and to achieve this the parent submarines which would tow the X-craft across to Norway needed to leave no later than 11 September. In the event, Enigma intercepts in the early hours of 9 September indicated that the German ships would be back in Altenfjord by that afternoon, and so the Allied operation, codenamed SOURCE, was able to go ahead as scheduled.[14]

Six X-craft (numbered *X-5* to *X-10*) were involved in the operation. It was intended that three would attack *Tirpitz* in Kaafjord, two would attack *Scharnhorst* at the entrance to Kaafjord, and one *Lützow* some miles away in Langefjord. After the force had sailed, further Enigma intercepts showed that *Scharnhorst* would not be at its berth on the night of 22 September (when the attack was planned), as it would be conducting gunnery trials from 21 to 23 September. This information was not passed on to the X-craft (possibly due to the restricted circulation of ULTRA). In the event, this did not matter, as two X-craft were lost in transit, and as a result *X-10* was re-tasked from *Scharnhorst* to *Tirpitz*. Although all but one of the craft were subsequently sunk, two did manage to place charges beneath or near *Tirpitz*, and several of their crew members were captured in time to experience the effects of their handiwork at first hand. At 8.12 a.m. on 22 September, Kaafjord was rocked by a series of huge explosions. The full effects of the charges were reduced by the fact that *Tirpitz* was swung on its moorings, so those laid under the bows detonated some distance from the ship. However, the effects were significant nonetheless. Decks and plates were twisted, and A and C turrets were lifted off their mountings. Significant flooding also occurred in lower compartments, and a number of the ship's sensitive gunnery and electronic systems were disabled. A degree of panic ensued among the ship's crew, as well as in the wider anchorage, as searches were made for further submarines.[15]

The immediate German response, and later assessments of the damage, were followed by the Admiralty via Enigma decrypts. A message reporting the capture of four submarine crew was intercepted at 8.50 a.m. and was in the hands of the OIC by just after 11 a.m. on 22 September.[16] This was followed by a message intercepted at 12.16 p.m. and deciphered the following day which described the ship flooded with 500 cubic metres of water.[17] Further messages revealed a request for a specialist electric-welding ship to be sent, as well as debate over how the X-craft had penetrated the anti-torpedo nets surrounding the battleship. These were all summarised in an OIC Special Intelligence Report circulated on 8 October.[18] Clearly, significant damage had been done to *Tirpitz*. The longer-term question for the Admiralty, however, was how long the ship would be out of commission. This became an even more pressing question after the sinking of the *Scharnhorst* in December, as the absence of any serviceable German capital ships in the Arctic would relieve the Home Fleet of a significant commitment in protecting the Arctic convoys until *Tirpitz* was repaired. In response, the OIC produced a second Special Intelligence Report in January 1944 examining all the available intelligence concerning repairs to the ship. Message traffic with repair companies in Germany, as well as within the *Kriegsmarine*, revealed that the electrical power systems in the ship were seriously disrupted. A coffer dam was also requested so that work could be carried out on the rudder and propeller shafts. A 100-ton floating crane was required (presumably to re-seat the turrets), as well as other gunnery repair materials. Meanwhile, large batches of crew were granted leave back to Germany, suggesting they would not be required to man the ship for some time. The OIC concluded that 15 March 1944 was the scheduled date by which the ship would be seaworthy, but that work on gunnery systems would still be required after that date.[19]

As the March 1944 deadline approached, both coast-watching and Enigma intercepts reported sea trials and other signs of *Tirpitz*'s renewed readiness for sea.[20] This indicated that the respite which had been offered to the Arctic convoys from surface attack was potentially at an end, and so the Admiralty took steps once again to deal with the threat. Not only would the Home Fleet sail a battleship and aircraft carrier covering force for the next convoy (JW 58), but this would be combined with an attempt to solve the problem at source by attacking *Tirpitz* again in Altenfjord, this time using carrier-borne aircraft. The previous 1942 Fleet Air Arm attack on *Tirpitz* had been carried out with Albacore torpedo bombers while it was at sea, but this was not possible in the anchorage in Kaafjord. Instead, bombing would be required, but the fleet's earlier aircraft, the Swordfish and Albacores, did not have the capacity to drop bombs of a weight which would have any effect on *Tirpitz*'s armoured decks. Fortunately, in 1943 the Fairey Barracuda monoplane had entered Fleet Air Arm service, and calculations suggested that a newly developed 1,600lb bomb dropped from that aircraft from at least 3,500 feet would reach a speed of descent capable of penetrating *Tirpitz*'s vitals and doing the necessary damage.

Plans were laid as early as December 1943 for what would become Operation TUNGSTEN. This involved an attack by over forty bombers, escorted by another eighty fighters, launched from no fewer than six aircraft carriers and escorted by a surface battlegroup from the Home Fleet. That an operation on such a scale was considered shows the seriousness with which the *Tirpitz* was taken at the Admiralty, but it also shows the confidence the Royal Navy had developed over the past years. It would earlier have been considered much too great a risk to place two fleet aircraft carriers in range of German land-based aircraft, but such was the weakness of the *Luftwaffe* in Norway by 1944 that this was not considered a problem. Nor did the German surface fleet or its submarines any longer present a credible threat to a British battlegroup.

The operation was scheduled for 4 April 1944, which would allow the battlegroup simultaneously to provide a covering force for convoy

JW 58. This would also offer an explanation for the presence of the ships at sea for German intelligence should the force be discovered. Meanwhile, intensive scrutiny of *Tirpitz's* activities was carried out via SIGINT, coast-watchers and air reconnaissance using Spitfires sent to Russia for the purpose. There were fears that the battleship might slip out to attack a convoy before the operation could be mounted, or that it might remove itself to another anchorage, or even back to Germany.[21] In contrast, Enigma revealed not only that *Tirpitz* would be in Altenfjord, but that on 3 April it would be outside the defensive nets, and away from its smoke generators and anti-aircraft defences, carrying out speed trials in the outer fjord. As a result, the attack was brought forward by twenty-four hours. Another Enigma message intercepted just before midnight on 2 April and forwarded to the Admiralty in the early hours of 3 April revealed the ship's departure time from Kaafjord as 5.30 a.m., returning at 6 p.m., and its destination as the Vargsund strait.[22]

At 4.30 a.m. on 3 April a force of forty-two Barracudas, divided into two waves an hour apart, departed from the fleet carriers HMS *Victorious* and *Furious*, plus the smaller escort carriers HMS *Emperor*, *Pursuer*, and *Searcher*. A further forty fighters accompanied each wave, while additional fighters from the escort carrier *Fencer* provided local cover for the battlegroup itself. The first wave arrived just after 5.30 a.m. as the battleship was in the process of unmooring and heading for sea, albeit still within Kaafjord. Surprise was complete, and in total the two attacks landed fifteen bombs on target, of which four were the 1,600lb type. Unfortunately, in their efforts to hit the ship the bomber pilots dropped from too low an altitude for the bombs to penetrate the armoured main-deck, but significant damage was done to the ship's upperworks, not least from strafing by the accompanying fighters, and heavy casualties were inflicted: 122 crew members were killed and a further 316 wounded.[23] At 7.43 a.m. *Tirpitz* signalled *Gruppe Nord* and Naval High Command in Berlin that it had been under attack from carrier-borne aircraft and had suffered 'several hits'. This information was on the desks of the OIC by 11.30 a.m. and must have caused a degree of satisfaction at the Admiralty.[24] Only four aircraft had been lost.

Unfortunately, Enigma then went quiet on any further facts about damage to *Tirpitz*. Initial estimates based on air-photo interpretation and agent reports put it out of action for five months. This was later amended to three, but no one knew for sure. No more Enigma intercepts describing the ship's condition were made until June, when a further message described the human casualties. As a result, the Home Fleet was tasked with repeating its attack. Three further operations were arranged: Operations PLANET on 24 April, BRAWN on 15 May and TIGER CLAW on 28 May. Unfortunately, all of these operations had to be cancelled due to adverse weather. By the end of May, priorities changed at the Admiralty, as the 6 June invasion of France ('D-Day') absorbed all resources, and Arctic convoys were once again suspended for the summer months. In addition, the clarity of the intelligence picture of Altenfjord suffered a blow when at the end of May Torstein Raaby was forced by increased German suspicions to withdraw from his observation of Kaafjord and escape via Sweden. His last contributions were weather reports supplied for the abortive May operations.[25]

Once the D-Day invasion forces had been successfully delivered to France, attention turned once again to the resumption of convoys to Russia, and in turn to the threat posed by *Tirpitz*. In July, information was received from another coast-watcher that the battleship was doing sea trials in Altenfjord. This led to a repeated effort by the Royal Navy and Fleet Air Arm. The Home Fleet had been reinforced by the carriers HMS *Formidable*, arrived from the Mediterranean, and the newly commissioned *Indefatigable*. These, along with *Furious* and an escorting surface battlegroup, sailed on 14 July on Operation MASCOT, and on 17 July a raid of similar size to the TUNGSTEN raid was launched. Unfortunately, by the time the aircraft arrived in Kaafjord the Germans had been given prior warning, and the target was thoroughly obscured by smoke from generators around the anchorage. No hits were achieved. It has been suggested that the warning was provided to the Germans via monitoring of the British battlegroup's own W/T communications. This possibility was raised by an Enigma intercept after the May operations, which suggested that Allied W/T was being heard by the enemy.[26] If so, this was a serious flaw in Allied operational security.

Three further efforts were made against *Tirpitz* by carrier aircraft. At the end of August Operation GOODWOOD was launched. On this occasion the plan was for the carrier strike-force to loiter for several days and make repeated attacks in quick succession. Bombers were launched on 22, 24 and 29 August, but again lack of wireless security gave away the presence of the battlegroup, and German smoke defences, as well as natural fog, foiled the attacks. Enigma traffic indicated that the attacking fleet had been identified as early as 21 August. Further intercepted traffic declared that damage to the ship in the raids had been 'insignificant';[27] however, one message was read requesting bomb-disposal personnel from the *Luftwaffe* base at Banak.[28] It was learned after the war that a single 1,600lb bomb had pierced *Tirpitz*'s armoured deck but had failed to detonate. It is possible to speculate about the consequences had this bomb exploded, but, unknown to the Admiralty, the strategic picture had already changed. In light of the Allied ability to defend convoys with carrier aircraft, and the weakness of the German air force in Norway, over the summer Admiral Dönitz decided that the battleship's seagoing days were over. It would be maintained as a floating battery for the defence of Norway against the anticipated Allied invasion, and its crew would be scaled down to provide manning only for the armament.[29]

Unaware of Dönitz's decision, the Allied commanders continued to be concerned by the *Tirpitz*'s potential to disrupt activity in northern waters and tie down the heavy units of the Home Fleet, which were badly needed to reinforce the Royal Navy in the Indian Ocean and Pacific. After the navy's lack of success, the task was passed to the RAF. A plan was devised to attack *Tirpitz* using heavy bombers carrying 12,000lb 'Tallboy' bombs. Unfortunately, Kaafjord was beyond the range of these aircraft for a return trip from the UK, so the bombers flew to Yagodnik near Archangel, from where they carried out the raid, before once again flying back to the UK. On 15 September 1944, twenty-seven Lancaster bombers from No. 617 Squadron and No. 9 Squadron commanded by Wing Commander J.B. Tait took off for Operation PARAVANE. Despite the smoke defences, one hit was achieved, blowing a 50-foot hole in the bows of the vessel and letting in over 1,000 tonnes of water.[30] The great ship nonetheless stayed afloat.

In September the German situation on north Norway continued to deteriorate. An armistice between the Finns and the Soviets removed one of the key obstacles to Soviet operations in the north. Fearing an invasion into Norway, the German army launched Operation *NORDLICHT*, a fighting withdrawal to prepared defence lines north of Tromsø. In fact, the operation continued into January 1945, but Altenfjord lay to the north of the limit of the planned retreat, so the German naval units there needed to be withdrawn at least to Tromsø, if not further south.[31] *Tirpitz* moved on 15 October to a new anchorage near Haaköy Island, opposite Tromsø. It was deliberately placed in water shallow enough that, if it sank, the main-deck would theoretically remain above water. Its departure was observed by coast-watchers, and also reported by Enigma, deciphered on 16 October.[32] Crucially, the move to Tromsø brought the ship within range of UK-based bombers, and so the RAF attack was renewed with a further raid (Operation OBVIATE) on 29 October. A near miss was achieved, the results of which were in the hands of the Admiralty more or less as soon as the bombers returned. A message from *Tirpitz* sent at 10.30 a.m. was read at 3.50 p.m. on 29 October: 'Near miss astern to port. 800 (tons of) water in the ship. No casualties. Slight damage to weapons.'[33] The bombers returned on 12 November (Operation CATECHISM) and this time were finally successful. Two direct hits and two near misses caused catastrophic damage and flooding, and at 9.52 a.m. on 12 November 1944 *Tirpitz* capsized, after one of its main turret magazines exploded. Over 900 of the crew died, trapped in the upturned hull.[34] Again, Enigma revealed the results of the attack within twenty-four hours, as several long messages were intercepted listing casualties and beginning the inquest into why, when the *Luftwaffe* had aircraft at cockpit-readiness on the nearby Banak airbase, no fighter cover was provided for the doomed battleship during the raid.[35]

The sinking of the 'Beast' made worldwide headlines, but an assessment of its long-term significance is more difficult. *Tirpitz* never engaged an Allied warship or sank a merchant vessel. It made only three sorties into Arctic waters in three years. Nonetheless, the shadow the ship cast over Allied convoy operations was vast, and it tied up significant Home Fleet resources for much of the war. The simple fact of it and its smaller sisters' presence as a 'fleet in being' in north Norway was critical to Allied thinking. The scale of concern to the Allies can be measured in the thirty-three separate air attacks made against the ship between 1940 and 1944, by over seven hundred aircraft.[36] By the time it sank, however, it is arguable that its influence had waned and it had ceased to be the threat it once was, a fact acknowledged by Admiral Dönitz when he confined it to the fjords in the summer of 1944.

Throughout *Tirpitz*'s presence in the Arctic, Allied intelligence was able to track its movements and measure its state of readiness to go to sea, and much of this was due to ULTRA. Arguably, the ship never made a move that was not reported in a timely fashion by the OIC and Bletchley Park. Even during the catastrophe of PQ 17, the flow of information concerning *Tirpitz* was ultimately correct, even though the decisions made on the basis of it have proved controversial. It has been argued that the intelligence provided tended to be 'historical' rather than predictive. As Ludovic Kennedy put it: 'Despite ULTRA they had rarely known for certain where *Tirpitz* was or would be; they could only tell (because of the time-lag between interception and decryption) where she had recently been.'[37]

As has been described in earlier chapters, however, in both of *Tirpitz*'s anti-convoy sorties, Operation *SPORTPALAST* in March 1942 and *RÖSSELSPRUNG* in July, the Admiralty was forewarned of German intentions once at sea, either via intelligence on the prior planning of the operations or through instructions to the ship intercepted once it had sailed. ULTRA was therefore able to report on future intentions as well as recent events. Similarly, the OIC reports produced after *Tirpitz* was damaged in Operation SOURCE, and again after the TUNGSTEN raid by the Fleet Air Arm, proved substantially correct in their assessments of the periods in which the ship would be unavailable for operations. Overall, the codebreakers at Bletchley Park and their colleagues at the OIC had reason to be pleased with their record against the battleship.

TECHNOLOGY AND TACTICS: THE SPRING CONVOYS 1944

Having followed the story of *Tirpitz* through to the end of 1944, it is now necessary to go back to the beginning of the year to look at how the convoys themselves progressed in the fourth year of the campaign. The literature of the Arctic campaign devotes little space to the final eighteen months, focusing in particular on the critical year of 1942, and this work is no exception; however, there are a number of notable features of the later convoys which are worthy of attention. There is also the risk that hindsight overshadows appreciation of what for the participants were still serious and bloody combats. Patrick Beesly summed this up nicely on the basis of his own experience in the OIC: 'The loss of the Scharnhorst transformed the strategic situation, and with hindsight everything that subsequently occurred in North Norway seems something of an anti-climax. *This was not the impression that those concerned on the British side had at the time.*'[38]

With *Scharnhorst* gone and *Tirpitz* under repair, the Allies took the opportunity to run four more convoy cycles between January and April 1944: JW/RA 56, 57, 58 and 59. Heavy covering forces were not required, as the German surface fleet was reduced to a few destroyers. This placed the burden on the U-boat fleet to interdict these sailings. On 27 December Admiral Dönitz directed that the U-boat force in Norway should be expanded to twenty-four boats, and six of these arrived in the course of January. However, in light of previous experience he can have had few illusions about their likely effectiveness.[39] Captain-of-U-boats Norway Rudolf Peters was also anxious about the prospects for his command, and he expressed his concerns on 31 December 1943. He listed a number of problems. These included the weather and lack of experienced crews, but, more particularly, he focused on Allied radar as a new problem:

1. Apparently the enemy sends search groups ahead of every convoy, which find our U-boat positions with the aid of radar and infra-red locations [*sic*], attack the boats, and report them. Acting on these reports the convoy has an opportunity of evading our patrol lines. This is what has apparently happened in several cases.
2. Another disadvantage is the fact that only some of the boats are equipped with 'Borkum' and 'Naxos' sets as well as 'Zaunkönig' torpedoes. They were thus very inferior to the enemy escorts and in most cases the sudden appearance of enemy patrol vessels took them by surprise.[40]

Peters was correct in that in the course of 1943 the British had introduced more and better radar systems, in particular airborne sets which operated in the *c*. 10cm wavelengths as opposed to the metre-plus wavelength systems used earlier. This meant that periscopes could be detected, as well as surfaced submarines. 'Borkum' and 'Naxos' were radar detectors which it was hoped would give the U-boats warning of attack, but neither was particularly effective, and crews were sceptical of their usefulness. The other technology he mentioned, 'Zaunkönig' ('wren'), was potentially more useful. This was the T5 acoustic-homing torpedo. When fired, this torpedo could pick up the propeller noise of a ship and steer towards the sound, theoretically making a hit much more likely. These weapons had first been tried in the Atlantic by the *Leuthen* wolfpack in September 1943, and they would be used in the Arctic for the first time against JW 56A and B.[41] Hopes were high for this weapon, but these were not to be realised, and the wide-scale reporting of their use via Enigma, which was insisted on by U-boat command, gave the Allies a very detailed understanding of their characteristics and effectiveness. The Naval Section U-boat torpedo stock book at Bletchley Park, compiled by Peggy Senior (described in Chapter 3) acquired a new column for the recording of T5 firings, and many are detailed therein.

The mismatch between German expectations and reality was revealed when convoy JW 56A sailed on 12 January 1944. The convoy immediately hit severe weather and was driven back to Iceland. Five ships stayed in Iceland, but the remaining fifteen sailed again on 21 January, followed by the second half of the convoy, JW 56B, which sailed with sixteen ships from Loch Ewe on 22 January. Despite evasive routing based on Enigma decrypts, the earlier convoy was picked up by a U-boat at the northern end of a patrol line of fifteen boats (wolfpack *Isegrim*, or 'wolf') deployed near Bear Island, and the rest of the force closed to the attack. In their attacks on JW 56A on 25 and 26 January, eight U-boats fired ten T5 torpedoes, as well as other types such as the earlier 'FAT' (*Federapparat Torpedo*), which followed a zig-zag course after launching. Three US Liberty ships were sunk, and the escorting destroyer HMS *Obdurate* was hit and damaged. In a subsequent attack on JW 56B on 29 and 30 January, nine U-boats fired a further twelve T5s, as well as other weapons. No merchantmen were hit, but the destroyer *Hardy* had its stern blown off and was sunk after the crew had been taken off. Thus, in the two sailings, three merchantmen had been lost and one destroyer sunk, with another damaged; one U-boat (*U-314*) had also been sunk by the convoy escorts.[42] The German account was quite different, as was revealed by an Enigma message sent from Captain-of-U-boats Norway on 1 February to his crews at sea:

> You have done your job well.
> Result to date of PQ25 and 26 [*sic*]
> 1) Sunk for certain: 7 destroyers, 4 steamships.
> 2) Torpedoed, probably sunk: 3 destroyers
> 3) Torpedoed: 6 steamships (Sinking not observed)
> 4) Probably hit: 6 destroyers, 1 steamship
> Carry on in this way.[43]

Peters was claiming at the most optimistic reading sixteen enemy warships sunk, along with eleven merchantmen, at a cost of one submarine. In fact, only four ships had been lost, and no merchant ships had been hit in the second convoy at all. The Admiralty responded to the losses by postponing the departure of the returning RA 56, which had been intended to sail simultaneously with the outward convoys. This was to allow the escorts from the outward passage to be used to cover the return trip. Thus, a combined RA 56 departed Kola on 2 February with thirty-seven merchant vessels accompanied by twenty-six warships. No losses were suffered.

For the next convoy, and with the endorsement of Admiral Fraser, the Admiralty reverted to a single large sailing of forty-two merchant ships with an escort of seventeen destroyers, as well as the escort carrier *Chaser* and light cruiser *Black Prince*. The situation in the Atlantic permitted a number of these destroyers to be brought from Western Approaches Command. These included the experienced HMS *Keppel*, who already had three U-boat sinkings to its name and would shortly add two more. JW 57 left Loch Ewe on 21 February. In response, the U-boat forces made a number of tactical changes. Although the Bear Island–North Cape narrows made a good hunting ground for the U-boats, once a convoy had passed the North Cape it had only a short period of sailing before reaching Murmansk. If the boats could attack further west, this might give them up to thirty-six hours more time for combat; but go too far west and they would be at risk from land-based air cover from Iceland. Admiral Peters moved his patrol lines to a position either side of the zero-degree meridian of longitude, to the east of Jan Mayen Island.[44] To achieve this, a longer north-to-south patrol line was required – and thus more boats. Fourteen U-boats from the *Werwolf* group were placed across the expected route of JW 57, a fact quickly revealed via Enigma intercepts. Priority was given to attacks on escort vessels. This was partly due to the fact that a T5 had more chance against a fast, and hence noisy, escort, separated from the convoy, than it did against multiple slow-moving ships in close formation, which would confuse the guidance system.

The passage of JW 57 was observed by *Luftwaffe* reconnaissance, and the convoy was shadowed fairly successfully from the air; however, this was of little help to the U-boats. The merchant ships passed to the south of their initial patrol line, and from then on Admiral Peters was forced repeatedly to try and place his boats across the path of the convoy while the submarines increasingly fell behind and had to play catch-up. A number of contacts were achieved with escort vessels, but no U-boat ever made contact with the merchant ships. Three days out, *U-990* managed to sink the destroyer HMS *Maharatta* (with the loss of all but seventeen of the crew), but that was the sole German success. In exchange, HMS *Keppel* sank *U-713*, and *U-601* tried unsuccessfully to fight it out on the surface with a Catalina aircraft flown from the Shetlands. It paid the price and was sunk by air-dropped depth charges. On the return leg – RA 57, which left Kola on 2 March – fifteen U-boats were sent against the convoy. One success was scored by *U-703*, which sank the British freighter *Empire Tourist*, but at a cost of three U-boats sunk over three days: *U-472*, *U-366* and *U-973*, all sunk by Swordfish aircraft from HMS *Chaser*, with the assistance in one case of the destroyer HMS *Onslaught*.[45]

In an environment which had become so hostile to U-boats, tactical intelligence from ULTRA became increasingly redundant. Commander Geoffrey Colpoys, Deputy Head of the OIC, captured this in his analysis of the attacks on JW 57. He pointed out that 'This intelligence [U-boat and aircraft contact reports] was passed to C. in C. H.F. but as the U-boats' efforts were comparatively feeble and he had such large escort forces at his command C. in C. saw no reason to order any diversions.'[46]

He went on:

> This convoy operation illustrates well the changed situation from the days of heavy losses and threats from air and surface attack as well as from U-boats. By themselves the U-boats seemed unable to press home any advantage. Occasionally one bold commander achieved a sinking, but when the escort forces reached the strength available for JW57, any U-boat who ventured near the convoy was almost invariably attacked by air or surface escorts before he could fire his torpedoes. This continuous threat to the U-boats is apparent throughout the above story and must have made the life of a U-boat commanding Officer in the Arctic a particularly hard one.[47]

Overall, Colpoys summarised the position thus: 'the situation had changed to a state where the question was "how many U-Boats were sunk?" rather than "how many ships were lost?".[48]

The next two convoys were even worse for the Germans. JW 58 sailed on 27 March, consisting of forty-nine merchant ships, escorted by two carriers, HMS *Activity* and *Tracker*, two light cruisers and another thirty smaller escorts. Against this, sixteen of the twenty-nine U-boats available were at sea. Also at sea was the fleet carrier battle-group sent to carry out Operation TUNGSTEN against *Tirpitz*, as described earlier in this chapter. Two days later the Allies claimed first blood, the sloop HMS *Starling* sinking *U-961*. Between 1 and 3 April, three more U-boats were sunk, two by aircraft, and one by HMS *Keppel*, taking its personal total to five. Six German aircraft were also shot down. In return, U-boat Command calculated that at least nine, and possibly fourteen, Allied ships had been sunk; in fact, the convoy had reached Kola without loss. Two return convoys followed, RA 58 of thirty-six empty merchantmen and RA 59 of forty-five ships, carrying personnel no longer required in Russia over the summer months. Only one ship was lost from these two convoys, the American Liberty ship *William S. Thayer*, but at a cost of three more U-boats sunk and further

German aircraft shot down.[49]

Churchill had promised Stalin 140 ship-loads of material over the winter of 1943–1944. In fact, between November and May, 188 merchant ships sailed to Russia. Of these, the German navy and air force were able to sink only five, along with two destroyers, at a cost of thirteen U-boats and a similar number of patrol aircraft. Taken from a force of thirty U-boats deployed to the two Norwegian flotillas, this represented a loss rate of 43 per cent. Historian Clay Blair summed up the bleak outlook for the *Kriegsmarine*: 'Throughout the war Dönitz repeatedly deplored the diversion of U-boats to the Arctic as a waste of naval assets. The outcome of those diversions in the winter of 1943–44 vividly proved his point. Moreover to the ruinous U-boat losses must be added the loss of *Scharnhorst* and the second crippling of *Tirpitz*.'[50]

As has been described, ULTRA had a significant part to play in the latter two events. In terms of the U-boat campaign in early 1944, the reading of Enigma played little tactical role, but as always, it remained key in understanding the wider strategic picture of the U-boat forces: serviceability and losses of boats, changes in doctrine and tactics, as well as the introduction of new technology such as the T5. In this role, it gave Allied commanders not only an operational understanding, allowing them to plan with confidence, but also the moral benefit of knowing just how on the ropes their enemy was by this stage of the war.

THE END OF THE ROAD: WINTER 1944–1945

Despite the less urgent need for SIGINT after the loss of the German capital ships, the pressure which Beesly described being felt in the OIC in the last fifteen months of the war also persisted at Bletchley Park into 1945. The resumption of Arctic convoys in August 1944 coincided with a series of belated improvements to German Enigma security. Arguably, had some of these changes happened earlier in the war, the consequences might have been severe for Hut 8's ability to read naval Enigma; however, they came too late to save the *Kriegsmarine*. By this stage of the war, Hugh Alexander's codebreakers had both the hard-won expertise in Enigma and the brute-force resources in British and US three- and four-rotor Bombe machines to tackle these new challenges.

Prior to the summer of 1943, the German U-boat fleet had managed with only three major Enigma keys: The *Heimisch* key (DOLPHIN at Bletchley Park), which continued to be used by U-boats in the Arctic after those in the Atlantic moved to the four-rotor *Triton* (SHARK) in February 1942, and a Mediterranean key, PORPOISE, which had been introduced around the same time as SHARK. However, from June 1943 these key networks started to be divided and subdivided until, by the end of the war, Hut 8 had identified sixteen different naval keys. Of concern for the Arctic was the division of DOLPHIN into two parts shortly after D-Day, on 17 June 1944. The key was subdivided, with one part used for the English Channel and another used for the North Sea and Arctic. At first, these were essentially the same key, but a *stichwort*, or keyword, was introduced for the Arctic traffic. This word was used to adapt the settings of the basic DOLPHIN key so that a different encryption setting was generated.[51] Since one of the new keys was derived from the basic settings of the other, this was not initially a huge problem; however, in September the Arctic key became entirely separate (codenamed NARWHAL at Bletchley Park). Fortunately, the *Kriegsmarine* continued to make the fundamental error of sending fleetwide messages word-for-word across the multiple keys, so Hut 8 could attack these using 'R.E.s', or re-encodements, where one key provided a crib for the next. Less fortunately, in September a German aircraft attempting to drop the month's keys to the German forces in Brest instead dropped them on nearby US troops. This ought to have been a benefit to Bletchley Park, but because the Germans knew they had done it, various emergency re-encryption procedures were introduced, which actually made breaking the various naval Enigma keys more difficult – proof that an additional 'pinch' was not always desirable when a breaking methodology was already successful.[52]

Worse was to follow when in November 1944 NARWHAL switched over to using all four Enigma rotors, instead of the previous procedure where the fourth rotor was retained in a neutral position to be compatible with the old M3 Enigma machines. All the principal naval keys were now four-rotor. Fortunately, such was the stock of four-wheel Bombe machines available, especially in Washington, D.C., where the

Americans had 113 machines in operation by November 1944 (GC&CS had another 51), that the greater number of Bombe runs required to find each key could be accommodated.[53] Drawing on his own experience in Naval Section, Harry Hinsley summed up this situation in his official history:

> Despite the fact that a four-wheel Enigma key (Narwhal) replaced the Home Waters key in the Arctic U-boat Command in September [*sic*], the naval decrypts continued to provide comprehensive intelligence about the strength and location of the U-boat patrol lines and to disclose the orders issued to them when convoys were sighted; Narwhal presented GC and CS with few difficulties as a result of its long experience with the Shark key.[54]

At the same time, a system of *Sonderschlüssel* – 'special keys' – was introduced, where keys were provided that were unique to individual flotillas, fortresses or even single U-boats. These keys carried so little traffic each that creating cribs for them was almost impossible and few were ever broken. Fortunately, this system was not widely rolled out, and most Arctic boats continued to use NARWHAL, which, in the words of A.P. Mahon (who had taken over from Hugh Alexander as Head of Hut 8), 'gave no special trouble' and continued to be broken through to the end of the war.[55] Indeed, in the final days of the conflict, the German government's own desperation proved its cryptanalytical undoing, as Mahon described: 'Our success was to a large extent due to the series of manifestoes put out by the German government which were re-encoded on all keys. Security at this stage became very bad and there were several re-encodements from plain language, the most remarkable being the repetition in the High Command Communique of Doenitz' final Order of the Day to his U Boats.'[56]

Clearly, at no point were Hut 8 or Naval Section at Bletchley Park in a position to relax or wind down their efforts until the end of hostilities. In fact, the final convoy, JW 67, sailed on 12 May, after the war had officially ended, but escorts were still provided against U-boats who might not have got the message, either physically or ideologically, to give up the fight. However, despite the obstacles belatedly thrown in their path, the naval codebreakers' success continued until the very last days.

Meanwhile, convoys to Russia resumed with JW 59 in August 1944. By this time, command changes had taken place on both sides. Bruce Fraser was replaced as C-in-C Home Fleet by Admiral Henry Moore. He was a cruiser man, having captained three light cruisers in the 1930s before beginning the war as commander of 3rd Cruiser Squadron. Various staff appointments followed before he took over the Home Fleet in June 1944.[57] On the other side of the North Sea, Admiral Peters was replaced as Commander-of-U-boats Norway by *Fregattenkapitän* Reinhard Suhren. Suhren was keen to take the battle to the enemy and was allocated more boats for the purpose, of which he had thirty-three by mid-1944. A number of these boats were fitted with new 37mm anti-aircraft guns. The addition of these weapons was the continuation of a policy begun in the Atlantic the previous year for the equipping of U-boats with air defence, in the form of multiple 20mm gun mounts. Instead of diving when contacted by an aircraft, the U-boats were ordered to fight through aggressively on the surface and attempt to shoot down their attacker. The dubious merits of this doctrine had already been demonstrated in the Atlantic, and the same would recur in the Arctic, as was shown by the sinking of *U-601* in February 1944. Nonetheless, Suhren went one step further – he considered that the advent of the 37mm meant that U-boats could stay surfaced in the face of attack by smaller escort vessels as well as aircraft. By fighting in packs and using T5 torpedoes and 37mm fire, escorts could be driven off and holes punched in the hitherto-solid defensive ring around the convoys. He explained the new doctrine in a lengthy message to all boats sent on 26 May 1944, and read by Bletchley Park the same day. He emphasised teamwork between U-boats: 'The difficulty of this task necessitates concerted action on the part of all boats. Faced with a number of targets all remaining on the surface, the enemy will not be able to cope with them all. Every boat on the surface splits up the defence further, and thus opens the way for other boats to get ahead. The old U-boat tradition seeks to prove itself anew in comradely cooperation attacking a common target.'[58]

Sadly for the crews involved, this dangerously overestimated the fighting power of a U-boat when stripped of its cloak of secrecy, and a high price would be paid for 'comradely cooperation' over the next twelve months.

JW 59 left Loch Ewe on 15 August with thirty-three merchant vessels and an escort of one cruiser and two escort carriers, *Vindex* and the American *Striker*, along with eighteen smaller escorts. A further distraction was provided by the carrier task group sent to attack *Tirpitz* on 22 August. First blood was claimed by the Germans when *U-354* attacked the carrier force and sank the frigate HMS *Bickerton*, as well as damaging the carrier *Nabob*. Meanwhile, *U-344* attacked the convoy, sinking the escort sloop HMS *Kite* (which the German captain claimed was a light cruiser). The Royal Navy struck back, aircraft from *Vindex* sinking *U-344*, and a group (once again including the redoubtable HMS *Keppel*), sank *U-354* when it joined the convoy attack fresh from its success against the carrier group. No merchant ships were damaged, and the convoy arrived at Kola on 28 August. Nine ships sailed in the return convoy RA 59A, escorted by the whole force which had covered JW 59, which left Kola the same day. This too arrived unscathed, while *Keppel*'s escort group and aircraft from *Vindex* accounted for a further U-boat, *U-394*.[59]

The next convoy cycle, JW and RA 60, sailed in mid-September. The outward journey was uneventful, but the returning empty ships accidentally overran the patrolling *U-310*, and it was able to sink two Liberty ships. At the same time, one U-boat, *U-921*, was lost, but the precise circumstances of the sinking were never resolved.[60] The next cycle, JW and RA 61, began on 20 October, this time with even more protection. A third escort carrier was added to the covering forces, and two surface escort groups were added to sweep ahead of the convoy and break up any U-boat patrol lines before the convoy reached them. This reflected a policy developed by the Admiralty, and in particular advocated by C-in-C Western Approaches, Admiral Max Horton, as early as spring 1944 that the Arctic convoys could be thought of as *offensive* operations, intended to sink U-boats and undermine the will of the *U-bootwaffe*, as much as defensive ones. He observed that the Arctic 'represents the only prolific area remaining where heavy losses can still be inflicted on both enemy U-boats and long-range aircraft'.[61]

One SIGINT-related factor which contributed to this was the practice adopted by the operational commander Admiral Dalrymple-Hamilton, who from JW 59 onwards flew his flag from the escort carrier *Vindex* rather than a cruiser, as had been previous practice. Previous chapters have described the problems raised when commanders of flag rank, and therefore indoctrinated into ULTRA, did not sail directly with the convoys but in shadowing cruiser forces or elsewhere, leaving the convoys themselves ignorant of the wider intelligence picture. Placing the Admiral at the heart of the convoy meant that he had both the land-based intelligence and the location of his seaborne assets at his fingertips, unlike Fraser or Burnett, who on previous runs had fought their battles only dimly aware of where the convoys actually were. There was also a practical advantage gained from the space and facilities aboard a larger ship, as Hinsley explained: 'Moreover the indoctrinated Admiral in command of the escorts flew his flag in one of the escort carriers instead of in a cruiser, and the much better location, display and communications facilities of that class of vessel enabled him to make proper and more effective use of the Sigint dispatched to him.'[62]

In the event, the hunting escort groups were frustrated by poor sonar conditions on the JW–RA 61 runs, and although several U-boat contacts were made, none were sunk. On the other side, the Germans had no success either, as no merchantmen or escorts were lost. A fast convoy, JW 61A, was also sailed, consisting of two liners full of Soviet prisoners of war being repatriated after capture as *Osttruppen* on the Western Front. These arrived unscathed, although the welcome the prisoners of war received from the Soviet authorities is probably best left to the imagination.

JW 62, the last convoy of 1944, sailed on 29 November. It faced a threat which had not been seen in the Arctic for two years, with the return of significant number of German torpedo bombers to north Norway. The *Luftwaffe* in Norway had been strengthened more gener-ally in the summer of 1944, but the increasingly effective Allied air and sea campaign against German coastal shipping around Norway absorbed most of the air force's attention. Indeed, such was the demand for air reconnaissance elsewhere that patrols over the Arctic were more or less abandoned, being carried out only when other intelligence suggested a convoy was imminent. However, the lack of success of the U-boats after August 1944 showed that Suhren's tactics were not working, or at the very least only worked if a convoy could be located in time to employ them. He also back-tracked on his surface attack theories, suggesting instead that convoys should be approached by night and that the U-boats should remain submerged ahead of the convoy and allow it to sail over them. To do this required air reconnaissance. As he put it: 'Results show as with earlier convoys, that it is impossible to make progress with present tactics when operating against a convoy strongly escorted by aircraft. Only the unobserved patrol line disposed ahead of a convoy promises success against merchant ships. For that purpose own armed air reconnaissance is essential. The U-boats are greatly hampered by destroyer groups as well as carrier aircraft.'[63]

The first time the *Luftwaffe* mounted a formal torpedo attack was against JW 62, but the aircraft failed to find the target. A second operation was launched against the returning RA 62, but despite losing two Ju 88 aircraft, no hits were achieved. The GCHQ history of the Arctic campaign summed up the German air force's efforts as follows: 'The features of this abortive effort are symptomatic of the entire final phase of the air campaign against Arctic convoys.'[64] It is hard to disagree with this sentiment.

Four convoy cycles, JW–RA 63, 64, 65 and 66, were run before the German surrender in May 1945, and a fifth, JW 67, departed later on 12 May. Attacks continued from the air, and by U-boats which increasingly turned to loitering outside the entrance to the Kola Inlet. Here they could be sure to find convoys which were otherwise untraceable without sufficient air reconnaissance. JW and RA 63 sailed undisturbed; JW 64 was successfully found and shadowed by the *Luftwaffe*, but an attack by forty-eight torpedo bombers failed when the wireless in the shadowing aircraft broke down and the bombers failed to find the target. As many as twelve U-boats waited off Kola, but these succeeded only in blowing the stern off the corvette *Denbigh Castle*, which was towed into the inlet but later abandoned. No other losses were sustained. The U-boats waited for the returning RA 64 to sail from Kola on 17 February, but despite sinking the corvette HMS

Bluebell and damaging the sloop HMS *Lark,* forcing it too to be towed ashore, and losing one U-boat, no merchant losses were inflicted. The convoy sailed on into some of the worst storms of the whole campaign. In the breaks in the weather, two torpedo-bomber attacks were launched, but only one straggler was hit, the *Henry Bacon.* It would be the last merchant ship lost to *Luftwaffe* attack in the campaign.[65]

JW 65 had a similar experience. The convoy sailed on 11 March but was not attacked until it reached Kola on 20 March. In the resulting fight, the sloop HMS *Lapwing* was sunk by a U-boat along with the merchant vessels *Thomas Donaldson* and *Horace Bushnell.* RA 65 was forced to fight through the U-boats outside Kola but suffered no losses, and nor did the outgoing JW 66, which sailed on 16 April.

Naval Section and the OIC continued to supply intelligence about the movements and patrol lines of the U-boats throughout the first four months of 1945, but once the tactics changed to wolfpacks simply waiting off the mouth of Kola Inlet, the result was what Harry Hinsley described as a 'straight fight', to which SIGINT could make little or no contribution.[66] In any case, the strength of the escort forces in these battles meant that little external help was required to fight the merchant ships through the cordon of U-boats, although this did come at some cost to the smaller escorts. The final fight took place on 29 April, when the returning RA 66 attempted to leave Kola Inlet. *U-968* sank the destroyer *Goodall,* and in return *U-286* and *U-307* were sunk by escorting frigates.[67] These would be the final losses of the Arctic convoy campaign on either side. Meanwhile, RA 66 sailed on otherwise unmolested to arrive in the Clyde on 8 May, the last day of the war.

CHAPTER ELEVEN

THE ARCTIC CONVOYS IN RETROSPECT

1941–1945

THE COST OF IT ALL

The key position that the Allied convoys to Russia hold in the mythology of the Second World War has been alluded to at the outset of this work. It is now worth considering some of those myths in comparison with the facts outlined in the foregoing chapters. The contribution of intelligence, and SIGINT in particular, to the protection of the convoys (and concomitant destruction of the *Luftwaffe* and *Kriegsmarine*) needs also to be assessed.

The Naval Staff History states that approximately 4 million tons of goods were shipped to the Soviet Union aboard the convoys, including over 5,000 tanks and 7,000 aircraft. Of this, around 300,000 tons was lost en route (7.5 per cent).[1] These figures are impressive; however, as Clay Blair pointed out, this represented less than a quarter (22.7 per cent) of the total stores delivered to the Russians, the rest travelling via the Persian Gulf or across the Pacific. In spite of this minority part in the process, the Arctic convoys are much the better known of the routes. As Blair argues:

However, the dangers of the Arctic Ocean and seas from the enemy and no less from the elements captured imaginations far more so than did the more perilous north Atlantic run. Moreover in part to assuage Stalin by highlighting the Arctic deliveries, the Allies propagandised the Murmansk convoys more than could be justified by the results achieved. Thus was left in some quarters the wrong impressions that not only were the Murmansk convoys the most hazardous and costly in terms of ships lost and seamen killed and missing, but also that deliveries to Kola inlet saved the Soviet Union from certain defeat.[2]

Whether the Soviet Union would have collapsed without Western help, particularly in 1942, is a counter-factual debate outside the scope of this book, as are the political implications of the campaign. However, a more localised analysis is possible. Was the continuation of the Arctic convoys in the face of the opposition of the enemy a viable operation of war? And if so, just how costly was it compared to similar operations, and why?

The simplest measure of the campaign is the number of ships lost. As with all historical data-sets, the exact numbers vary according to the counting criteria. The Naval Staff History gives the following figures for the convoys. In total, 40 outbound convoys sailed, amounting to a total of 811 ship-journeys. Of these, 33 ships turned back due to weather or mechanical defect, and 58 were sunk by enemy action (7.2 per cent). On the return leg, 36 convoys sailed for a total of 717 ship-journeys. Of these, 29 were lost (4 per cent), including 1 which went aground and 5 which were lost in a British minefield. This gives a total of 87 ships lost out of 1,528 sailings, or an average of 5.7 per cent.[3] Other scholars have reached different totals, by including vessels making independent journeys, giving 98 ships lost overall,[4] or by another count 103.[5] However, these numbers are close enough that the approximate figure is not in doubt.

Compared with the campaign in the Atlantic, the Arctic convoys were a more costly venture in terms of ships lost. A calculation has been made by Italian naval historian Fabio De Ninno of losses suffered by Allied merchant shipping across the North Atlantic at the height of the U-boat war in 1942–1943. He calculated that, across the northern Atlantic in those two years, 16,855 successful ship-journeys were made, for the loss of 308 ships: a loss rate of 1.79 per cent.[6] Thus, at its worst, the Atlantic run was only about a third as dangerous as its Arctic equivalent. Overall, in the Atlantic, losses work out at around 0.3 per cent, which is lower still. However, the Arctic was not the most costly supply run attempted by the Royal Navy. The attempts to supply Malta in 1940–1942 claim that title. Of 110 voyages by merchant ships to Malta in 35 separate operations, 79 arrived, 3 to be sunk soon after reaching the island and 1 sunk on a return voyage. Six of seven independent sailings failed. This equates to a merchant ship loss rate of over 30 per cent. In addition, the navy lost a battleship, two aircraft carriers, four cruisers, a fast minelayer, twenty destroyers and minesweepers and forty submarines in operations supporting the Malta convoys.[7] This compares with eighteen warships lost in the Arctic (along with one Polish submarine). Thus, the Arctic convoys were by no means the most perilous activity undertaken by Britain's Merchant and Royal Navies in the Second World War. The losses were also not evenly distributed chronologically. While 1942 was by any measure a terrible year in the Arctic, later Allied winter convoy campaigns in 1943–1944 and 1944–1945 saw light losses and significant damage inflicted on the enemy. To fully understand the nature of these losses, it is useful to break them down according to the cause of the sinkings, and the circumstances surrounding them. The value of intelligence needs also to be factored in. As intelligence historian Andrew Boyd described it: 'British knowledge of the overall threat they faced was uniformly excellent. However exploiting this intelligence tactically in fighting convoys through was more difficult, with each German threat posing different challenges.'[8] These challenges can be assessed individually.

THE U-BOAT THREAT

The traditional popular perception is that U-boats were the greatest threat to convoys. It is true that more merchantmen were lost to submarine attack in the Arctic than from any other cause, with forty-one ships lost in this way. However, that number is still fewer than half the total of ships lost, and air attack accounted for almost as many (thirty-seven ships). Admiral Dönitz was never convinced that his submarines were best used in the north, and, as we have seen, he several times argued for their removal. Ironically, they reached their highest numbers at the time when they were least effective due to Allied counter-measures, in 1944–1945. Clay Blair has calculated that just over a hundred individual U-boats served in the Arctic between 1941 and 1945.[9] That gives a ratio of only 1 ship sunk for every 2 submarines deployed in the campaign as a whole, which is not a particularly impressive record when it is considered that the overall U-boat fleet of 1,168 boats commissioned during the war sank 3,304 merchant vessels in total, or around 3 per boat on average.[10] Losses to the *U-bootwaffe* were also severe. Again, numbers vary, but figures of between thirty-eight and forty-one boats lost in the Arctic are often quoted.[11] This equates to an exchange of one U-boat sunk for every merchant ship sunk, not a ratio that would be considered sustainable by any navy. This also equates to a loss rate overall of around 40 per cent, again a high price to pay in boats and crews for only a modest benefit.

The U-boat effort against the Arctic convoys is a story of ever-diminishing returns. No sustained effort was made in 1941, but in the first half of 1942 the wolfpacks presented a genuine threat to the convoys, sinking twenty-four ships. However, this compares with sinkings in single figures for every other year of the war. At the outset, Allied escort resources were stretched and tactics primitive. As the war progressed and resources became more plentiful, assisted with better technology, convoy attack became harder and harder for the U-boats. Two key factors were in play. The first was air power. The addition of escort aircraft carriers to the convoys from PQ 18 onwards extended the search radius available to escort commanders exponentially. Even the few aircraft available on the early escort carriers could force U-boats to dive, depriving them of both speed and situational awareness just when they were closing in on their targets. This combined later with centimetric radar (both ship- and air-borne), which made even submarines at periscope depth vulnerable. German tactics also placed them at a further disadvantage, as collective 'wolfpack' attacks relied on either a U-boat or aircraft to shadow the convoy for a period of hours or days to allow other boats to close in for the attack. Once these shadowers were vulnerable to detection and attack, either in the air or on the surface, contact was often lost with a convoy before an attack could develop. Official Historian Stephen Roskill summed up the usefulness of the carriers:

> The need for escort carriers to accompany convoys, in order to provide anti-submarine patrols and fighter defence, had not been foreseen before the war; and the ships of that class were in fact all war-time improvisations. Yet wherever they appeared – on the Gibraltar route, in the north Atlantic, or in the Arctic – they at once proved their worth; and nowhere did they justify themselves more abundantly than in the stormy, ice-bound waters of the far north.[12]

The second factor working against the U-boats was the presence of 'fighting escorts' and, later, veteran Atlantic escort groups accompanying convoys. These were able to work along the route in advance of the convoys themselves, seeking out U-boat patrol lines and actively engaging them, attempting to blow a hole through the line of submarines through which the convoy could pass. Even in 1945, when the submarines congregated en masse off Kola Inlet, preliminary attack by escort groups allowed convoys to pass unscathed. This was on several occasions combined with deception operations, where the escorts would attack up the main seaway while the convoy passed by on an alternative, recently de-mined route.

All of these various measures combined to be increasingly effective. A final statistic about U-boat sinkings of merchantmen worth considering is that only around 60 per cent of the sinkings were of ships within escorted convoys. Seventeen ships (out of the forty-one lost) were sunk while straggling or otherwise separated from their escorts. In a particularly stark example, convoy PQ 17 was shadowed by U-boats and aircraft intermittently from 1 July 1942, but only three ships were lost (to air attack). All of the ten ship sinkings subsequently attributed to U-boats occurred after the convoy had scattered on the evening of 4 July and the ships were sailing independently. Even in this early period, a coherent, well-escorted convoy was a tough nut for U-boats to crack, and by late 1944 the nut had become almost impervious.

Given the challenges facing the U-boats, where does SIGINT fit into the picture? As has been described, throughout the campaign a significant proportion of U-boat wireless traffic was successfully intercepted and decrypted. However, the value of this material was variable. The delays in decryption meant that, on a good day, messages were read within a few hours, but on a bad day, the wait could be thirty-six hours or more. Frank Birch calculated that an average decryption delay for Home Waters traffic (DOLPHIN) in August 1942 was twenty hours and thirty minutes.[13] This meant that the tactical value of the intelligence was relatively limited. This was combined with a lack of sea-room, especially in the choke point around the North Cape, that meant that evasive routing of convoys to avoid U-boat patrol lines was not always possible in the way that it was, for example, in the Atlantic. Nonetheless, the constant communication that was maintained within U-boat groups, and with their shore-based controllers, meant that the Admiralty nearly always had some warning of where patrol lines were being formed across the path of the convoys, and how many boats were involved. In 1944 and 1945 in particular, this allowed the escort groups to seek out the patrol lines ahead of the convoy itself and make pre-emptive attacks.

The real value of U-boat SIGINT was more strategic. Long-term analysis of traffic allowed the Admiralty to keep a good understanding of the size of the enemy submarine fleet, its losses and state of readiness and its current doctrine and tactics. The latter was important, for example, when the policy of submarines fighting aircraft on the surface was promulgated to the U-boat fleet in 1943. The ability of Bletchley Park to monitor the success or otherwise of the T5 torpedo is another example. Again, Frank Birch summarised this benefit:

But what you will get cumulatively day after day on all subjects in all areas is a very complete picture and a very comprehensive knowledge. This is your background; it is solid and reliable and it grows more so. Your foreground, on its own, will continue to be sketchy and incomplete. [. . .]

This background should include a wide and detailed picture of the organisation, disposition and systems of the enemy's naval forces and auxiliaries [. . .] It is in the sustained synthesis of this material rather than in the chancy windfalls of current intelligence, that the essential value of the Special Intelligence source lies.[14]

THE GERMAN AIR FORCE

As has already been remarked on above, nearly half of the merchant ship losses inflicted on the Arctic convoys were from air attack, a total of thirty-seven ships. Of these losses, almost exactly half were inflicted by bombers and the other half by torpedo aircraft. However, it is notable that all but one of these sinkings occurred in a short period between March and July 1942. The explanation is simple: this was the only period when the *Luftwaffe* deployed a significant air-striking force to north Norway, consisting in particular of torpedo-bomber aircraft. The German air force was, as has been discussed, extremely slow to pick up on the potential of torpedo bombers, and it was not until 1942 that they had a viable strike force. The impact of that force was immediate. The massed torpedo attacks on convoys PQ 16, 17 and 18 showed the potential damage these aircraft could inflict, and although the cost in aircraft was high, the hit rate was also correspondingly devastating. Dividing the results, as was done with U-boats, into those ships lost while escorted and those lost while straggling or otherwise alone is also instructive. All but one of the ships sunk by aerial torpedo were in escorted convoys. This stems from the fact that, using tactics like the 'golden comb', it was possible to place a large number of torpedoes in a dense wave into a closely packed concentration of ships. Hits were almost inevitable, especially as doctrine required convoys to close up together when under air attack so as best to shelter under the anti-aircraft-gun umbrella of their escorts. Dive bombers, by contrast, were able to target unescorted ships more effectively, accounting for ten unescorted vessels and nine within convoys. Medium bombing from higher altitudes was almost entirely ineffective, except when used as a diversion in concert with a low-level torpedo attack.

In the first half of the campaign, the Allies had little or no effective defence against air attack. Existing naval escort vessels were equipped for air defence, but only a few specialist ships existed, and the navy was forced to build auxiliary anti-aircraft ships as a stop-gap. The smaller escorts also struggled to carry enough ammunition to fight off more than a couple of serious attacks. Only when carrier-borne fighter cover became available did the convoys have an effective air-defence capability, and as was explained above, this was also achieved via stop-gap measures: building impromptu escort carriers on merchant ship hulls. The CAM ships, with their catapulted Hurricane fighters, can be viewed only as what they were – a desperate emergency measure which had little overall effect. From an Allied point of view, therefore, it is fortunate that the *Luftwaffe* withdrew its torpedo bombers in later 1942. Had they remained in strength in the north, their impact would potentially have been very significant. As it was, the air threat was one of the factors which limited convoy sailings in the light summer months, but even at other times of year they had the potential to cause significant damage. Although it is beyond the scope of this work, the impact of land-based air power on naval operations in the Mediterranean was extremely significant, on both sides, as the losses in the Malta convoys described earlier testify. The dominance of air operations in the Pacific, where, lacking land bases, many of the aircraft were carrier-based, also demonstrates the significance of this arm in seaborne operations.

As with the U-boat fleet, intelligence was able to provide a thorough strategic understanding of the air picture. This was derived not only from Naval SIGINT but also from the prolific and more easily broken *Luftwaffe* wireless networks which were the domain of Bletchley Park's Huts 6 and 3, as well as minor codes analysis done in Josh Cooper's Air Section. The Admiralty was kept regularly informed of the scale of the air threat and the make-up of the enemy striking forces and their base locations. At a tactical level, however, once again SIGINT was less useful. As Andrew Boyd observed: 'By contrast, intelligence helped less in countering German air force attacks, which did most of the damage. German air force Enigma provided excellent coverage of order of battle and capability, notably the airborne torpedo threat, but its intercepts were rarely timely or precise enough to warn of specific attacks.'[15]

One solution to this, as has been described, was to place intercept teams (HEADACHE teams) aboard ship to provide local interception of both air-to-air and air-to-ground W/T and R/T chatter. These units were effective in picking up incoming raids, but the short distance between the bases at Bardufoss and Banak and the convoys off Bear Island, combined with the intercept range of VH/F signals, meant that the warnings given of incoming raids were typically counted in minutes, not hours, and there was little that the convoy commanders could do to counter them beyond standing wearily once again to action stations.

One area of *Luftwaffe* activity which did produce a significant SIGINT dividend was interception of communications to and from reconnaissance aircraft, especially the long-range FW 200 Condors. The sighting reports that these aircraft provided, and the homing signals that shadowing aircraft provided for U-boats, meant that both Bletchley Park and H/F-D/F units afloat often had a good indication of whether or not the enemy knew the whereabouts of a convoy, and if and when contact was lost. This was an asset to commanders both at sea and on shore, especially once German strategic thinking with regard to the protection of their surface ships was understood by the Allies. Enemy surface operations could be effectively ruled out unless the German air force had a good understanding of the operational situation, and of which Allied task forces were, or were not, at sea. This brings us to our last category of threat to the convoys: the enemy surface fleet.

THE GERMAN SURFACE FLEET

In the end, the surface units of the *Kriegsmarine* had a minimal material effect on the Arctic convoys, sinking only three merchant ships in the whole campaign. Their effect on the Royal Navy was more significant, with the cruisers HMS *Edinburgh* and *Trinidad*, the destroyer *Achates* and the minesweeper *Bramble* all lost as a result of combat with German surface ships. Significant damage was also inflicted on other warships in these engagements. However, the importance of the German surface units, and in particular the capital ships, lies more in their *potential* for destruction, and the strangle-hold this placed on Allied operations until the final destruction of *Tirpitz* in November 1944. The possibility of a sortie by a German surface task force had to be taken into account in the planning of each convoy, and a substantial part of the Home Fleet, including its principal battleships, as well as its often sole fleet aircraft carrier, were required to sail as covering forces each time a convoy cycle was undertaken. This placed a huge strain on Royal Navy resources, as is reflected in the suspension of Arctic operations on each occasion that ships were required for major operations elsewhere, such as operations TORCH or OVERLORD. The British heavy units also required their own escorts, further depleting the force of destroyers available for close escort of the convoys themselves. The hard-pressed Royal Navy cruiser squadrons were also called upon to accompany many of the convoys, and it was this branch of the service that did much of the surface fighting and took the greatest losses.

And yet, despite all this expenditure of effort, it is arguable that the Admiralty never really developed an effective strategy for dealing with the German surface threat. The danger from U-boats, and more particularly from German land-based air power, meant that the Royal Navy was extremely reluctant to commit any vessel larger than a destroyer east of Bear Island. This inevitably meant that the last and most dangerous portion of the convoys' route was available for German surface operations with very low risk of interference from Allied heavy units – a fact that the German Naval High Command was eager to exploit. Two factors worked in the Allies' favour. The first was simple good luck. For example, during Operation *SPORTPALAST* in March 1942, *Tirpitz* and its destroyers missed finding convoys PQ 12 and QP 8 due to bad weather and the mischance that the convoy was delayed on its route and not where it 'should' have been. On a different day with different weather, a much more disastrous outcome for the Allies might have resulted. Again, during Operation *OSTFRONT* in December 1943, Captain Johannesson's German destroyer flotilla came within a whisker of encountering convoy JW 55B, while its cruiser covering force was away dealing with *Scharnhorst*. Once more, disaster was narrowly avoided. Napoleon is said to have remarked that the first quality he wanted in his generals was luck; the same might be said for Allied convoy commodores.

The second factor was the German navy's strategic reluctance to engage its forces in direct combat with the Royal Navy. As the Naval Staff History described it: 'So long as the *Tirpitz* was battleworthy, the problem was never really solved, though in practice things worked out better than could have been expected. But this was due to the restrictions imposed on the German forces by Hitler, rather than to the intrinsic value of British protective measures.'[16]

This malign influence worked at two levels – the first was the *Führer's* and the *OKM's* reluctance to sanction operations in the first place, but the second was the shadow this cast over the at-sea commanders' tactical decision-making. In December 1942, Operation *REGENBOGEN* was initially executed to perfection by Admiral Kummetz, and convoy JW 51B was at his mercy, when he was intimidated into retreat by a greatly inferior force. This is not to detract from the bravery and skill of the Royal Navy destroyer and cruiser forces he faced, but by any normal measure he should have wrought havoc in that convoy. Similarly, the fate of the *Scharnhorst* a year later was sealed in part by the reluctance of Admiral Bey to pursue his mission, and by his misguided attempt to preserve his forces from attack, which in the end produced the opposite result.

It was in these surface operations that SIGINT was perhaps at its most useful, both strategically and tactically. At the long-term level, ULTRA and its supporting intelligence sources (coast-watchers and air reconnaissance) were able to keep close tabs on the locations of the German heavy units and their state of readiness for sea. The monitoring of the cycles of damage to, and repair of, *Tirpitz* are a case in point. The ship was tracked from the moment it left its slips in 1938 until its capsize in 1944. There was rarely a moment when the OIC did not have a good idea where it was, or at least where it had recently been. The story is the same for the other capital ships, including *Scharnhorst*, as well as the cruiser and destroyer squadrons. Part of the reason for this was the vice-like grip that German Naval High Command insisted on keeping over its Norwegian assets. Wireless traffic approving every movement of these vessels, as well as ancillary messages arranging mine-sweeper and air cover for their activities, meant that there was plentiful SIGINT available whenever any activity by the German surface fleet was in prospect. Equally, and arguably crucially, in the case of *Tirpitz* and PQ 17, the *absence* of this ancillary W/T activity was also a good indicator of the state of German operations. When an operation by the heavy units was planned, prior information was often also available concerning the nature of those plans. In this regard, the intelligence provided by Swedish interception of German landline communications provided a vital advantage, occasionally giving chapter and verse of the German plans, as was the case in Operation *RÖSSELSPRUNG* in July 1942.

The German fear of interception of their big ship operations by a British surface battlegroup also generated a quantity of useful SIGINT. As was described above, monitoring of German air reconnaissance efforts looking for the Home Fleet gave a good advance indicator of whether the *Kriegsmarine* thought it safe to put to sea. And so long as the task groups of the Home Fleet could remain undetected, it was a good bet that the German capital ships would remain in the fjords until they could be assured of non-interference by their Allied equivalents. Again, analysis of this intelligence often relied on inference from the absence of traffic rather than positive evidence of messages, but once the OIC understood the enemy mindset, this intelligence could be considered fairly reliable.

Once the German ships were at sea, the SIGINT picture was less clear. The primary difficulty was simply the time taken to decrypt traffic, which could be highly variable according to the point in the German key cycle at which operations took place. This was exacerbated by the short sailing distance from Altenfjord to the convoy routes, which could be covered by a German battleship in less than twelve hours. In order to understand the usefulness of ULTRA in these battles, a clear picture of the 'boom-and-bust' flow of SIGINT to the Admiralty has to be taken into account. Sometimes this worked in the Allies' favour; at other times, such as on 4 July 1942, it didn't. A second problem was the combination of security in the distribution of intelligence and confusion of command between land and sea. ULTRA was limited to officers of flag rank. This meant that, as we have seen, it was often the case that those at the sharp end, especially convoy commodores and destroyer flotilla commanders, remained in ignorance of the 'big picture', while their shadowing forces in battleships and cruisers had a much better idea what was going on.

Even for senior commanders, however, the picture was not always clear. As has been described, in March and again in July 1942, Admiral Tovey suffered from a partial flow of ULTRA to him while at sea; some information was shared and some was not. At the same time, he was obliged to make his own tactical decisions at some points but was directly commanded by the Admiralty at others. He further muddied the waters with his own ship-board SIGINT, which, lacking the experience of the analysts ashore, often reached erroneous conclusions. This situation improved as the war progressed. When Admiral Fraser sailed to sink the *Scharnhorst* in December 1943, he was both provided with good timely SIGINT and also left to make his own tactical decisions without back-seat driving from his superiors. A route was also found to provide ULTRA information in veiled form to more junior commanders so that they were also kept apprised of the tactical picture. One difficulty Fraser did have was exercising command and control of his own forces. He was obliged to break with normal communications security protocols on several occasions, exchanging positional information with his various groups of ships. Inquiries at the time by the Admiralty exonerated this conduct, but that may be because he won the battle. Had things turned out differently, he might have been subject to much more rigorous scrutiny. It also seems clear that, in this case, the German signals interception arrangements failed to exploit the intelligence which could have been generated by Fraser's W/T indiscretions.

Indeed, at this point some reference should be made to German SIGINT efforts. The story of ULTRA is often told as if it were a one-sided affair, with complete Allied success and utter German failure. However, as we have seen, this was by no means the case. The Germans had their share of genius codebreakers, and in the *B-Dienst* the German navy was equipped with a seasoned and efficient SIGINT agency. It was able to read Allied naval codes throughout much of the Arctic campaign. Often this took longer than it did at Bletchley Park, so the information was not as tactically 'hot' as it could have been, but, nonetheless, the Germans were able to predict the timetable of the Arctic convoys with fair accuracy, often referring to them by their correct convoy codes. They were also able to monitor Allied air activity and infer from it the timing of sorties by the Home Fleet. They also used D/F effectively on the Home Fleet battlegroups attacking the *Tirpitz* later in the war, even after their ability to read Allied codes had been substantially reduced. And yet, their ability to respond in a nimble way to intelligence information never seems to have fully developed. This was not just the case in the Arctic, or indeed in the war at sea. German intelligence efforts were stifled throughout the conflict by over-complex command structures, inter-service rivalries and ultimately by a leadership driven more by dogma and ambition than by strategic reality. A lot of battles were lost and good intelligence squandered by an institutional resistance to bad news. Thus, the *Kriegsmarine*, and the wider *Wehrmacht*, never reaped the full benefit of their intelligence capability. Had the climate been different, men such as Wilhelm Tranow might now be much more widely remembered, in addition to their opponents across the Channel such as Turing, Hinsley and Birch.

'WHEN THE SEA SHALL GIVE UP HER DEAD'

It would be remiss to complete this study without consideration of the human cost of the Arctic campaign. Again, popular culture has characterised these operations as especially lethal and unpleasant. This is probably because the weather and the coldness of the seas conjures an image of particular horror. The reality, however, is that being cast adrift from a sinking ship is no more pleasant in a warm sea than a cold one, and death comes equally to all those trapped in a sinking wreck wherever it goes down. The plight of merchant seamen is also singled out as if their lack of agency in combat makes their loss somehow more tragic. The figures for losses in the Arctic are as follows: 829 merchant seamen lost their lives on the convoys, while the Royal Navy lost 1,840 men. Although fewer Royal Navy ships were sunk, their crews were typically much larger than those of merchant ships, and the sinking of a single destroyer could result in substantial loss of life. Overall, the Allied loss amounted to 2,669 men. It should also be remembered that, in an era of mass conscription, many, if not most, of the Royal Naval personnel at sea in the Arctic were 'Hostilities Only' sailors, who had no more choice in being there or affinity for the sea than their colleagues in the merchant service.

On the German side, the death toll was much higher. The sinking of *Sharnhorst* and *Tirpitz* led to the deaths of over 3,000 men. More sailors died in the sinking of the *Scharnhorst* alone (1,932) than the Royal Navy lost in the whole campaign, Total surface ship crew losses amounted to 3,712. As has already been mentioned, the loss-rate for U-boat crews was worse still. Although they form a minority of the German casualties, 1,884 U-boatmen were killed in the campaign, a number proportionally higher than their surface colleagues, and about 40 per cent of the U-boats serving in the north were sunk. It is sobering to consider that of the ten U-boats which formed wolfpack *Eisteufel* which attacked PQ 17 in 1942, nine had been sunk by 1945, eight with all hands. Of the 417 crewmen aboard those nine boats, only four survived.[17]

It would be invidious to base conclusions on the success or failure of the campaign, and victory or defeat, on the respective losses of the two sides. But there is little doubt that in human and material terms the *Kriegsmarine* came off worse in the Arctic campaign compared with the Royal Navy. The fact also remains that more than 90 per cent of the tonnage of goods supplied to the Soviets, and the ships in which it was carried, arrived safely. Sceptics both at the time and since 1945 have questioned whether the continuation of convoys to Russia was a rational or worthwhile operation of war. In terms of the 'Safe and Timely Arrival' of the merchant shipping, which was so often cited as the navy's primary purpose, the campaign was broadly a success. Official Historian Stephen Roskill summed this up: 'The balance of success therefore plainly lay very much on the Allied side; and as the Royal Navy conducted all the operations, and provided almost all the escorts, that service may feel justifiably proud of an achievement as great as any recorded in its long history.'[18]

Writing in 1961, Roskill was not able to disclose the role SIGINT, and ULTRA in particular, played in the campaign, as these matters would remain secret for another fifteen years. However, there is little question that the Allied SIGINT operation, from the Y interceptors ashore and afloat, via the codebreakers of Hut 8, the analysts of Naval Section or the plotters in the OIC, made a significant contribution to the success of the overall campaign.

Frank Birch rather ruefully remarked in his history of Naval SIGINT:

> There lingered until the end of the war in certain elevated and rari-fied atmospheres several of the old popular superstitions about Sigint. A familiar one was the belief that codes and ciphers were broken by a few freakish individuals with a peculiar kink, no help,

and very little material except damp towels around their heads. Another was the quite common notion that 'if you knew the enemy's code, you knew what he was up to; if you didn't, you didn't'. It was not quite as simple as that.[19]

SIGINT in the Arctic was neither 'simple' nor flawless in its contributions to the battle. Problems arose both in the development of the intelligence itself and in its application by users ashore and afloat, but in the end it proved its value beyond any doubt. It is impossible to tell the story of the Russian convoys, or indeed the war at sea from 1939 to 1945, without thorough consideration of it.

ENDNOTES

1 THE WAR IN THE ARCTIC

1. J. Broome, *Convoy is to Scatter: The Story of PQ17* (1972), p. 192.
2. Broome, *Convoy is to Scatter*, p. 15.
3. Broome, *Convoy is to Scatter*, p. 229.
4. M. Llewellyn-Jones (ed.), *The Royal Navy and the Arctic Convoys: A Naval Staff History* (2007).
5. F.H. Hinsley, *British Intelligence in the Second World War: Its Influence on Strategy and Operations*, 5 volumes (1979–1981).
6. For example: M.G. Walling, *Forgotten Sacrifice: The Arctic Convoys of World War II* (2016); J.R. McKay, *Surviving the Arctic Convoys: The Wartime Memoirs of Leading Seaman Charlie Erswell* (2021).
7. For example: the documentary *PQ17: An Arctic Convoy Disaster* (BBC Productions, 2014).
8. For example: B. Edwards, *The Road to Russia: Arctic Convoys 1942* (2015); M. Lardas, *Arctic Convoys 1942: The Luftwaffe Cuts Russia's Lifeline* (2022).
9. For example: H. Sebag-Montefiore, *Enigma: The Battle for the Code* (2004); D. Kahn, *Seizing the Enigma: The Race to Break the German U-boat Codes, 1939–1943* (1992).
10. TNA Series DEFE3.
11. TNA Series ADM223.
12. Individual convoy reports are in TNA ADM237.
13. TNA HW43/10–43/25.
14. TNA HW11/14–11/37.
15. TNA HW11/36.
16. W. Churchill, *The Second World War*, Vol. 4: *The Hinge of Fate* (1951), p. 237.
17. M.L. Hadley, *Count Not the Dead: The Popular Image of the German Submarine* (1995), p. 1.
18. C. Blair, *Hitler's U-Boat War*, Vol. 1: *The Hunters, 1939–1942* (1996), p. xi.
19. C. Blair, *Hitler's U-Boat War*, Vol. 2: *The Hunted, 1939–1942* (1998), p. 707.
20. R. Woodman, *Arctic Convoys 1941–1945* (1994), p. 40.

21. P. Beesly, *Very Special Intelligence: The History of the Admiralty's Operational Intelligence Centre, 1939–1945* (1977), p. 125.
22. H. Anderson & L. Griffiths, 'G.C. & C.S. Naval History, Vol. 7: German Navy – The U-Boat Arm' (unpublished GCHQ typescript), BPT Archives, p. 35.
23. https://uboat.net/types/viic.htm (accessed 22 September 2021).
24. http://www.ww2incolor.com/forum/showthread.php/4537-German-Torpedo-Bombers-What-Were-they (accessed 20 June 2019).
25. https://www.dlbs.de/de/Projekte/Focke-Wulf-Condor/index.php (accessed 13 February 2023).
26. L. Griffiths, 'G.C. & C.S. Naval History, Vol. 23: Northern Waters' (unpublished GCHQ typescript, BP Archive D-6188-006), p. 59.
27. https://www.junobeach.org/canada-in-wwII/articles/submarines-attack-in-the-st-lawrence/western-approaches-tactical-policy-april-1943 (accessed 21 September 2021).
28. Woodman, *Arctic Convoys*, p. 32.
29. Woodman, *Arctic Convoys*, pp. 33–4.
30. Captain's confidential report by Admiral Sir John D. Kelly, 14 September 1933, https://web.archive.org/web/20180327144828/http://www.admirals.org.uk/admirals/fleet/toveyjc.php (accessed 21 September 2021).
31. Woodman, *Arctic Convoys*, p. 33.
32. F.H. Hinsley, *British Intelligence in the Second World War: Its Influence on Strategy and Operations*, Vol. 2 (1981), p. 214.

2 DOLPHIN AND OTHER ENIGMAS

1. Internet Movie Database, https://www.imdb.com/title/tt0028468 (accessed 9 April 2021).
2. R. Erskine, 'Birch, Francis Lyall [Frank]', *Oxford Dictionary of National Biography*, http://www.oxforddnb.com/view/10.1093/ref:odnb/9780198614128.001.0001/odnb-9780198614128-e-61099;jsessionid=B26F663B8BE74229E076E17C95EB3826.
3. GCHQ, 'Key Personalities at Bletchley Park 1939–1945' (unpublished typescript), BP Archives, p. 25.
4. F. Birch, *This Freedom of Ours* (1937).
5. Internet Movie Database, https://www.imdb.com/name/nm0083257 (accessed 2 February 2021).
6. W. Clarke, 'History of GCCS and its Naval Section, 1919–1945' (unpublished typescript), TNA HW3/16.
7. Handwritten letter, Birch to Clarke 3/9/1939, TNA HW8/21.
8. F. Birch, 'G. C. & C. S. Naval Sigint, Vol. 1: The Organisation and Evolution of British Naval Sigint' (unpublished typescript, 1952), TNA HW43/10, p. 96.
9. F. Birch, 'A History of British Sigint, 1914–1945, Vol. 1' (unpublished typescript), TNA HW43/1, pp. 62, 72.
10. GCHQ, 'Key Personalities at Bletchley Park', p. 25.
11. Kahn, *Seizing the Enigma*.
12. Barbara Abernethy, in M. Smith, *Station X: The Codebreakers of Bletchley Park* (1998) p. 26.

13. BPT Oral History Project, Mrs M. Morgan (née Darby), WRNS 3rd Officer, Bletchley Park, February 1942–July 1945. Hut 4, Block A, Naval Section, NS IX. Interviewed 21 Jan 2016.

14. P. Fitzgerald, *The Knox Brothers* (1978) p. 93.

15. BPT Oral History Project, Mrs Phyllis Drinkwater (née Garrett), Bletchley Park, 1942–1945. Block A, Naval Section, NS IX, signal distribution. Interviewed 12 April 2014.

16. J. Ferris, *Behind the Enigma: The Authorised History of GCHQ Britain's Secret Cyber-Intelligence Agency* (2020), p. 70.

17. English Heritage, 'Bletchley Park Buckinghamshire Architectural Investigation, Reports and Papers B/010/2004' (unpublished typescript, 2004), BP Archives, p. 130.

18. GCHQ, 'History of Bletchley Park Huts and Blocks 1939–45' (unpublished typescript), BP Archives, p. 13.

19. GC&CS organisational table, 4 August 1940, TNA HW14/6.

20. Miles Tandy, personal communication.

21. Birch, 'G. C. & C. S. Naval Sigint, Vol. 1', pp. 108–10.

22. Kahn, *Seizing the Enigma*, pp. 31–4.

23. Crypto Museum, https://www.cryptomuseum.com/crypto/enigma/m3/index.htm (accessed 9 April 2021).

24. Crypto Museum, https://cryptomuseum.com/crypto/enigma/i/index.htm (accessed 9 April 2021).

25. Olaf Ostwald, personal communication, 31 March 2021.

26. C. Alexander, 'Cryptographic History of Work on the German Naval Enigma' (unpublished typescript), TNA HW25/1, p. 5.

27. Numbers derived from H. Fletcher, 'Hut 6 Bombe Register', Vols 1–2, TNA HW25/19–20.

28. A.P. Mahon, 'The History of Hut Eight 1939–1945' (unpublished GCHQ typescript), TNA HW25/2, p. 24.

29. Birch, 'G. C. & C. S. Naval Sigint, Vol. 1', pp. 108–71.

30. GCHQ, 'History of Bletchley Park Huts and Blocks 1939–45'.

31. Mahon, 'The History of Hut Eight', p. 14.

32. C. Morris, 'Navy Ultra's Poor Relations', in F.H. Hinsley & A. Stripp (eds), *Codebreakers: The Inside Story of Bletchley Park* (1993), p. 243.

33. Kahn, *Seizing the Enigma*, pp. 106–12.

34. R. Erskine, 'Captured Kriegsmarine Enigma Documents at Bletchley Park', in *Cryptologia*, 32:3 (2008), p. 206.

35. Kahn, *Seizing the Enigma*, p. 117.

36. GCHQ, 'History of NS VI (Technical Intelligence)', TNA HW3/137, p. 10.

37. F. Birch, 'History of Naval Sigint, Vol. 4' (unpublished typescript), TNA HW43/15, p. 214.

38. Kahn, *Seizing the Enigma*, p. 136.

39. Birch, 'History of Naval Sigint, Vol. 4', p. 223.

40. Birch, 'History of Naval Sigint, Vol. 4', p. 225.

41. A.P. Mahon, 'History of I.D.8 G August 1939–December 1942' (unpublished GCHQ history), TNA HW3/134, p. 73.

42. Birch, 'History of Naval Sigint, Vol. 4', p. 228.

43. GC&CS, 'Technical intelligence and Captured documents', TNA HW50/15, p. 16.

44. GC&CS, 'Technical intelligence and Captured documents', p. 18.

45. Morris, 'Navy Ultra's Poor Relations', pp. 231–45.
46. Hinsley, *British Intelligence in the Second World War*, Vol. 2, p. 204.

3 THE BIG PICTURE

1. Sebag Montefiore, *Enigma*, p. 52.
2. F.H. Hinsley, 'BP, Admiralty, and Naval Enigma', in Hinsley & Stripp (eds), *Codebreakers*, p. 77.
3. Hinsley, 'BP, Admiralty, and Naval Enigma', p. 77.
4. Hinsley, 'BP, Admiralty, and Naval Enigma', p. 79.
5. Kahn, *Seizing the Enigma*, p. 145.
6. BPT Oral History Project, Caroline Chojecki (née Rowett), Foreign Office Civilian, Hut 4 and Block B, Naval Section NS IV, intelligence research on U-boats, unpublished typescript memoir.
7. Beesly, *Very Special Intelligence*, p. 127.
8. T. Insall, *Secret Alliances: Special Operations and Intelligence in Norway 1940–1945* (2019; paperback edn, 2021), p. 143.
9. Insall, *Secret Alliances*, p. 218.
10. BPT Oral History Project, E.M. Senior, Foreign Office Civilian, Block A, Naval Section, NS VI, Technical Intelligence, producing dictionary of technical terms. Interviewed June 2013.
11. BPT Oral History Project, G. Acason, WRNS, Block A, Naval Section, NS IV, U-boat signals index. Interviewed October 2014.
12. GC&CS, 'Historical Memorandum No. 33 The History of N.S. VI (Technical Intelligence)', TNA HW3/137, p. 5.
13. GC&CS, 'Historical Memorandum No. 33', p. 21.
14. GC&CS, 'Historical Memorandum No. 33', p. 51.
15. GC&CS, 'Historical Memorandum No. 33', p. 6.
16. GC&CS, 'Historical Memorandum No. 33', p. 10.
17. GC&CS, 'Historical Memorandum No. 33', p. 71.
18. GCHQ, 'History of the British Plot' (unpublished typescript), TNA HW3/145.
19. BPT Oral History Project, J. Tocher, WRNS Block A, Naval Section, NS IV, Watch head in British plot team maintaining plot of allied and enemy shipping. Interviewed July 2013.
20. BPT Oral History Project, J. Tocher. Interviewed July 2013.
21. BPT Oral History Project, S. Willson, WRNS, Block A(N), Naval Section, NS IV P, maintained British plot. Interviewed July 2015.
22. Birch, 'G. C. & C. S. Naval Sigint, Vol. 1', p. 22.
23. Birch, 'G. C. & C. S. Naval Sigint, Vol. 1', p. 21.
24. Birch, 'G. C. & C. S. Naval Sigint, Vol. 1', p. 18.
25. Birch, 'G. C. & C. S. Naval Sigint, Vol. 1', pp. 30–1.
26. Birch, 'G. C. & C. S. Naval Sigint, Vol. 1', p. 36.
27. Birch, 'A History of British Sigint, Vol. 1', p. 39.
28. Mahon, 'History of I.D.8 G August 1939–December 1942', p. 2.
29. Hinsley, 'BP, Admiralty, and Naval Enigma', p. 78.
30. Beesly, *Very Special Intelligence*, p. 39.
31. F.H. Hinsley, *British Intelligence in the Second World War: Its Influence on Strategy and Operations*, Vol. 1 (1979), pp. 141–3.
32. Hinsley, 'BP, Admiralty, and Naval Enigma', p. 78.

33. Birch, 'G. C. & C. S. Naval Sigint, Vol. 1', p. 141.
34. Beesly, *Very Special Intelligence*, p. 100.
35. Alec Dakin, 'The Z Watch in Hut 4, Part I', in Hinsley & Stripp (eds), *Codebreakers*, p. 50.
36. Dakin, 'The Z Watch in Hut 4, Part I', pp. 52–3.
37. Birch, 'G. C. & C. S. Naval Sigint, Vol. 1', p. 47.
38. Birch, 'A History of British Sigint, Vol. 1', p. 283.
39. Birch, 'G. C. & C. S. Naval Sigint, Vol. 1', p. 142.
40. GC&CS, 'Notes for Naval Section Output', TNA HW50/15.
41. Birch, 'G. C. & C. S. Naval Sigint, Vol. 1', p. 246.
42. D. Kahn, *Hitler's Spies: German Military Intelligence in World War II* (1978), p. 213.
43. Kahn, *Hitler's Spies*, p. 213.
44. Kahn, *Hitler's Spies*, p. 214.
45. Kahn, *Hitler's Spies*, p. 215.
46. Kahn, *Hitler's Spies*, p. 215.
47. Kahn, *Hitler's Spies*, p. 216.
48. Hinsley, *British Intelligence in the Second World War*, Vol. 2, pp. 635–40.
49. National Security Agency, 'Battle of the Atlantic, Volume III: German Naval Communications Intelligence, SRH-024', http://www.ibiblio.org/hyperwar/ETO/Ultra/SRH-024/index.html#index (accessed 27 June 2019).
50. *BdU* War Diary, 28 September 1941, quoted in R. Erskine & F. Weierud, 'Naval Enigma: M4 and its Rotors', in *Cryptologia*, 11:4 (1987), p. 235.
51. *BdU* War Diary, 24 October 1941, quoted in Erskine & Weierud, 'Naval Enigma', p. 235.
52. K. Dönitz, *Memoirs: Ten Years and Twenty Days* (1958; paperback edn, 1990), p. xv.

4 *TIRPITZ*: THE BATTLE THAT NEVER WAS

1. This account of the Fleet Air Arm attack is drawn from J. Sweetman, *Tirpitz: Hunting the Beast* (2000; paperback edn, 2004), pp. 29–30.
2. Convoy compositions are taken from www.convoyweb.org.uk.
3. Woodman, *Arctic Convoys*, p. 36.
4. Hinsley, *British Intelligence in the Second World War*, Vol. 2, p. 200.
5. Blair, *Hitler's U-boat War*, Vol. 1, p. 356.
6. J. Winton, *ULTRA at Sea* (1988), p. 58.
7. S.W. Roskill, *The War at Sea, 1939–1945*, Vol. 2: *The Period of Balance* (1956), p. 116.
8. Griffiths, 'G.C. & C.S. Naval History, Vol. 23', p. 52.
9. https://www.axishistory.com/books/364-germany-kriegsmarine/kriegsmarine-flottenstreitkraefte/6425-admiral-nordmeer (accessed 12 August 2021).
10. Woodman, *Arctic Convoys*, p. 40.
11. General Admiral Boehm, post-war essay quoted in H. Anderson & L. Griffiths, 'G.C. & C.S. Naval History, Vol. 2: German Navy – Organisation' (unpublished GCHQ typescript), BP Archives, p. 63.
12. PG/35193, quoted in Griffiths, 'G.C. & C.S. Naval History, Vol. 23', p. 60.
13. Woodman, *Arctic Convoys*, p. 53.
14. Woodman, *Arctic Convoys*, p. 58.
15. Griffiths, 'G.C. & C.S. Naval History, Vol. 23', pp. 62–3.
16. Sweetman, *Tirpitz*, p. 3.

17. Winton, *ULTRA at Sea*, p. 53.
18. Sweetman, *Tirpitz*, pp. 5–12.
19. ZTPG 28271 and ZTPG 28274, 15 January 1942, TNA DEFE3/79.
20. ZTPG 28279, 15 January 1942, TNA DEFE3/79.
21. Sweetman, *Tirpitz*, p. 24.
22. https://www.kbismarck.com/prinzeugen.html (accessed 11 August 2021).
23. ZTPG 35405, 21 February 1942, TNA DEFE3/86.
24. Admiralty to C-in-C Home Fleet, 1826A/17 February, TNA ADM223/109.
25. https://www.kbismarck.com/prinzeugen.html (accessed 11 August 2021).
26. Blair, *Hitler's U-boat War*, Vol. 1, p. 356.
27. Hinsley, *British Intelligence in the Second World War*, Vol. 2, p. 205.
28. Hinsley, *British Intelligence in the Second World War*, Vol. 2, p. 205.
29. Roskill, *The War at Sea*, Vol. 2, p. 124.
30. Woodman, *Arctic Convoys*, p. 68.
31. Roskill, *The War at Sea*, Vol. 2, p. 119.
32. Woodman, *Arctic Convoys*, p. 72.
33. ZTPG/36827, 6 March 1942, TNA DEFE3/87.
34. Admiralty to C-in-C Home Fleet, 1518A/7 March, TNA ADM223/109.
35. C-in-C's Report, TNA ADM199/347, para. 10, quoted in Hinsley, *British Intelligence in the Second World War*, Vol. 2, p. 205.
36. Admiralty to C-in-C Home Fleet, 0057A/8 March, TNA ADM223/109.
37. Admiralty to C-in-C Home Fleet, 1225A/8 March, TNA ADM223/109.
38. Hinsley, *British Intelligence in the Second World War*, Vol. 2, p. 209.
39. Admiralty to C-in-C Home Fleet, 1500A/8 March, TNA ADM223/109.
40. ZTPG 37124, 8 February 1942, TNA DEFE3/88.
41. Admiralty to C-in-C Home Fleet, 2331A/8 March, TNA ADM223/109.
42. Admiralty to C-in-C Home Fleet, 0148A/9 March, TNA ADM223/109.
43. Hinsley, *British Intelligence in the Second World War*, Vol. 2, p. 210.
44. Admiralty to C-in-C Home Fleet, 0248A/9 March, TNA ADM223/109.
45. Sweetman, *Tirpitz*, p. 29.
46. Woodman, *Arctic Convoys*, p. 77.
47. Sweetman, *Tirpitz*, p. 34.
48. Woodman, *Arctic Convoys*, p. 80.
49. C-in-C's Report, TNA ADM199/347, para. 7, quoted in Hinsley, *British Intelligence in the Second World War*, Vol. 2, p. 206.
50. *Tirpitz* War Diary, 1–15 March 1942, http://www.kbismarck.com/archives/tp-ktb1-15mar42.pdf (accessed 19 August 2021).
51. ZTPG 36977, 7 March 1942, TNA DEFE3/87.
52. *Tirpitz* War Diary, 1–15 March 1942.
53. *Tirpitz* War Diary, 1–15 March 1942, emphasis in original.
54. Beesly, *Very Special Intelligence*, p. 129.
55. Admiralty to C-in-C Home Fleet, 1007A/9 March, TNA ADM223/109.
56. Admiralty to C-in-C Home Fleet, 0640A/10 March, TNA ADM223/109.
57. ZTPG 36843, 6 March 1942, TNA DEFE3/87.
58. ZTPG 36853, 6 March 1942, TNA DEFE3/87.
59. For example, ZTPG/36856-8, 6 March 1942, TNA DEFE3/87.
60. Griffiths, 'G.C. & C.S. Naval History, Vol. 23', pp. 65–6.
61. Roskill, *The War at Sea*, Vol. 2, p. 124.
62. Beesly, *Very Special Intelligence*, p. 80.

63. Birch, 'G.C. & C.S. Naval Sigint, Vol. 1', p. 298.
64. Hinsley, *British Intelligence in the Second World War*, Vol. 2, p. 209.

5 THE SHIP THAT SANK ITSELF

1. http://www.naval-history.net/WW2aBritishLosses10tables.htm (accessed 9 May 2022).
2. https://en.wikipedia.org/wiki/Fiji-class_cruiser (accessed 10 March 2022).
3. Llewellyn-Jones, *The Royal Navy and the Arctic Convoys*, p. 24.
4. Woodman, *Arctic Convoys*, p. 85.
5. Griffiths, 'G.C. & C.S. Naval History, Vol. 23', p. 67.
6. Griffiths, 'G.C. & C.S. Naval History, Vol. 23', p. 67.
7. Admiralty to C-in-C Home Fleet, 1905A/20 March, TNA ADM223/109.
8. Llewellyn-Jones, *The Royal Navy and the Arctic Convoys*, p. 24.
9. ZTPG 38391, 38392, 38403, 19 March 1942, TNA DEFE3/89.
10. Roskill, *The War at Sea*, Vol. 2, p. 125.
11. ZTPG 38961, 20 March 1942, TNA DEFE3/89.
12. Admiralty message 1336A/23, referenced in Llewellyn-Jones, *The Royal Navy and the Arctic Convoys*, p. 24.
13. ZTPG38878, 38901, 20 March 1942, TNA DEFE3/89.
14. Llewellyn-Jones, *The Royal Navy and the Arctic Convoys*, p. 25.
15. ZTPG 39459, 39488, 25 March 1942, TNA DEFE3/89.
16. Admiralty to C-in-C Home Fleet, 2326A/26 March, TNA ADM223/109.
17. ZTPG 39544, 25 March 1942, TNA DEFE3/89; Admiralty 0001A/27 March 1942, TNA ADM223/109.
18. ZTPG 39738, 39749, 39754, 26 March 1942, TNA DEFE3/89.
19. Admiralty to C-in-C Home Fleet, 1645A/27, 1825A/27, 1826A/27 1827A/27 and 2148A/27 March, TNA ADM223/109.
20. Llewellyn-Jones, *The Royal Navy and the Arctic Convoys*, p. 25.
21. ZTPG 40028, 40030, 40047, 28 March 1942, TNA DEFE3/89.
22. ZTPG 40037, 28 March 1942, TNA DEFE3/89.
23. Woodman, *Arctic Convoys*, p. 90.
24. Woodman, *Arctic Convoys*, pp. 92–5.
25. Llewellyn-Jones, *The Royal Navy and the Arctic Convoys*, pp. 30–31.
26. Llewellyn-Jones, *The Royal Navy and the Arctic Convoys*, p. 32.
27. Griffiths, 'G.C. & C.S. Naval History, Vol. 23', p. 68.
28. Griffiths, 'G.C. & C.S. Naval History, Vol. 23', p. 69.
29. ZTPG 40488, 2 April 1942, TNA DEFE3/89 and ZTPG 41114, 4 April 1942, TNA DEFE3/90, summarised in Admiralty to C-in-C Home Fleet, 1931B/5, TNA ADM223/110.
30. ZTPG 42094, 8 April 1942, TNA DEFE3/91.
31. Llewellyn-Jones, *The Royal Navy and the Arctic Convoys*, p. 34.
32. Woodman, *Arctic Convoys*, p. 114.
33. Woodman, *Arctic Convoys*, p. 115.
34. Llewellyn-Jones, *The Royal Navy and the Arctic Convoys*, p. 34
35. ZTPG 42569, 11 April 1942, TNA DEFE3/93.
36. Woodman, *Arctic Convoys*, p. 108.
37. ZTPG 42617, 12 April 1942, TNA DEFE3/93.
38. ZTPG 42628, 12 April 1942, TNA DEFE3/93.

39. ZTPG 42958, 42959, 13 April 1942, TNA DEFE3/93.
40. ZTPG 43402, 15 April 1942, TNA DEFE3/94.
41. ZTPG 43942, 18 April 1942, TNA DEFE3/94.
42. Quoted in Llewellyn-Jones, *The Royal Navy and the Arctic Convoys*, p. 35.
43. Griffiths, 'G.C. & C.S. Naval History, Vol. 23', p. 71.
44. Admiralty to C-in-C Home Fleet, 1900B/26, 1604B/27 and 1739B/28 April 1942, TNA ADM223/110.
45. Griffiths, 'G.C. & C.S. Naval History, Vol. 23', p. 72.
46. Griffiths, 'G.C. & C.S. Naval History, Vol. 23', p. 76.
47. ZTPG 46093, 30 April 1942, TNA DEFE3/97.
48. Woodman, *Arctic Convoys*, p. 129.
49. Quoted in Llewellyn-Jones, *The Royal Navy and the Arctic Convoys*, p. 36.
50. ZTPG 46085, 30 April 1942, TNA DEFE3/97.
51. ZTPG 46087, 30 April 1942, TNA DEFE3/97.
52. ZTPG 46716, 1 May 1942, TNA DEFE3/97.
53. Llewellyn-Jones, *The Royal Navy and the Arctic Convoys*, p. 38.
54. ZTPG 46508, 1 May 1942, TNA DEFE3/97.
55. ZTPG 46517, 1 May 1942, TNA DEFE3/97.
56. Woodman, *Arctic Convoys*, p. 126.
57. Llewellyn-Jones, *The Royal Navy and the Arctic Convoys*, p. 42.
58. ZTPG 46915, 3 May 1942, TNA DEFE3/97.
59. ZTPG 46549, 3 May 1942, TNA DEFE3/97.
60. Llewellyn-Jones, *The Royal Navy and the Arctic Convoys*, p. 44.
61. Griffiths, 'G.C. & C.S. Naval History, Vol. 23', p. 79.
62. Griffiths, 'G.C. & C.S. Naval History, Vol. 23', p. 80.
63. Griffiths, 'G.C. & C.S. Naval History, Vol. 23', p. 81.
64. Llewellyn-Jones, M, *The Royal Navy and the Arctic Convoys*, p. 46.
65. Quoted in Llewellyn-Jones, *The Royal Navy and the Arctic Convoys*, p. 46.
66. Admiralty to C-in-C Home Fleet, 0020A/27 March 1942, TNA ADM223/109.
67. Admiralty to C-in-C Home Fleet, 1827/27 March 1942, TNA ADM223/109.
68. Admiralty to C-in-C Home Fleet, 0506B/13 April 1942, TNA ADM223/110.
69. Admiralty to C-in-C Home Fleet, 2357B/14 April 1942, TNA ADM223/110.
70. Admiralty to C-in-C Home Fleet, 1553B/21 April 1942, TNA ADM223/110.
71. ZTPG 46133 and 46175, 29 April, TNA DEFE3/97.
72. Admiralty to C-in-C Home Fleet, 0020A/27 March 1942, TNA ADM223/109.
73. Admiralty to C-in-C Home Fleet, 1645A/27, 1825A/27, 1826A/27, 2148A/27 March 1942, TNA ADM223/109.
74. ZTPG 40030, 40106, 40124, 28 April 1942, TNA DEFE3/91.
75. ZTPG 42570, 11 April 1942, TNA DEFE3/93.
76. ZTPG 42954, 13 April 1942, TNA DEFE3/93; Admiralty to C-in-C Home Fleet, 1542B/14 April 1942, TNA ADM223/110.
77. ZTPG 46091, 30 April 1942, TNA DEFE3/97.
78. Admiralty to C-in-C Home Fleet, 1402B/1 May 1942, TNA ADM223/110.

6 'CONVOY IS TO SCATTER'

1. 'A History of the R/T "Y" Organisation Ashore and Afloat July 1940 to May 1945', TNA HW8/99.

2. This quotation and other information concerning Jack Purvis is derived from his written memoir, donated to Bletchley Park Trust by his son, J. Purvis.

3. Llewellyn-Jones, *The Royal Navy and the Arctic Convoys*, p. 47.

4. Adm. Sir J.C. Tovey, 'Convoys to North Russia, 1942', Supplement to *London Gazette*, 13 October 1950, p. 5143.

5. Llewellyn-Jones, *The Royal Navy and the Arctic Convoys*, p. 49.

6. R.G. Onslow, quoted in Roskill, *The War at Sea*, Vol. 2, p. 131.

7. https://uboat.net/ops/wolfpacks/216.html (accessed 16 June 2022).

8. Admiralty to C-in-C Home Fleet 1645B/19 May, TNA ADM223/111.

9. Admiralty to C-in-C Home Fleet 1231B/23 May, TNA ADM223/111.

10. ZTPG 51643, 23 May 1942, TNA DEFE3/101, reported in Admiralty to C-in-C Home Fleet 0058B/25 May, TNA ADM223/111.

11. Llewellyn-Jones, *The Royal Navy and the Arctic Convoys*, p. 50.

12. Woodman, *Arctic Convoys*, p. 147.

13. Llewellyn-Jones, *The Royal Navy and the Arctic Convoys*, p. 51.

14. *BdU* War Diary, 3 June 1942, quoted in Llewellyn-Jones, *The Royal Navy and the Arctic Convoys*, p. 51.

15. Blair, *Hitler's U-boat War*, Vol. 1, p. 658.

16. Beesly, *Very Special Intelligence*, p. 130.

17. Griffiths, 'G.C. & C.S. Naval History, Vol. 23', p. 82.

18. Hinsley, *British Intelligence in the Second World War*, Vol. 2, p. 213.

19. Beesly, *Very Special Intelligence*, p. 132.

20. https://en.wikipedia.org/wiki/Order_of_battle_for_Convoy_PQ_17 (accessed 14 August 2019).

21. Hinsley, *British Intelligence in the Second World War*, Vol. 2, p. 213.

22. Admiralty to C-in-C Home Fleet, 1729B/22 June 1942, TNA ADM223/111.

23. ZTPG 59109, 1 July 1942, TNA DEFE3/110.

24. Hinsley, *British Intelligence in the Second World War*, Vol. 2, p. 215.

25. ZTPG 59351, 2 July 1942, TNA DEFE3/110.

26. Griffiths, 'G.C. & C.S. Naval History, Vol. 23', p. 83. See also ZTPG 59371, 1 July 1942, TNA DEFE3/110.

27. ZTPG 59368, 1 July 1942, TNA DEFE3/110.

28. ZTPG 59366, 2 July 1942, TNA DEFE3/110.

29. Admiralty to C-in-C Home Fleet, 1313B/2 July 1942, TNA ADM223/111.

30. ZTPG 59381, 2 July 1942, TNA DEFE3/110.

31. Admiralty to C-in-C Home Fleet, 1017B/3 July 1942, TNA ADM223/111.

32. Griffiths, 'G.C. & C.S. Naval History, Vol. 23', p. 84.

33. Beesly, *Very Special Intelligence*, p. 133.

34. ZTPG 59447, 3 July 1942, TNA DEFE3/110.

35. Admiralty to C-in-C Home Fleet, 1754B/3 July 1942, TNA ADM223/111.

36. ZTPG 59915, 3 July 1942, TNA DEFE3/110.

37. ZTPG 59972, 3 July 1942, TNA DEFE3/110.

38. Griffiths, 'G.C. & C.S. Naval History, Vol. 23', p. 85.

39. Woodman, *Arctic Convoys*, p. 204.

40. Beesly, *Very Special Intelligence*, p. 133.

41. Beesly, *Very Special Intelligence*, p. 137.

42. This account is summarised in Hinsley, *British Intelligence in the Second World War*, Vol. 2, pp. 217–19. A copy of the original report is also held in Bletchley Park Trust Archives D-1655-009.

43. ZTPG 59863 and ZTPG 59864, 3 July 1942, TNA DEFE3/110.
44. ZTPG 59868, 3 July 1942, TNA DEFE3/110.
45. ZTPG 59870, 4 July 1942, TNA DEFE3/110.
46. Hinsley, *British Intelligence in the Second World War*, Vol. 2, Appendix 11, p. 688.
47. Beesly, *Very Special Intelligence*, p. 134.
48. ZTPG 59910, 4 July 1942, TNA DEFE3/110.
49. ZTPG 59892, 4 July 1942, TNA DEFE3/110.
50. ZTPG 59900, 4 July 1942, TNA DEFE3/110.
51. Hinsley, *British Intelligence in the Second World War*, Vol. 2, Appendix 11, p. 688.
52. ZTPG 59899, 4 July 1942, TNA DEFE3/110.
53. Woodman, *Arctic Convoys*, p. 209.
54. Woodman, *Arctic Convoys*, p. 213.
55. Admiralty Message 2111B, 4 July 1942, TNA ADM237/168.
56. Admiralty Message 2123B, 4 July 1942, TNA ADM237/168.
57. Admiralty Message 2136B, 4 July 1942, TNA ADM237/168.
58. Woodman, *Arctic Convoys*, p. 216.
59. Hinsley, *British Intelligence in the Second World War*, Vol. 2, Appendix 11, p. 688.
60. For example, ZTPG 60062 and ZTPG 60063, 4 July 1942, TNA DEFE3/110.
61. Hinsley, *British Intelligence in the Second World War*, Vol. 2, p. 222.
62. ZTPG 60237, 5 July 1942, TNA DEFE3/110.
63. Hinsley, *British Intelligence in the Second World War*, Vol. 2, Appendix 11, p. 689.
64. Hinsley, *British Intelligence in the Second World War*, Vol. 2, p. 221.
65. ZTPG 60448, 6 July 1942, TNA DEFE3/110.
66. Beesly, *Very Special Intelligence*, pp. 124 and 141.
67. Hinsley, *British Intelligence in the Second World War*, Vol. 2, p. 222.
68. Llewellyn-Jones, *The Royal Navy and the Arctic Convoys*, p. 70.
69. ZTPG 60438, 5 July 1942, TNA DEFE3/110.
70. ZTPG 60448, 6 July 1942, TNA DEFE3/110.
71. Hinsley, *British Intelligence in the Second World War*, Vol. 2, p. 214.
72. Woodman, *Arctic Convoys*, p. 139.
73. Beesly, *Very Special Intelligence*, p. 137.

7 'THE GOLDEN COMB'

1. P.C. Smith, *Convoy PQ18: Arctic Victory* (1975; paperback edn, 1977).
2. A. Cunningham, *A Sailor's Odyssey* (1951), p. 140.
3. R. Hill, *Destroyer Captain* (1975; paperback edn, 1979), p. 56.
4. J. Tovey, writing in foreword to D. Pope, *73 North: The Battle of the Barents Sea* (1958; paperback edn, 2005), pp. x–xi.
5. W. Churchill, *The Second World War*, Vol. 4, p. 238.
6. Llewellyn-Jones, *The Royal Navy and the Arctic Convoys*, p. 72.
7. 'Report on G.A.F. "Y" Activity – P.Q.18 H.M.S. Scylla – September 1942', TNA HW14/53.
8. Llewellyn-Jones, *The Royal Navy and the Arctic Convoys*, p. 72.
9. Smith, *Convoy PQ18: Arctic Victory*, p. 129.
10. Llewellyn-Jones, *The Royal Navy and the Arctic Convoys*, p. 74.
11. Smith, *Convoy PQ18: Arctic Victory*, p. 130.
12. Griffiths, 'G.C. & C.S. Naval History, Vol. 23', p. 85.

13. Schmundt was transferred in August 1942; the post was occupied by *Konteradmiral* August Thiele in a caretaker role before *Konteradmiral* Otto Klüber took over permanently in September, https://www.oocities.org/~orion47/WEHRMACHT/KRIEGSMARINE/Konteradmirals/KLUEBER_OTTO.html (accessed 17 August 2022).
14. Woodman, *Arctic Convoys*, p. 262.
15. ZTPG 73200, 73201, 73203, 9 September 1942, TNA DEFE3/192.
16. Admiralty to C-in-C Home Fleet, 1839A/10 September, TNA ADM223/111.
17. Llewellyn-Jones, *The Royal Navy and the Arctic Convoys*, p. 76.
18. Llewellyn-Jones, *The Royal Navy and the Arctic Convoys* p. 77.
19. ZTPG 74191, 74192, 74198, 74199, 74204, 13 September 1942, TNA DEFE3/193.
20. Admiralty to C-in-C Home Fleet, 1229A and 1518A/13 September, TNA ADM223/112.
21. https://uboat.net/allies/merchants/ship/2170.html (accessed 17 August 2022).
22. Llewellyn-Jones, *The Royal Navy and the Arctic Convoys*, p. 79.
23. ZTPG 74428, 74433, 74533, 14 September 1942, TNA DEFE3/193.
24. Admiralty to C-in-C Home Fleet, 1306A and 1550A/15 September, TNA ADM223/112.
25. ZTPG 74638, 14 September 1942, TNA DEFE3/193.
26. https://uboat.net/allies/merchants/ship/2170.html.
27. ZTPG 74870, 17 September 1942, TNA DEFE3/193.
28. Llewellyn-Jones, *The Royal Navy and the Arctic Convoys*, p. 82.
29. https://uboat.net/allies/merchants/ship/2170.html.
30. https://uboat.net/allies/merchants/ship/2170.html.
31. ZTPG 75260, 20 September 1942, TNA DEFE3/194.
32. ZTPG 75289, 20 September 1942, TNA DEFE3/194.
33. Admiralty to C-in-C Home Fleet, 0743A/20, 0916A/20 and 1123A/20 September 1942, TNA ADM223/112.
34. Hinsley, *British Intelligence in the Second World War*, Vol. 2, p. 222.
35. Hinsley, *British Intelligence in the Second World War*, Vol. 2, p. 224.
36. Birch, 'G.C. & C.S. Naval Sigint, Vol 1', p. 87.
37. Admiralty to C-in-C Home Fleet, 0310A/11 September 1942, TNA ADM223/112.
38. Admiralty to C-in-C Home Fleet, 0740A/11 September 1942, TNA ADM223/112.
39. Admiralty to C-in-C Home Fleet, 1603A/11 September 1942, TNA ADM223/112.
40. Hinsley, *British Intelligence in the Second World War*, Vol. 2, p. 225.
41. ZTPG 74188, 20 September 1942, TNA DEFE3/193.
42. Admiralty to C-in-C Home Fleet, 2325A/13 September 1942, TNA ADM223/112.
43. ZTPG 74198, 20 September 1942, TNA DEFE3/193.
44. Admiralty to C-in-C Home Fleet, 1125A/15 September 1942, TNA ADM223/112.
45. Admiralty to C-in-C Home Fleet, 0400A/16 September 1942, TNA ADM223/112.
46. Hinsley, *British Intelligence in the Second World War*, Vol. 2, p. 226.
47. Admiralty to C-in-C Home Fleet, 1739A/17 September 1942, TNA ADM223/112.
48. Admiralty to C-in-C Home Fleet, 1142A/19 September 1942, TNA ADM223/112.
49. Llewellyn-Jones, *The Royal Navy and the Arctic Convoys*, p. 80.
50. Les Sayer, quoted in M. Arthur, *Lost Voices of the Royal Navy: Vivid Eyewitness Accounts of Life in the Royal Navy from 1914 to 1945* (paperback edn, 2005), pp. 392–4.
51. ZTPG 73215, 9 September 1942, TNA DEFE3/192.
52. ZTPG 73995, 12 September 1942, TNA DEFE3/192.
53. ZTPG 74878, 16 September 1942, TNA DEFE3/193.

54. ZTPG 75135, 18 September 1942, TNA DEFE3/194.
55. J. Tovey, despatch, quoted in Llewellyn-Jones, *The Royal Navy and the Arctic Convoys*, p. 85.
56. Report by Admiral Burnett, quoted in Llewellyn-Jones, *The Royal Navy and the Arctic Convoys*, p. 85.
57. Report by Admiral Burnett, quoted in Llewellyn-Jones, *The Royal Navy and the Arctic Convoys*, p. 85.
58. 'Report on G.A.F "Y" Activity – P.Q.18 H.M.S. Scylla – September 1942', TNA HW14/53.
59. 'Y Operations on Board HMS Scylla with PQ18', TNA HW/14/55.
60. 'Y Operations on Board HMS Scylla with PQ18', TNA HW/14/55.
61. 'Report on G.A.F "Y" Activity – P.Q.18 H.M.S. Scylla – September 1942', TNA HW14/53.
62. Llewellyn-Jones, *The Royal Navy and the Arctic Convoys*, p. 86.
63. Admiralty to C-in-C Home Fleet 1325A/5 November 1942, TNA ADM2298/112.
64. https://uboat.net/ops/wolfpacks/240.html (accessed 23 August 2022).
65. Woodman, *Arctic Convoys*, p. 307.
66. Admiralty to C-in-C Home Fleet 1354A/20 November 1942, TNA ADM2298/113.
67. Admiralty to C-in-C Home Fleet 1550A/20 November 1942, TNA ADM2298/113.
68. Blair, *Hitler's U-Boat War*, Vol. 2, p. 22.

8 RAEDER'S LAST GAMBLE

1. From Caroline Chojecki (née Rowett) lecture at RMA Sandhurst 1992, BP Archives.
2. Caroline Chojecki (née Rowett) lecture at RMA Sandhurst 1992.
3. TNA PRO HW14/1.
4. Unless otherwise stated, this section is drawn from English Heritage, 'Bletchley Park Buckinghamshire Architectural Investigation, Reports and Papers B/010/2004', Vol. 2, 8.1 and 8.2.
5. TNA HW14/22.
6. Memorandum from F. Birch, 7 November 1941, TNA HW8/23.
7. Birch, 'G. C. & C. S. Naval Sigint, Vol. 1', p. 221.
8. Birch, 'G. C. & C. S. Naval Sigint, Vol. 1', p. 241.
9. Caroline Chojecki (née Rowett) lecture at RMA Sandhurst 1992.
10. S. Budiansky, *Blackett's War: The Men who Defeated the Nazi U-boats and Brought Science to the Art of Warfare* (2013), pp. 222–6.
11. Tovey, 'Convoys to North Russia, 1942', pp. 5151–2.
12. N. Falconer, 'On the Size of Convoys: An Example of the Methodology of Leading Wartime OR Scientists', in *Operational Research Quarterly*, 27:2, part 1 (1976), p. 317.
13. Tovey, 'Convoys to North Russia, 1942', p. 5152.
14. Hinsley, *British Intelligence in the Second World War*, Vol. 2, p. 528.
15. Hinsley, *British Intelligence in the Second World War*, Vol. 2, p. 526.
16. Llewellyn-Jones, *The Royal Navy and the Arctic Convoys*, p. 88.
17. ZTPG 93689, 93694, 17 December 1942, TNA DEFE3/212, and ZTPG 04205, 94206, 17 December 1942, TNA DEFE3/213.
18. Tovey, 'Convoys to North Russia, 1942', p. 5152.
19. ZTPG 96334, 27 December 1942, TNA DEFE3/215.

20. Admiralty to C-in-C Home Fleet, 1236A/29 December 1942, TNA ADM223/114.
21. Griffiths, 'G.C. & C.S. Naval History, Vol. 23', p. 99.
22. Pope, *73 North*, p. 111.
23. ZTPG 96742, 30 December 1942, TNA DEFE3/215.
24. Pope, *73 North*, p. 117.
25. ZTPG 96682, 30 December 1942, TNA DEFE3/215.
26. Admiralty to C-in-C Home Fleet, 2015A/30 December 1942, TNA ADM223/114.
27. Llewellyn-Jones, *The Royal Navy and the Arctic Convoys*, p. 93.
28. Roskill, *The War at Sea*, Vol. 2, p. 293.
29. C-in-C to Admiral Burnett, 1127A/27, quoted in Llewellyn-Jones, *The Royal Navy and the Arctic Convoys*, p. 92.
30. The following account of the action of 31 December is largely drawn from Llewellyn-Jones, *The Royal Navy and the Arctic Convoys*, pp. 93–101.
31. 'Senior Officer Force R's Report No. H.D.0571A of 6th January 1943', TNA ADM199/73.
32. Woodman, *Arctic Convoys*, p. 329.
33. S. Kerslake, *Coxswain in the Northern Convoys* (1984), http://www.naval-history.net/WW2Memoir-RussianConvoyCoxswain07.htm (accessed 12 October 2022).
34. Tovey, 'Convoys to North Russia, 1942', p. 5154.
35. Roskill, *The War at Sea*, Vol. 2, pp. 292–3.
36. Report of Commander Kinloch, quoted in Llewellyn-Jones, *The Royal Navy and the Arctic Convoys*, p. 103.
37. Extract from log of *Hipper*, NID 24/X9/45, quoted in Llewellyn-Jones, *The Royal Navy and the Arctic Convoys*, p. 103.
38. ZTPG 96704, 30 December 1942, TNA DEFE3/215.
39. Griffiths, 'G.C. & C.S. Naval History, Vol. 23', p. 104.
40. ZTPG 96732, 31 December 1942, TNA DEFE3/215.
41. Beesly, *Very Special Intelligence*, p. 205.
42. ZTPG 96789, 1 January 1943, TNA DEFE3/215.
43. ZTPG 96803, 31 December 1942, TNA DEFE3/215.
44. ZTPG 96805, 31 December 1942, TNA DEFE3/215.
45. ZTPG 96850, 31 December 1942, TNA DEFE3/215.
46. ZTPG 96912, 31 December 1942, TNA DEFE3/215.
47. Griffiths, 'G.C. & C.S. Naval History, Vol. 23', p. 102.
48. Woodman, *Arctic Convoys*, p. 330.
49. Dönitz, *Memoirs*, p. 311.
50. J. Winton, *The Death of the Scharnhorst* (1983; paperback edn, 2000), p. 13.
51. Hinsley, *British Intelligence in the Second World War*, Vol. 2, p. 531.
52. Broadcast quoted in Blair, *Hitler's U-Boat War*, Vol. 2, p. 156.
53. Llewellyn-Jones, *The Royal Navy and the Arctic Convoys*, p. 105 nn.
54. Woodman, *Arctic Convoys*, p. 333.
55. Llewellyn-Jones, *The Royal Navy and the Arctic Convoys*, pp. 106–7.
56. Llewellyn-Jones, *The Royal Navy and the Arctic Convoys*, Appendix A.

9 'WE WILL FIGHT TO THE LAST SHELL'

1. Mrs Sheila Allen (née Holding), Bletchley Park 1942–1945, Naval Section, WAAF Teleprinter Operator, Personal Memoir, BPT Roll of Honour.

2. Mrs Sheila Allen (née Holding), Bletchley Park 1942–1945, Naval Section, WAAF Teleprinter Operator, Personal Memoir, BPT Roll of Honour.
3. ZTPG 194163, 194164 and 194168, 24 December 1943, TNA ADM223/36.
4. ZTPG 1946576 and 194726, 25 December 1943, TNA ADM223/36.
5. ZTPG 195207, 26 December 1943, TNA ADM223/36.
6. Winton, *The Death of the Scharnhorst*, p. 16.
7. Winton, *The Death of the Scharnhorst*, p. 19.
8. Admiral Fraser, quoted in W. Churchill, *The Second World War*, Vol. 5: *Closing the Ring* (1952), p. 145.
9. S.W. Roskill, *The War at Sea, 1939–1945*, Vol. 3: *The Offensive, Part 1* (1960), pp. 57–8.
10. Hinsley, *British Intelligence in the Second World War*, Vol. 2, pp. 533–4.
11. Hinsley, *British Intelligence in the Second World War*, Vol. 2, p. 536.
12. F.H. Hinsley, *British Intelligence in the Second World War: Its Influence on Strategy and Operations*, Vol. 3, Part 1 (1984), pp. 254–5.
13. Winton, *ULTRA at Sea*, p. 78.
14. Roskill, *The War At Sea*, Vol. 3: *The Offensive, Part 1*, p. 72.
15. Llewellyn-Jones, *The Royal Navy and the Arctic Convoys*, p. 108.
16. Winton, *The Death of the Scharnhorst*, p. 46.
17. Griffiths, 'G.C. & C.S. Naval History, Vol. 23', p. 119.
18. Dönitz, *Memoirs*, p. 373.
19. Winton, *The Death of the Scharnhorst*, p. 51.
20. Llewellyn-Jones, *The Royal Navy and the Arctic Convoys*, p. 110.
21. Beesly, *Very Special Intelligence*, p. 210, referring to ZTPG 192806, 192819, 20 December 1943, TNA ADM223/36.
22. Admiralty ULTRA Message 0752A/20 December 1943, TNA ADM223/187, referencing ZTPG 192799, 20 December 1943, TNA ADM223/36.
23. Admiralty ULTRA Message 1020A/20 December 1943, TNA ADM223/187, referencing ZTPG 192850, 20 December 1943, TNA DEFE3/368.
24. Admiralty ULTRA Message 2330A/21 December 1943, TNA ADM223/187, referencing ZTPG 193540, 21 December 1943, TNA ADM223/36.
25. Winton, *The Death of the Scharnhorst*, p. 62.
26. ZTPG 194018, 194066, 194272, 22 December 1943, TNA ADM223/36.
27. G. Colpoys, 'Admiralty Use of Special Intelligence in Operations' (unpublished typescript), TNA ADM223–8, p. 108.
28. Admiralty ULTRA Message 1025A/24 December 1943, TNA ADM223/187.
29. Report of Commander in Chief Home Fleet, 31 December 1943, ADM199/913, p. 2.
30. A. Konstam, *The Battle of the North Cape: The Death Ride of the Scharnhorst, 1943* (2009; paperback edn, 2021), p. 51.
31. Konstam, *The Battle of the North Cape*, p. 51.
32. Admiralty ULTRA Message 0550A/25 December 1943, TNA ADM223/187, referencing ZTPG 194759, 25 December 1943, TNA ADM223/36.
33. Winton, *The Death of the Scharnhorst*, p. 68.
34. ZTPG 194810, 194814, 194820, 25 December 1943, TNA DEFE3/370.
35. ZTPG 195189, 194876, 25 December 1943, TNA ADM223/36.
36. Admiralty ULTRA Message 0217A/26 December 1943, TNA ADM223/187.
37. Konstam, *The Battle of the North Cape*, p. 70.
38. Account quoted in Winton, *The Death of the Scharnhorst*, p. 70.

39. Quoted in F. Busch, *The Drama of the Scharnhorst: A Factual Account from the German Viewpoint* (1956), p. 94.
40. Dönitz, *Memoirs*, p. 378.
41. Llewellyn-Jones, *The Royal Navy and the Arctic Convoys*, p. 112.
42. Winton, *The Death of the Scharnhorst*, p. 92; Busch, *The Drama of the Scharnhorst* p. 114.
43. Beesly, *Very Special Intelligence*, p. 216.
44. The following battle narrative is based on Llewellyn-Jones, *The Royal Navy and the Arctic Convoys*, pp. 112–14, and Winton, *The Death of the Scharnhorst*, pp. 92–136.
45. ZTPG 195300, 26 December 1943, TNA DEFE3/371.
46. Admiral B. Fraser, quoted in Winton, *The Death of the Scharnhorst*, p. 147.
47. Colpoys, 'Admiralty Use of Special Intelligence in Operations', p. 106.
48. Cunningham, *A Sailor's Odyssey* p. 592.
49. Griffiths, 'G.C. & C.S. Naval History, Vol. 23', p. 126.
50. BPT Oral History Project, Peggy Huntington (née Munn), Foreign Office Civilian, Block C, Hollerith operator. Interviewed December 2011.
51. BPT Oral History Project, Peggy Huntington.
52. BPT Oral History Project, Joan Joslin (née Glover), Foreign Office Civilian, Block C, Hollerith Operator. Interviewed May 2014.

10 KILLING THE 'BEAST'

1. H. Denham, *In Memoriam Hugh Alexander*, https://web.archive.org/web/20160305204303/https://www.nsa.gov/public_info/_files/cryptologic_spectrum/in_memoriam.pdf (accessed 5 January 2023).
2. 'National Chess Centre', https://jlpmemorystore.org.uk/content/being_a_partner/leisure/leisure-general/national_chess_centre (accessed 5 January 2023).
3. BPT Oral History Project, Merial 'Jo' Dunn (née Matthews) WRNS Bombe operator, later Bombe controller. Interviewed May 2014.
4. Miss Wenda Reynolds, Temporary Civil Servant, Administration & Personnel Section, Bletchley Park, 1941–1945, Oral history interview, BPT Archive.
5. Rolf Noskwith, Foreign Office civilian, Hut 8 Crib Room, Bletchley Park, Oral History Project, BPT Archive.
6. Denham, *In Memoriam Hugh Alexander*.
7. Sweetman, *Tirpitz*, p. xviii.
8. Winton, *ULTRA at Sea*, p. 54.
9. Insall, *Secret Alliances*, p. 310.
10. L. Kennedy, *Menace: The Life and Death of the Tirpitz* (1979; paperback edn, 1981), pp. 76ff.
11. Insall, *Secret Alliances*, p. 229.
12. Kennedy, *Menace*, p. 94.
13. OIC Special intelligence report SI 655, 5 August 1943, TNA ADM223/98.
14. Hinsley, *British Intelligence in the Second World War*, Vol. 3, Part 1, p. 259.
15. Kennedy, *Menace*, pp. 110–11.
16. ZTPG 166196, 22 September 1943, TNA DEFE3/342.
17. ZTPG 166543, 22 September 1943, TNA DEFE3/342.
18. OIC Special intelligence report SI 724, 8 October 1943, TNA ADM223/170.
19. OIC Special intelligence report SI 840, 27 January 1944, TNA ADM223/171.

20. Hinsley, *British Intelligence in the Second World War*, Vol. 3, Part 1, p. 273.
21. Hinsley, *British Intelligence in the Second World War,*, Vol. 3, Part 1, p. 274.
22. ZTPG 227242, 2 April 1944, TNA DEFE3/403.
23. Kennedy, *Menace*, p. 126.
24. ZTPG 227320, 3 April 1944, TNA DEFE3/403.
25. Hinsley, *British Intelligence in the Second World War*, Vol. 3, Part 1, p. 276.
26. Hinsley, *British Intelligence in the Second World War*, Vol. 3, Part 1, p. 276.
27. ZTPG 277428, 24 August 1944, TNA DEFE3/453.
28. ZTPG 277439, 24 August 1944, TNA DEFE3/453.
29. Dönitz, *Memoirs*, p. 386.
30. Kennedy, *Menace*, p. 131.
31. C. Mann & C. Jörgensen, *Hitler's Arctic War: The German Campaigns in Norway, Finland and the USSR 1940–1945* (2002; paperback edn, 2016), pp. 175ff.
32. ZTPG 292762, 15 October 1944, TNA DEFE3/468.
33. ZTPG 297791, 29 October 1944, TNA DEFE3/473.
34. Kennedy, *Menace*, p. 142.
35. ZTPG 303336, 303341, 303342, 12 November 1944, TNA DEFE3/479.
36. Sweetman, *Tirpitz*, p. 241.
37. Kennedy, *Menace*, p. 39.
38. Emphasis added. Beesly, *Very Special Intelligence*, p. 218.
39. Blair, *Hitler's U-Boat War*, Vol. 2, p. 472.
40. War Diary of Captain U-Boats, Norway, 31 December 1943, https://archive.org/details/wardiaryofcaptain1943germ/page/941/mode/2up (accessed 30 December 2022).
41. Griffiths, 'G.C. & C.S. Naval History, Vol. 23', p. 129.
42. Blair, *Hitler's U-Boat War*, Vol. 2, p. 514.
43. ZTPG 206042, 1 February 1944, TNA DEFE3/382.
44. Griffiths, 'G.C. & C.S. Naval History, Vol. 23', p. 131.
45. Blair, *Hitler's U-Boat War*, Vol. 2, p. 515.
46. Colpoys, 'Admiralty Use of Special Intelligence in Operations', p. 141.
47. Colpoys, 'Admiralty Use of Special Intelligence in Operations', p. 143.
48. Colpoys, 'Admiralty Use of Special Intelligence in Operations', p. 139.
49. Blair, *Hitler's U-Boat War*, Vol. 2, p. 517.
50. Blair, *Hitler's U-Boat War*, Vol. 2, p. 518.
51. Alexander, 'Cryptographic History of Work on the German Naval Enigma', p. 6.
52. Alexander, 'Cryptographic History of Work on the German Naval Enigma', p. 77.
53. 'B.T.M. 3-Wheel bombes and B.T.M. and W.W. 4-Wheel Bombes', TNA HW25/17.
54. F.H. Hinsley, *British Intelligence in the Second World War: Its Influence on Strategy and Operations*, Vol. 3, Part 2 (1988), p. 490.
55. Mahon, 'The History of Hut Eight', p. 108.
56. Mahon, 'The History of Hut Eight', p. 114.
57. https://www.unithistories.com/officers/RN_officersM5.html#Moore_HR (accessed 6 January 2023).
58. ZTPG 246322, 22 May 1944, TNA DEFE3/422.
59. Blair, *Hitler's U-Boat War*, Vol. 2, p. 600.
60. Blair, *Hitler's U-Boat War*, Vol. 2, p. 600.
61. A. Lambert, 'Seizing the Initiative: The Arctic Convoys 1944–45', in N. Rodger (ed.), *Naval Power in the Twentieth Century* (1996), p. 155.

62. Hinsley, *British Intelligence in the Second World War*, Vol. 3, Part 2, p. 490.
63. *F. d. U Noordmeer* War Diary, quoted in Griffiths, 'G.C. & C.S. Naval History, Vol. 23', p. 152.
64. Griffiths, 'G.C. & C.S. Naval History, Vol. 23', p. 152.
65. Blair, *Hitler's U-Boat War*, Vol. 2, p. 678.
66. Hinsley, *British Intelligence in the Second World War*, Vol. 3, Part 2, p. 493.
67. Blair, *Hitler's U-Boat War*, Vol. 2, p. 680.

11 THE ARCTIC CONVOYS IN RETROSPECT

1. Llewellyn-Jones, *The Royal Navy and the Arctic Convoys*, p. 129.
2. Blair, *Hitler's U-Boat War*, Vol. 2, p. 682.
3. Llewellyn-Jones, *The Royal Navy and the Arctic Convoys*, p. 147.
4. B. Schofield, *The Russian Convoys* (1964), p. 223.
5. Arnold Hague, quoted at https://www.warsailors.com/freefleet/shipstats.html#arcticfacts (accessed 9 January 2023).
6. F. De Ninno, 'The Mediterranean Battle of the Convoys: Some Revaluations', https://www.academia.edu/11047405/The_Mediterranean_battle_of_the_convoys?auto=download (accessed 18 November 2020).
7. R. Woodman, *Malta Convoys 1940–1943* (2003), pp. 470–1.
8. A. Boyd, *British Naval Intelligence through the Twentieth Century* (2020), p. 496.
9. Blair, *Hitler's U-Boat War*, Vol. 2, pp. 785–6.
10. Data from https://uboat.net/allies/merchants (accessed 9 January 2023).
11. Blair, *Hitler's U-Boat War*, Vol. 2, pp. 785–6.
12. S.W. Roskill, *The War at Sea, 1939–1945*, Vol. 3: *The Offensive, Part 2, 1st June 1944–14th August 1945* (1961), p. 262.
13. Birch, 'G.C. & C.S. Naval Sigint, Vol. 1', p. 84.
14. Birch, 'G.C. & C.S. Naval Sigint, Vol. 1', p. 18.
15. Boyd, *British Naval Intelligence through the Twentieth Century*, p. 498.
16. Llewellyn-Jones, *The Royal Navy and the Arctic Convoys*, p. 130.
17. Data from https://uboat.net/boats/listing.html (accessed 12 January 2023).
18. Roskill, *The War at Sea*, Vol. 3: *The Offensive, Part 2*, p. 262.
19. Birch, 'G.C. & C.S. Naval Sigint, Vol. 1', p. 7.

BIBLIOGRAPHY

UNPUBLISHED ARCHIVAL SOURCES

The National Archives (TNA), Kew, London

In addition to the particular documents listed below, a large volume of decrypted wireless message traffic was also examined. The texts of messages deciphered at GC&CS and passed on to the Admiralty via teleprint ('ZTPG' traffic) are held in Series DEFE3. Messages passed to the fleet at sea from the Admiralty are held in Series ADM223. Individual messages cited in the text are referenced in the endnotes.

ADM Series

ADM199/73	'Senior Officer Force R's Report No. H.D.0571A of 6th January 1943'
ADM199/913	Report of Commander-in-Chief Home Fleet, 31 December 1943
ADM223/8	Colpoys, G. 'Admiralty Use of Special Intelligence in Operations'
ADM223/98	OIC Special intelligence report SI 655, 5 August 1943
ADM223/109	Admiralty to C.-in-C. Home Fleet, 1826A/17 February 1942
ADM223/170	OIC Special intelligence report SI 724, 8 October 1943
ADM223/171	OIC Special intelligence report SI 840, 27 January 1944

HW Series

HW3/16	Clarke, W. 'History of GCCS and its Naval Section, 1919–1945'
HW3/134	Mahon, A.P. 'History of I.D.8 G August 1939–December 1942'
HW3/137	'History of NS VI (Technical Intelligence)'
HW3/137	GC&CS, 'Historical Memorandum No. 33 The History of N.S. VI (Technical Intelligence)'
HW3/145	GCHQ, 'History of the British Plot'
HW8/21	Handwritten letter, Birch to Clarke, 3 September 1939
HW8/99	'A History of the R/T "Y" Organisation Ashore and Afloat July 1940 to May 1945'
HW14/53	'Report on G.A.F. "Y" Activity – P.Q.18 H.M.S. Scylla – September 1942'

HW14/55	'Y Operations on Board HMS Scylla with PQ18'
HW25/1	Alexander, C. 'Cryptographic History of Work on the German Naval Enigma'
HW25/2	Mahon, A.P. 'The History of Hut Eight 1939–1945' (GCHQ)
HW25/17	'B.T.M. 3-Wheel bombes and B.T.M. and W.W. 4-Wheel Bombes'
HW25/19–20	Fletcher, H. 'Hut 6 Bombe Register', Vols 1–2
HW43/1	Birch, F. 'A History of British Sigint, 1914–1945, Vol. 1'
HW43/10	Birch, F. 'G. C. & C. S. Naval Sigint, Vol. 1: The Organisation and Evolution of British Sigint' (GCHQ, 1952)
HW43/15	Birch, F. 'History of Naval Sigint, Vol. 4'
HW50/15	GC&CS, 'Technical intelligence and Captured documents'
HW50/15	GC&CS, 'Notes for Naval Section Output'

Bletchley Park Trust (BPT) Archives

Anderson, H. & L. Griffiths. 'G.C. & C.S. Naval History, Vol. 2: German Navy – Organisation' (GCHQ typescript)

Anderson, H. & L. Griffiths. 'G.C. & C.S. Naval History, Vol. 7: German Navy – The U-Boat Arm' (GCHQ typescript)

Griffiths, L.A. 'GC & CS Naval History, Vol. 23: Northern Waters' (GCHQ typescript)

GCHQ, 'Key Personalities at Bletchley Park 1939–1945' (GCHQ typescript)

GCHQ, 'History of Bletchley Park Huts and Blocks 1939–45' (GCHQ typescript)

English Heritage, 'Bletchley Park Buckinghamshire Architectural Investigation, Reports and Papers B/010/2004' (typescript, 2004)

INTERNET RESOURCES

National Security Agency, 'Battle of the Atlantic, Volume III: German Naval Communications Intelligence, SRH-024', http://www.ibiblio.org/hyperwar/ETO/Ultra/SRH-024/index.html#index

Denham, H. *In Memoriam Hugh Alexander*, https://web.archive.org/web/20160305204303/https://www.nsa.gov/public_info/_files/cryptologic_spectrum/in_memoriam.pdf

Captain's confidential report by Admiral Sir John D. Kelly, 14 September 1933, https://web.archive.org/web/20180327144828/http://www.admirals.org.uk/admirals/fleet/toveyjc.php

Tirpitz War Diary, 1–15 March 1942, http://www.kbismarck.com/archives/tp-ktb1-15mar42.pdf

Erskine, R. 'Birch, Francis Lyall [Frank]', *Oxford Dictionary of National Biography*, http://www.oxforddnb.com/view/10.1093/ref:odnb/9780198614128.001.0001/odnb-9780198614128-e-61099;jsessionid=B26F663B-8BE74229E076E17C95EB3826

OTHER WEBSITES CONSULTED

https://uboat.net/
http://www.ww2incolor.com/
https://www.imdb.com/

https://www.cryptomuseum.com/
www.convoyweb.org.uk
https://www.axishistory.com/

BLETCHLEY PARK TRUST (BPT) ORAL HISTORY PROJECT

Acason, G., WRNS, Block A, Naval Section, NS IV, U-boat signals index. Interviewed October 2014.

Allen, S. (née Holding), Naval Section, WAAF Teleprinter Operator, Block A, Naval Section. Typescript memoir.

Chojecki, C. (née Rowett), Foreign Office Civilian, Hut 4 and Block B, Naval Section NS IV, intelligence research on U-boats. Typescript memoir.

Drinkwater, P. (née Garrett), Foreign Office Civilian, Block A, Naval Section, NS IX, signal distribution. Interviewed 12 April 2014.

Dunn, M. (née Matthews), WRNS Bombe operator, later Bombe controller.

Huntington, P. (née Munn), Foreign Office Civilian, Block C, Hollerith operator. Interviewed December 2011.

Joslin, J. (née Glover), Foreign Office Civilian, Block C, Hollerith Operator. Interviewed May 2014.

Morgan, M. (née Darby), WRNS 3rd Officer, Hut 4, Block A, Naval Section, NS IX, secretarial support to senior personnel. Interviewed 21 Jan 2016.

Noskwith, R., Foreign Office Civilian, Hut 8 Crib Room, Enigma decryption. Interviewed June 2012.

Purvis J., RAF Flt Lt, Air Section liaison officer with convoy PQ 17. Typescript memoir.

Reynolds E., Foreign Office Civilian, Mansion and Hut 9, Administration & Personnel Section. Interviewed May 2014.

Senior, E., Foreign Office Civilian, Block A, Naval Section, NS VI, Technical Intelligence, producing dictionary of technical terms. Interviewed June 2013.

Tocher, A., WRNS Block A, Naval Section, NS IV, Watch head in British plot team maintaining plot of allied and enemy shipping. Interviewed July 2013.

Willson, S., WRNS, Block A(N), Naval Section, NS IV P, maintained British plot. Interviewed July 2015.

PUBLISHED BOOKS AND ARTICLES

Arthur, M. *Lost Voices of the Royal Navy: Vivid Eyewitness Accounts of Life in the Royal Navy from 1914 to 1945* (paperback edn, London: Hodder & Stoughton, 2005)

Beesly, P. *Very Special Intelligence: The History of the Admiralty's Operational Intelligence Centre, 1939–1945* (London: Hamish Hamilton, 1977)

Birch, F. *This Freedom of Ours* (Cambridge: Cambridge University Press, 1937)

Blair, C. *Hitler's U-Boat War,* Vol. 1: *The Hunters, 1939–1942* (New York: Random House, 1996)

Blair, C. *Hitler's U-Boat War,* Vol. 2: *The Hunted, 1939–1942* (New York: Random House, 1998)

Boyd, A. *British Naval Intelligence through the Twentieth Century* (Barnsley: Pen & Sword Books, 2020)

Broome, J. *Convoy is to Scatter: The Story of PQ17* (London: Futura, 1972; paperback edn, 1974)

Budiansky, S. *Blackett's War: The Men who Defeated the Nazi U-boats and Brought Science to the Art of Warfare* (London: Vintage, 2013)

Busch, F. *The Drama of the Scharnhorst: A Factual Account from the German Viewpoint*, tr. E. Brockett & A. Ehrenzweig (London: Robert Hale, 1956)

Churchill, W. *The Second World War*, Vol. 4: *The Hinge of Fate* (London: Cassell, 1951)

Churchill, W. *The Second World War*, Vol. 5: *Closing the Ring* (London: Cassell, 1952)

Cunningham, A. *A Sailor's Odyssey* (London: Hutchinson, 1951)

Dakin, A. 'The Z Watch in Hut 4, Part I', in F.H. Hinsley & A. Stripp (eds), *Codebreakers: The Inside Story of Bletchley Park* (Oxford, Oxford University Press, 1993; paperback edn, 1994)

Dönitz, K. *Memoirs: Ten Years and Twenty Days*, tr. R. Stevens (London: Weidenfeld & Nicolson, 1958; paperback edn, London: Frontline Books, 1990)

Edwards, B. *The Road to Russia: Arctic Convoys 1942* (Barnsley: Pen & Sword Books, 2015)

Erskine, R. 'Captured Kriegsmarine Enigma Documents at Bletchley Park', in *Cryptologia*, 32:3 (2008), pp. 199–219

Erskine, R. & F. Weierud. 'Naval Enigma: M4 and its Rotors', in *Cryptologia*, 11:4 (1987), pp. 235–44

Falconer, N. 'On the Size of Convoys: An Example of the Methodology of Leading Wartime OR Scientists', in *Operational Research Quarterly*, 27:2, part 1 (1976), pp. 315–27

Ferris, J. *Behind the Enigma: The Authorised History of GCHQ Britain's Secret Cyber-Intelligence Agency* (London: Bloomsbury, 2020)

Fitzgerald, P. *The Knox Brothers* (Newton Abbot: Readers Union, 1978)

Hadley, M. *Count Not the Dead: The Popular Image of the German Submarine* (Montreal: McGill-Queen's University Press, 1995)

Hill, R. *Destroyer Captain* (London: Kimber, 1975; paperback edn, London: Grenada Publishing, 1979)

Hinsley, F.H. 'BP, Admiralty, and Naval Enigma', in F.H. Hinsley & A. Stripp (eds), *Codebreakers: The Inside Story of Bletchley Park* (Oxford: Oxford University Press, 1993; paperback edn, 1994)

Hinsley, F.H. *British Intelligence in the Second World War: Its Influence on Strategy and Operations*, Vol. 1 (London: HMSO, 1979)

Hinsley, F.H. *British Intelligence in the Second World War: Its Influence on Strategy and Operations*, Vol. 2 (London: HMSO, 1981)

Hinsley, F.H. *British Intelligence in the Second World War: Its Influence on Strategy and Operations*, Vol. 3, Part 1 (London: HMSO, 1984)

Hinsley, F.H. *British Intelligence in the Second World War: Its Influence on Strategy and Operations*, Vol. 3, Part 2 (London, HMSO: 1988)

Insall, T. *Secret Alliances: Special Operations and Intelligence in Norway 1940–1945* (London: Biteback, 2019; paperback edn, 2021)

Kahn, D. *Hitler's Spies: German Military Intelligence in World War II* (London: Hodder & Stoughton, 1978)

Kahn, D. *Seizing the Enigma: The Race to Break the German U-boat Codes, 1939–1943* (London: Souvenir Press, 1992; paperback edn, Annapolis, MD: Naval Institute Press, 2012)

Kennedy, L. *Menace: The Life and Death of the Tirpitz* (1979; paperback edn, London: Sphere Books, 1981)

Kerslake, S. *Coxswain in the Northern Convoys* (London: William Kimber, 1984)

Konstam, A. *The Battle of the North Cape: The Death Ride of the Scharnhorst, 1943* (Barnsley: Pen & Sword Maritime, 2009; paperback edn, Barnsley: Pen & Sword Books, 2021)

Lambert, A. 'Seizing the Initiative: The Arctic Convoys 1944–45', in N. Rodger (ed.), *Naval Power in the Twentieth Century* (London: Palgrave Macmillan, 1996)

Lardas, M. *Arctic Convoys 1942: The Luftwaffe Cuts Russia's Lifeline* (London: Osprey Publishing, 2022)

Llewellyn-Jones, M. (ed.). *The Royal Navy and the Arctic Convoys: A Naval Staff History* (London: Routledge, 2007)

Mann, C. & C. Jörgensen. *Hitler's Arctic War: The German Campaigns in Norway, Finland and the USSR 1940–1945* (2002; paperback edn, Barnsley: Pen & Sword Books, 2016)

McKay, J.R. *Surviving the Arctic Convoys: The Wartime Memoirs of Leading Seaman Charlie Erswell* (Barnsley: Pen & Sword Books, 2021)

Morris, C. 'Navy Ultra's Poor Relations', in F.H. Hinsley & A. Stripp (eds), *Codebreakers: The Inside Story of Bletchley Park* (Oxford, Oxford University Press, 1993; paperback edn, 1994)

Pope, D. *73 North: The Battle of the Barents Sea* (London: Weidenfeld & Nicolson, 1958; paperback edn, Ithaca, NY: McBooks Press, 2005)

Roskill S.W. *The War at Sea, 1939–1945*, Vol. 2: *The Period of Balance* (London: HMSO, 1956)

Roskill, S.W. *The War at Sea, 1939–1945*, Vol. 3: *The Offensive, Part 1* (London: HMSO, 1960)

Roskill, S.W. *The War at Sea, 1939–1945*, Vol. 3: *The Offensive, Part 2, 1st June 1944–14th August 1945* (London: HMSO, 1961)

Schofield, B. *The Russian Convoys* (paperback edn, London: Pan Books, 1964)

Sebag-Montefiore, H. *Enigma: The Battle for the Code* (London: Wiley, 2004; paperback edn, London: Cassell, 2004)

Smith, M. *Station X: The Codebreakers of Bletchley Park* (London: Pan Macmillan, 1998; paperback edn published as *The Secrets of Station X: How the Bletchley Park Codebreakers Helped Win the War*, London: Biteback, 2011)

Smith, P.C. *Convoy PQ18: Arctic Victory* (London: William Kimber, 1975; paperback edn, London: New English Library, 1977)

Sweetman, J. *Tirpitz: Hunting the Beast* (Annapolis, MD: Naval Institute Press, 2000; paperback edn, Cheltenham: The History Press, 2004)

Tovey, Adm. Sir J.C. 'Convoys to North Russia, 1942', Supplement to *London Gazette*, 13 October 1950, https://www.thegazette.co.uk

Walling, M.G. *Forgotten Sacrifice: The Arctic Convoys of World War II* (London: Osprey Publishing, 2016)

Winton, J. *The Death of the Scharnhorst* (Chichester: Antony Bird Publications, 1983; paperback edn, London: Cassell, 2000)

Winton, J. *ULTRA at Sea* (London: William Heinemann, 1988)

Woodman, R. *Arctic Convoys 1941–1945* (London: John Murray, 1994)

Woodman, R. *Malta Convoys 1940–1943* (2000; paperback edn, London: John Murray, 2003)

INDEX

INDEX